solitude & company

Esta es la única foto mía
tomada por Conguleto mientras
escribía Cien años de soledad

Gabriel García Márquez in Mexico D.F. 1966,
writing *One Hundred Years of Solitude*.

solitude & company

the life of **GABRIEL GARCÍA MÁRQUEZ** *told with help from his friends, family, fans, arguers, fellow pranksters, drunks, and a few respectable souls*

SILVANA PATERNOSTRO

Translated from the Spanish by Edith Grossman

Seven Stories Press

New York ✳ Oakland ✳ London

Seven Stories Press
140 Watts Street
New York, NY 10013
sevenstories.com

Library of Congress Cataloging-in-Publication Data

Names: Paternostro, Silvana, author. | Grossman, Edith, 1936- translator.
Title: Solitude & company : the life of Gabriel García Márquez told with help
    from his friends, family, fans, arguers, fellow pranksters, drunks, and a
    few respectable souls / Silvana Paternostro ; translated from the Spanish
    by Edith Grossman.
Other titles: Soledad & Compañía. English | Solitude and company
Description: New York : Seven Stories Press, 2019.
Identifiers: LCCN 2018045522| ISBN 9781609808969 (hardcover) | ISBN
    9781609808976 (ebook)
Subjects: LCSH: García Márquez, Gabriel, 1927-2014. | García Márquez,
    Gabriel, 1927-2014--Friends and associates.
Classification: LCC PQ8180.17.A73 Z825513 2019 | DDC 863/.64 [B] --dc23
LC record available at https://lccn.loc.gov/2018045522

Book design by Jon Gilbert

Printed in the United States of America

9 8 7 6 5 4 3 2 1

Contents

A. C.

AFTER *CIEN AÑOS DE SOLEDAD*

To Gabriel García Márquez
and George Plimpton,
teachers, *in memoriam*

I am consoled, however, that at times oral history might be better than written, and without knowing it we may be inventing a new genre needed by literature: fiction about fiction.

Gabriel García Márquez, *Living to Tell the Tale*

Prologue

In November 2000, the magazine *Talk*, recently founded by Tina Brown, asked me to prepare an oral history of Gabriel García Márquez. They wanted two thousand words; badly counted and with photographs, that amounted to three or four pages. That is, something short. Definitely not his biography.

I was hired because although I've lived in New York since 1986, I was born in Barranquilla, and therefore was a neighbor of the imaginary world of Macondo. Besides, in the winter 1996 issue of *The Paris Review*, I had published "Three Days with Gabo," a detailed chronicle of a journalism workshop García Márquez offered in Cartagena that I attended as a student.

I proposed that instead of interviewing the heads of state, movie stars, and immensely wealthy men with whom he associated on a daily basis, I would travel to Colombia to talk with those who knew him before he became the legendary Latin American author. When I said I would even talk to the characters who appear in *One Hundred Years of Solitude*, referring to a group of friends he had immortalized as "the pranksters of La Cueva" and the "first and last friends that he ever had in his life," they immediately sent me a plane ticket that I found very funny, because printed on the front of the folder that held the ticket was the image of Mickey Mouse. *Talk* was financed by the Disney Corporation.

"After Colombia, I have to go to Mexico," I risked telling the editor. "That was where he wrote the novel."

"Whatever you need," was the answer.

The piece was never published. *Talk* closed because the formula of mixing show business with journalism and literature was not an obvious success. "What other magazine puts a bare-chested Hugh Grant on the cover and devotes six pages to a serious section on books?" the editor who had asked me for it told me not long ago. "Only Tina would have asked for an oral history of Gabriel García Márquez."

Thanks to Tina's daring, however, I was able to produce twenty-four tapes, ninety minutes on each side, of people talking about Gabriel García Márquez. I published a few pieces carved out of those conversations. In 2002, when *Living to Tell the Tale*, his book of memories, was published in Spanish, the magazine *El malpensante* (*The Evil-Minded*) came out with a more Colombian and more extensive version of what I had prepared for *Talk*. I called it "Solitude & Company," the name that at one point García Márquez was going to give to a film production company he wanted to set up with some Colombian partners. With the same title I published another version in the edition of *The Paris Review* commemorating its fiftieth anniversary, which in turn was translated and published in Mexico by the magazine *Nexos* in its spring 2003 issue. Almost a decade went by before I decided, in March 2010, that it was time to listen to those tapes again and transform them into this book.

When I finished listening to them, though, I realized that what I had was not enough for a book. I needed to fill in gaps. Which is why I began a second round of interviews with those who I thought would provide context and chronology to the first voices.

Solitude & Company is divided into two parts. In the first, "B.C.: Before *Cien años de soledad*," his siblings speak, as well as those who were his buddies before he became the universally loved Latin American icon. Those who knew him when he still didn't have a proper English tailor nor an English biographer—two things I heard him say are the marks of a writer's success—and didn't accompany presidents and multimillionaires (as on the night I saw him cut the baby-blue inaugural ribbon at the Museo Soumaya, Carlos Slim's gift to Mexico City, which reminded me of the interviews I had prepared for *Talk*). This first part gathers together the voices of those irreverent and hopeful times when a boy from the provinces decided to become a writer. This is the story of how he did it. Here we witness the formation of the creator venerated throughout the world. In the second part, "A.C.: After *Cien años de soledad*," a prize-winning García Márquez appears, a celebrated man.

A great deal has been written about García Márquez, but no matter how much is written, the author's prose, the censorship of his memories, and the analysis of his biographer weigh heavily. Oral history, the formal name of this genre, allows those who were very close to him to describe for us the man who became the most important writer in Latin America, the lover of power, and defender to the end of Fidel Castro. It allows them to tell us how they welcomed him, helped him, and watched him create himself; it permits them to make us feel how much they love him or how much he annoyed them; just them, without other narrators or descriptions as intermediaries.

This book, then, is a ticket to a celebration where everybody talks, everybody shouts, everybody has an opinion and even tells lies. That is the essence of oral history, along the lines of *Edie: American Girl* by Jean Stein and George Plimpton, and *Truman Capote: In Which Various Friends, Enemies, Acquaintances and Detractors Recall His Tur-*

bulent Career by Plimpton. This format, which fell from the skies with that imperative phone call from Tina Brown, is formidable because it is amusing and light, yet profoundly true.

But you must keep in mind that each morsel of dialogue deals with the version of the person who is speaking. Reading it is as fun as attending a fiesta and stopping to listen to the guests talk about García Márquez, and, as at the best parties, some speak more than others. The shouters are here, the super-analytical, the pranksters, the singers, the vulgar, and even those who have had too much to drink. At this party we are with the company that made possible the solitude that García Márquez needed to write his *One Hundred Years of Solitude*.

To write this book I didn't speak to García Márquez. That is exactly what oral history demands. That is, it is written with the voices of others. Oral history involves talking to someone about a person without that person being present, and even more important, recording those conversations. To begin working, I organized the tapes in the order in which the interviews had been held. Then, I started to listen to the interviews I had conducted and recorded more than a decade before. Through the headphones I heard my own laughter, but at the same time new questions jumped out at me. For example, I chuckled listening to the people from my native Barranquilla, but I also realized that outside of Colombia, no one understands what "nursing at a rooster's tit" means. Then I understood that I had to resolve not only how to explain Barranquillan argot, but also the fact that I was talking to people of advanced age. Their memory would fail and they would stammer when they couldn't remember something. And since I wasn't going to give them back their memories, I left in their voices the tenderness of their declining years.

Music, especially the *vallenato*, an accordion-infused country blues, played an important part in those first conversations, and more than once the interviewees broke into song, and so I let them sing here, too. I also include the machista logic of the judge García Márquez consulted so that he could tell him what had happened on that fateful Sunday when, as a young man, the magistrate had witnessed what the world knows today as "the chronicle of a death foretold." I also include a lot of explanations about Barranquilla, because it is not only fertile ground for the so-called magical realism; it is also where García Márquez met his first and last friends, the wise Catalonian along with Alfonso, Álvaro, Germán, and a few others of the "arguers" who appear in the last chapter of *One Hundred Years of Solitude*. When I arrived in Barranquilla with my tape recorder these faithful friends had all passed away but I was lucky to find two survivors to tell me what they were like when they took care of García Márquez. This book is an homage to friendship, a recognition of his friends because in Barranquilla he certainly had the very best.

Looking for more accounts of friendship, I wanted to communicate with María Luisa Elío and Jomí García Ascot. *One Hundred Years of Solitude* is dedicated to them. All the Gabologists and Gabolaters in Colombia knew by heart the works and miracles of the "arguers" that appear in the novel, but no one could tell me anything about these two people, obviously important in the life of the author. Other than that they lived in Mexico City.

I arrived in Mexico City, with another ticket from Disney, registered at the Casa Durango, and began my search. Carlos Monsiváis told me they were a Spanish couple; told me that Jomí, the husband, had died and gave me the phone number of the señora. The next day a very attractive and elegant lady in a gray-blue pantsuit that matched the color of her eyes and scarf received me in the library of a house to the south of the city. She was as generous with her stories as she had been with Gabriel García Márquez, when for hours she listened to him, simply the friend of a friend at a dinner party, recount the story of the book he was planning to write. That idea turned into *One Hundred Years of Solitude*, and the first edition is dedicated to her. I am sure she recounted the story of that dinner party at many other dinner parties. That afternoon María Luisa Elío told me as I turned on my tape recorder that this was the first formal, taped interview of that memory.

There are certain individuals who are not as close to García Márquez, and a few who never met him. However, their commentary on moments in Colombia's history that marked the life of the writer, like the assassination of Jorge Eliécer Gaitán on April 9, 1948, and the historical period known as the Violence unleashed by this event, are essential to understanding the history of García Márquez and of his books. Nereo López, the official photographer of the Colombian delegation sent to Stockholm when García Márquez received the Nobel Prize, moved to New York in 1997 when he was eighty "to open up his horizons," and I took advantage of his admirable audacity to have him talk to me about the days when García Márquez was just another colleague and Colombia was bleeding to death. His vivid recollections brought history to life.

Here a García Márquez appears without the self-censorship of *Living to Tell the Tale*, and without the weight of the more than seven hundred pages of the excellent biographies by Dasso Saldívar and Gerald Martin. It is a rich, rare historical document that retrieves the collective memory of his life and reflects on the work of being a writer; of how he comes to the necessary Rilkean pact with solitude. It is a book that demonstrates how friendship and circumstances, but above all discipline and dedication, are necessary in order to triumph.

His close friend the Argentinian writer Tomás Eloy Martínez confessed to me that in order to be Gabo's friend, you had to take an *omertá*, as if you were in the mafia. "You have to never write about him," he told me one afternoon on his patio in New Jersey. García Márquez recounts that in Paris, when he was young and poor, he had seen Ernest Hemingway in a park. Instead of approaching him and beginning a conversation, he decided to shout his name from the other side of the little square, raise his hand, and signal with that gesture how much he respected him. I understood the fear he felt, for it is very difficult to let oneself be tempted by proximity.

I have written this book from a distance and in the same spirit. It is a human portrait of someone who turned into a legend. I firmly believe we are bigger, more important, more eternal, and even more saintly than myths. García Márquez is great without our having to accept the comfortable tales that he had no errors, defects, defeats, recklessness, loves, or enmities. If we do that, we will only contribute to an empty foolishness.

To enjoy this book one must put aside the notion that everything in life has a single truth. Oral history contrasts each person's truth. That is part of its charm. Come to this party with that in mind and holding a whiskey on the rocks, or a glass of champagne, which is what I am told Gabo himself preferred. If you are in for the full experience, walk to your bookshelf and take out your copy of *One Hundred Years of Solitude*, or go to your nearest bookstore and buy it. Read it again, or for the first time, now that you've heard the fun facts and indiscretions, the behind-the-scenes of what is described as "probably the finest and most famous work—a classic of world literature for all time." The last two chapters will fill you with delight as you understand the winks he made to his friends. I hope you will laugh out loud when you read, for example, that "Álvaro frightened the crocodiles with his noisy laughter and Alfonso invented outlandish stories about the bitterns who had pecked out the eyes of four customers who misbehaved the week before, and Gabriel was in the room of the pensive mulatto girl who did not collect in money but in letters to a smuggler boyfriend who was in prison on the other side of the Orinoco because the border guards had caught him and had made him sit on a chamberpot that filled up with a mixture of shit and diamonds." You will understand why he always contested those who said he had a great imagination with a simple sentence: everything in his fiction is based on facts.

ONE HUNDRED YEARS
OF SOLITUDE

The Earthquake of 1967

GREGORY RABASSA: It happened the way earthquakes happen. We can't predict earthquakes, even though we know they're going to happen.

EMMANUEL CARBALLO: An astonishing case in the history of literature in Spanish. It's something genetic. There are genes that predestine you to be a great writer, and he worked very hard. He didn't devote himself to literature gratuitously, but he worked very hard. Very, very disciplined. He left all his jobs, borrowed money, sold things, and shut himself up in his house for eight months to write. His entire family, his wife, his sons, his friends, we all made an empty space around him because he was frenetically dedicated to one thing. They lived very modestly in a small apartment, there were no luxuries there, they spent only what was necessary.

Everyone agreed that he should have peace, time, and affection. And thanks to that—principally to his family and his friends—the novel was written. I was the person who read the novel from the time he began to write it until he finished it, and because I was reading and commenting chapter after chapter every week, by the time he brought over the next chapter I had nothing to correct, nothing to replace, because all my suggestions were already there in the novel.

MARÍA LUISA ELÍO: He gave me pieces to read. What Gabo had written at night, he would read us parts the next day . . . And from that first moment you realized it was a marvel. He knew it.

GUILLERMO ANGULO: No, he didn't know. In fact, he was very doubtful that it would be a good novel. When it was published, he sent me a copy. I read it. I liked it a great deal. He sent me another copy. I don't have my copy because I had to pass it on to Germán Vargas, and Germán Vargas had to pass it on to Plinio. And I ought to tell you something that I don't believe anyone has told you and that no one is going to tell you: Plinio reprimanded him because it was anti-Communist. "What? The country's full of problems and you're writing a fairy tale?"

MARÍA LUISA ELÍO: One isn't a fool and I can be very cutting where literature is concerned. I mean, whomever it is can be a very famous writer, and if I don't like it, I don't like it. So I read it and I knew that this Señor García Márquez was very great. I didn't doubt it for a second . . .

I thought the book was really good. But I'll be frank with you: to *that* degree, no.

SANTIAGO MUTIS: They lost control of the situation. Abroad and in Colombia too. Because Gabo became an event, a phenomenon. Everyone kneeled down before him. I don't know whether Gabo tells this or Tomás Eloy Martínez. One week after they published the novel there, Gabo travels to Buenos Aires not because of *One Hundred Years of Solitude* but to be a judge at a fiction competition. One night they go to the theater, and when Gabo goes in someone recognizes him, the entire audience gets up and applauds him. That's where it began. And it hasn't stopped! It didn't stop. Ever. That is, they never left him alone.

RODRIGO MOYA: On November 29, 1966, Gabriel García Márquez visits me in my home in the Condesa Building, accompanied by his wife Mercedes, so that one of my photographs would illustrate the first edition. I took the photographs in my house, which had a good deal of natural light. He arrived wearing a plaid jacket. He loved those plaids. He looked impassive but he certainly was conscious of the camera. He was conscious that he had created a masterpiece. He had already written a great deal, he had already had success, and throughout the work you can breathe the certainty that only geniuses have. I had that impression then. Of course, not the magnitude. Gabo was just thirty-nine years old. But a foretelling of what was to come.

B.C.

BEFORE *CIEN AÑOS DE SOLEDAD*

Photo of wedding between Gabriel
Eligio and Luisa Santiaga.

I

The Son of Luisa Santiaga
and Gabriel Eligio

*How the son of the telegraph operator in Aracataca begins
to collect stories in the cradle*

RAFAEL ULLOA: Gabo wasn't born in 1928, but in 1927. He says
he was born in '28 to coincide with the slaughter on the banana
plantations,* but it was his brother who was born in '28.

LUIS ENRIQUE GARCÍA MÁRQUEZ: Until 1955 I thought I had
come into this world on September 8, 1928, after my mother's
nine months of pregnancy. But it happened that in that year of
1955, Gabito wrote *The Story of a Shipwrecked Sailor* in *El Espectador* and he had difficulties with the government of General Rojas
Pinilla. Then he had to leave the country, for which he needed a
certain document, and in that document, I don't know why, it was
stated that Gabito was born on March 6, 1928—that is, the same
year I was born, something which left me in a difficult situation:
either being the only six-month premature baby on record who

---

* On December 5 and 6, 1928, in the town of Ciénaga, near Santa Marta (also close to
Aracataca where García Márquez was born), the Colombian army shot at a group of workers
of the United Fruit Company protesting poor working conditions. It is known as the Banana
Massacre. The event looms so large in García Márquez's own history that he changed the
year of his birth to coincide with the year of the incident. He writes about the massacre in
One Hundred Years of Solitude, claiming that the army killed three thousand workers. In a
twist that feels appropriate for "magical realism," it is this account that entered the annals of
Colombian history.

weighed ten pounds two ounces, or almost his twin. He never corrected the date, but the one who was born in 1928, in Aracataca, Magdalena, was me. Gabito was born on March 6 of '27.

RAMÓN ILLÁN BACCA: Luisa, Gabo's mother, was a well-regarded person. They were what we would call well-regarded people. What were well-regarded people back then? They were people valued by the people of the provincial upper class, because we're talking about the upper-class people of Santa Marta. As the Bogotanos would say: "You're decent people from the hot land." Luisa studied at the Colegio de la Presentación in Santa Marta, which was the secondary school for the high class. But they were just well regarded. That is, they were people invited to some parties and not to others. It all depends on what party it was. Señor García, his father, I don't think he was even well regarded.

RAFAEL ULLOA: Gabriel Eligio García is the father. My mother is first cousin to García Márquez's father. So my mother told me a little about family issues. And I'm a great fan of García Márquez. I've read all his books. I'm from Sincé, of course. It's the hometown of this gentleman's father. Sincé, spelled with a *c*. The town was called San Luis de Sincé. But for people it was Sincé.

CARMELO MARTÍNEZ: Luisa Santiaga, Gabito's mother, was a white lady, short, with a wart right here. White. The same age as my mother. My mother was born in 1904 and Luisa in the same year. She's about ninety-six years old. She doesn't know anything anymore.

RAFAEL ULLOA: Carlos H. Pareja is from Sincé and is related to Gabito's father. And, well, Carlos had good connections. He helped Gabo's father so he could begin to study medicine but he ran out of dough and then, since he was in a bad situation, they told him: "Don't fuck around, do something. Find a job." And then he was appointed telegraph operator in Aracataca. When he went there he fell in love with Luisa Santiaga Márquez, who was the daughter of Colonel Márquez. His mother was a very peaceful woman, Luisa Santiaga Márquez. She was a good friend of my mother's.

JAIME GARCÍA MÁRQUEZ: They say that Gabriel Eligio García, my father, came to Aracataca as a telegraph operator and saw Luisa, my mother, one day and liked the girl right away. One day he approached her and said: "After carefully analyzing the women I've met in Aracataca, I have reached the conclusion that the one who suits me best"—that's how he said it, suits me—"is you. I want to marry you, think it over; but if you decide not to, tell me and don't worry, because I'm not dying for you." I think what happened was that he was dying of fear that she would turn him down, and to protect himself he made that ridiculous declaration. And I think so because we're all the same: very affectionate with our women.

RAMÓN ILLÁN BACCA: Not even the colonel, Luisa's father, wanted Gabriel Eligio. He was on a lower level, and the people cared a great deal about these levels back then because they were small places and everyone lived closer together.

LUIS ENRIQUE GARCÍA MÁRQUEZ: From the beginning, the marriage was nomadic. They married in Santa Marta, went to Riohacha for their honeymoon and settled there; they returned to Aracataca when Gabito was about to be born, and then, when I was about four months old, we went to Barranquilla; all that moving around in just two and a half years, between June 1926, when they married, and January 1929, when we went to Barranquilla. As you know, Gabito stayed in Aracataca with our grandparents.

CARMELO MARTÍNEZ: He was raised by his maternal grandparents, who didn't call him Gabrielito but Gabito, and so he was called Gabito. I call him Gabito. Not Gabo.

RAFAEL ULLOA: Besides, Colonel Márquez was a liberal and had fought in the War of a Thousand Days.* And this guy [Gabriel Eligio], who was from Sincé, was a Goth [a Conservative]. "Don't fuck with me, I don't want anything to do with that sonuvabitch Goth here. Send the girl to another town." Then, since Gabriel Eligio was a telegraph operator, he began to send Luisa messages along the telegraph wires and in the end they married because they couldn't hide.

PATRICIA CASTAÑO: In 1926, when this Señor García arrives in Aracataca as a telegraph operator and they [Luisa Santiaga's family]

---

* The War of a Thousand Days is the name given to a civil armed conflict that lasted about one thousand days, from 1989 to 1902. Colombia was a country of two political parties: the Conservative Party, close to the feudal ways of traditional landowners and the clergy, and the Liberal Party of the rising mercantile class, which believed in liberal ideas and the separation of state and religion. The conflict began when the Liberals accused the ruling Conservative Party of fraudulent elections. Up until very recently, the division between the Liberals and the Conservatives was such that people didn't marry outside party lines. Everyone knew if a family was Liberal or Conservative. García Márquez grew up in a Liberal household. His grandfather Nicolás García fought in the war. García Márquez has said that all the Liberal characters including Aureliano Buendía, the founder of Macondo, take after his beloved grandfather.

In *No One Writes to the Colonel*, the colonel is a retired veteran who awaits his government pension and was present at the signing of the Treaty of Neerlandia, the peace treaty that ended the war.

begin to oppose him, they decide to take this trip so that this gentleman will forget about her and they can introduce her to her family that had remained in Barrancas, and to her new friends. They leave Aracataca and go down toward Valledupar, they go around the Sierra. And they pass through Valledupar and through Patillal until they come to Barrancas. It's the first time that Tranquilina [Gabo's grandmother] goes back there. It was very far. It looked as if it were on the corner, but it was very far and they spent two or three months getting there. There wasn't even a highway. We're talking about 1926 or '27. They traveled by mule along horse paths at the edge of the Sierra, and they stayed there. They kept in touch through the telegraph operators. There I heard that she kept the telegrams under the fireboxes in the stove. Who would have thought of looking for them there? Imagine that beneath every firebox there was something like a metal plate. And she placed the letters beneath that firebox. She knew that messages went from telegraph office to telegraph office. Back then they were called Marconi. She knew that in the telegraph office was his message that arrived on yellow paper.

We went to Barrancas with Gerald Martin, the English biographer, and several of García Márquez's siblings. They took us to the places where there are pools in the river, where they had outings, and there are references in her letters to their going on an excursion to the river. Then yes, that trip was marvelous and the most impressive thing is that fireboxes still exist. There are fireboxes in a back corner of some houses. You still find people who cook on these fireboxes or who keep the firebox on the floor.

AIDA GARCÍA MÁRQUEZ: Gabito's arrival united the family, because when my father came from Riohacha to Aracataca, Gabito had been born and thanks to that they gave him a warm welcome;

and so everything was arranged, and since my grandparents were the godparents at the baptism, they also became compadres. My grandfather Nicolás began to call my father "my compadre Gabriel Eligio." And then it happened that the grandson was staying, staying to live in my grandparents' house. Then Luis Enrique was born and my parents went to live in Barranquilla, where Margot was born, who was always sick because she ate dirt (like Rebeca in *One Hundred Years of Solitude*). My granny went to Barranquilla to visit and she thought Margot was undernourished, so then she told my mother to let her take her, that she would give her iron and take care of her, and so Margot began living with my grandparents too. In Barranquilla my father had a successful pharmacy; my mother went back and forth between Aracataca and Barranquilla to visit my grandparents and to see Gabito and Margot.

CARMELO MARTÍNEZ: Gabriel García Martínez was dark, Indian dark, not black dark. A very imaginative man. Gabito's imagination was due to his father's imagination. He was a very interesting man. Imaginative.

RAFAEL ULLOA: His father was also half a doctor. In the family there were always not only pharmacists but herbalists and some witches. There was a man in our family, on the Paternina side, that they say prepared certain pomades and then . . . "What a powerful pomade, it works against every poison." He would spread the pomade on his hand and let a snake bite him. Of course, the snake had no poison, but he performed his pantomime in the crowded square. He lived around Sincé. Gabito uses that guy in his stories.

CARMELO MARTÍNEZ: Besides, his father was a Conservative like me.

RAFAEL ULLOA: Very few people know that his father almost wasn't really García but Martínez. They should be Martínez, not García. He should be Gabriel Martínez Márquez not Gabriel García Márquez. You know that in the past, in the small towns, there was a problem. Many children were born out of wedlock and Gabo's father was born out of wedlock, and so he took his mother's name, García. Argemira García was the daughter of a Señor García who had arrived in Sincé with Lozana Paternina. This Lozana Paternina was the sister of my grandfather, my mother's father. And so I knew Gabito. When they gave him the Nobel Prize, the story came out. But they killed it because . . . don't fuck around, he's a huge writer. How do you say he's an illegitimate child now out there?

JAIME GARCÍA MÁRQUEZ: Besides being a telegraph operator, an occupation that was so ephemeral that sometimes it seems to me it wasn't even real and that it's an invention of Gabito's, my father was a versatile man who recited verses and played the violin.

MARGARITA DE LA VEGA: When I met his father he was one of those men who sat—they do it much less now, in Cartagena, what with all the tourism—in the Plaza de Bolívar, that is, the square that's outside the Palace of the Inquisition and the city hall. The one where they have a folklore dancer now every afternoon. The locals would sit there and talk, especially at dusk and things like that. My father never sat there because he didn't have the time, he would converse at other times, because he was a doctor, and his office was nearby. And an uncle, for example, who was the wastrel of the family and didn't do anything, passed his time sitting there.

Luis Carlos López, "One-Eyed López," the great poet, would sit there and tell stories. Back then it was a kind of bohemian thing, the people who would sit there and sometimes drink rum too. García Márquez's father loved to tell stories and he sat there too.

He lived in a lot of places and failed a lot of times. He had many professions. He was a telegraph operator. In other words, he's the character in *Love in the Time of Cholera*. The one who comes to town and is the telegraph operator and falls in love with Gabo's mother, who at that moment is the daughter of the man with the best reputation in town. We're talking now about Aracataca, not Cartagena. And one who has distinguished family names. Colonel Márquez. The Márquez Iguarán is a family with a certain tradition in the town. The Iguarán comes from the Guajira region. The Márquez comes from Santa Marta and from Fundación, and then she's the prettiest girl in town. And she was very pretty. I met her when she was an old woman and you still could see how pretty she had been. He was homelier. Even as an old man you could see he was homelier. He took some long-distance courses in pharmacy and he was a pharmacist. Then he became a homeopathic practitioner.

CARMELO MARTÍNEZ: He died here in Cartagena, buying paychecks. They never pay the teachers. Other people buy their paychecks at a discount. And that's how they live.

JOSÉ ANTONIO PATERNOSTRO: If the person was going to earn a hundred, the buyer would say: "Fine, I'll give you eighty. Here it is, and you tell the company to pay me a hundred and I'll earn the difference." That's the deal. It's called buying paychecks. The buyer of the paycheck anticipates the person's salary.

That's how they used to do it. In the park. In the square of the town. Men would need the money, so they'd find someone who tells them: "I'll give it to you but let's go here." In Cartagena it was the Plaza de Bolívar, outside the city hall and the Palace of the Inquisition. Then they'd buy the paycheck, they'd go to the government paymaster's office and say: "Don't you pay them. He's signed this over to me and you pay me." It was perfectly legal. I'll give you an example: Marco Fidel Suárez, who was president of Colombia. Marco Fidel Suárez was a poor man, son of a washerwoman, and, they say, of General Obando. Marco Fidel Suárez was elected president and his mother fell gravely ill. They hadn't paid him his president's salary, and he negotiated the salary for two or three months with a moneylender who was in Bogotá back then, and who lent him the money. He instructed the paymaster of the Presidency of the Republic at that time not to pay him but to pay so-and-so.

They threw Suárez out of the presidency because the politicians of the day considered it undignified for the president to sell his paycheck.

CARMELO MARTÍNEZ: Since the world began that's existed. Of course it has, honey.

RAMÓN ILLÁN BACCA: I'll dare to say that everything about Brussels and García Márquez is based on hearsay because his family wasn't one of those that went to Brussels. He didn't have money or land. In *One Hundred Years of Solitude*, one of the Buendías goes to Brussels at the end, right? It was the fashion to go to study in

Brussels. But that was information he had heard, it didn't come from his family. My aunts had lived ten years in Brussels, and before Brussels, they were sent to Antwerp.

Tranquilina would sometimes spend the night in my aunts' house, one of those ancestral houses where there was food for everyone who came by. Huge tables. Prepared for when a compadre from Aracataca or Guacamaya would arrive because they had a farm, or were related to the overseer, or something like that. Since the people had to come on the morning train to spend the afternoon doing their work and then could catch the train the next day to go back to Aracataca. They couldn't do everything in the same day. Then they would have to spend the night in Santa Marta. Then that was their connection to my aunts' house. When García Márquez brought out *One Hundred Years of Solitude,* my aunts' response was this: "Ay, who would have thought that Tranquilina's grandson would be so intelligent?" That was the response.

2

Raised by Grandparents

In which his first eight years living with his grandparents
are explained, and what happens to him when
his grandfather, the colonel, dies

MARGOT GARCÍA MÁRQUEZ: In Aracataca we lived with my grandfather, my grandmother, Gabito, and our aunt Mama, whose real name was Francisca Mejía, the first cousin of our grandfather Nicolás Ricardo Márquez Mejía. She never married and was a person of strong character. For example, she was the one who kept the keys to the church and the keys to the cemetery. One day they came to ask for the keys to the cemetery because they had to bury a dead person. Aunt Mama went to look for the keys, but she began to do something else and forgot about them. About two hours later she remembered, but the dead person had to wait until she appeared with the blessed keys. Nobody dared to say anything to her there. Aunt Mama was also the one who baked the hosts for the church, which she did in my grandfather's house. I remember that Gabito and I were happy to eat the trimmings from the hosts.

EDUARDO MÁRCELES DACONTE: Until he was eight years old, García Márquez lived in Aracataca. Well, let me tell you that the relationship between García Márquez and my family is a long-standing one. García Márquez's grandfather was a good friend of my grandfather, Antonio Daconte. The colonel would go to my grandfather's store, in what was called the Four Corners, the important part of Aracataca. They would sit in a little room my grandfather had to the side of his store. He wasn't the one doing the selling in the store. That grandfather was the colonel waiting for his pension that never arrived. He was the colonel who took part in the Thousand-Day War. This was at the beginning of the century and so he had been promoted to colonel. He often visited my grandfather and drank black coffee, and they exchanged ideas there and talked about the things that were happening in the world, in the country. My grandfather had a regular get-together. Three or four thermoses, filled with black coffee, some cups and sugar and everything, and people came and visited him and sat in the chairs he had there. So one of these people was García Márquez's grandfather. Sometimes García Márquez's grandfather brought his grandson to my grandfather's.

MARGOT GARCÍA MÁRQUEZ: Ah! Our grandfather was happy with us. They say he laughed a lot over this story about Gabito, which they told me afterward. When he was very little he was sitting in the doorway of the house to watch the soldiers march past on their way to the banana plantations. Once he came running in, very excited, and he said to our grandfather: "Papa Lelo! Papa Lelo! The bolgers went by" (he meant soldiers, but he still didn't speak very well). "Well, well, my boy, and what did they say to you?" Grandfather asked him. 'Hiya, cute little Gabi." A liar since he was born.

IMPERIA DACONTE: He was adorable. Little, good-looking. We were more or less the same age. He was the only boy who lived with the colonel. Our courtyard was very big. Since the house is so big, the part of the yard in the next street was García Márquez's courtyard. We would go to his house very often for guavas; he had an immense yard of fruit trees. His grandmother, old Tranquilina, would give us lots of fruit, guavas and everything.

MARGOT GARCÍA MÁRQUEZ: Until Gabito was born, Grandfather Nicolás passed for a very serious, very reserved man, and so my mother treated him with a great deal of respect and even with some distance. But as soon as his grandson was born he melted, he changed. His seriousness went to the devil. He became loving, affectionate, he played with us, sat us on his knee, got down on all fours so we could ride him, as if he were a donkey. His friends protested: "How can you do something like that, Nicolás Márquez: look how you've ended up!" Grandfather loved Gabito so much that he decided to celebrate his birthday every month. A party every month to celebrate him. He invited his friends to toast Gabito's "birthmonth." He brought us animals as presents; we had parrots, macaws, troupials, there was even a sloth in the courtyard, which was planted with fruit trees. The sloth lived hanging from the jackfruit tree, which was as tall as a palm, and the animal climbed to the top and began to throw down fruits, which were like custard apples. Grandmother parboiled them and everybody came by to eat. They tasted like potatoes.

EDUARDO MÁRCELES DACONTE: Don't forget that his parents had twelve children.

MARGOT GARCÍA MÁRQUEZ: Every day Grandfather took us to visit my mother. This is what we did: in the afternoon, Aunt

Mama changed our clothes, our shoes, and made us look good. I remember that Grandmother would say: "Now, Nicolasito, take them so their mother can see them." And our grandfather took Gabito and me, each of us holding one of his hands, for a little turn (as our grandfather said), and when we passed my mother's house, he would stop for a while, caressing Luis Enrique and Aida, picking up Ligia and Gustavo (the family kept growing), talked about something or other with my father, and then continued the little turn.

I remember that Gabito and I always arrived nice and clean, recently combed (we always wore shoes and socks, they never allowed us to go barefooted in case worms crawled in, in case animals bit us, in case something stuck to us), and we found those crazy siblings, especially Luis Enrique and Aida, as mischievous, disobedient, quarrelsome as they were, out roaming the streets all day.

IMPERIA DACONTE: The colonel went every night to visit my father. Since he had a shop and all, there was a lot of activity in that house. They'd put out a tray with lots of little cups of black coffee. And all Father's friends would go there at night to drink coffee. I don't know what they talked about because I was very little. García Márquez was there, very small, and so were we.

EDUARDO MÁRCELES DACONTE: My grandfather, Antonio Daconte, when he came to Aracataca from Italy, must have been very good-looking. He had five wives, just imagine, he even married two sisters. That is, first one, then he divorced and married the other one. That's why I'm explaining these things to you, so you can see where they come from, often even things Gabo forgot about because this would have been interesting. My grandfather came and married María Calle first and with her he had five sons. Then he divorced María Calle and married Manuela, who's my grandmother and was younger. The two sisters never talked to each other again. If one saw the other coming down the street, she crossed to the other side. But never again, until they died, they never spoke again . . . With María he had five sons. Galileo, Amadeo, Antonio, Pedro, Rafael. And with my grandmother Manuela he had five daughters.

His daughters were Elena, Yolanda, María, Imperia. Imperia is my mother . . . Elena is Nena Daconte, the name of the character in the story "The Trail of Your Blood in the Snow." She's my mother's sister. She liked the idea that he used her name, but she also didn't make a big deal about it.

MARGOT GARCÍA MÁRQUEZ: Well . . . but I'll go on with the story of the little turn, which continued from my mother's house down to the Turks' corner, which was the place where the politicians met, and Grandfather spent some more time talking there. Gabito didn't leave him, he was always listening to what they were talking about; in the meantime, I began to look in the windows of the Turks' grocery stores. There were four corners and I went from one to the other looking in windows. Since then I have the habit of looking in store windows. Even today it fascinates me to walk and look in store windows.

EDUARDO MÁRCELES DACONTE: Back then my grandfather, as I was telling you, had a very big, very pretty house on the corner, and it was like the meeting place for people in Aracataca. My grandfather also imported billiards and what they called *buchácara*, or pool. The wooden house is still there. I hope they never knock it down. In the courtyard, which was where they showed movies, they now have costume parties, bring in an orchestra, and rent it out for carnival dances. One of the columns that Gabo wrote in *El Espectador* he dedicated to my grandfather. There he talks about how he went to visit my grandfather and went over to the large water jar and tried to see, to take out the water and see where the elves were. The jars are made of clay and are used to keep water cool and often they have something like a filter over them. They keep them anywhere. They have glasses and the dipper to take out the water and the water jar on a wooden base. The stand. Aha. They came and poured in the water. I remember that back then there was no aqueduct in Aracataca, what we had were water sellers, they were the ones who brought in water on burros, they got it in the ditch (there was no pollution back then) and took the water coming directly from the river. There was no danger at all. By then there was an aqueduct, but for a long time I remember that you bought two cans, three cans of water. "Give me four cans of water." The cans were those cans of lard where they attached a wooden crosspiece in the middle with nails. The story is that he remembered that when he was little they had told him that little people lived at the bottom of all the water jars. So he would go and try to get them out. He would go put his glass deep in the jug trying to find the elves. It has a name that escapes me for the moment, but he wrote a very good column about this subject. And I remember that my grandfather's water jar was really immense, and all the cousins would go running there to get water. A delicious, cool water. A water that tasted of I don't know what, I've never had that taste of water again, it was mossy, it tasted of moss, of dampness, I don't know. Because there's water that's metallic in a way . . .

MARGOT GARCÍA MÁRQUEZ: The little turn ended at bedtime and we went home to go to bed. Then, yes, my grandmother, who had been busy all day with household matters, put me in the bed, taught me to pray, sang to me, and told me stories until I fell asleep.

EDUARDO MÁRCELES DACONTE: There was no electricity in Aracataca. I was very small and I remember that people used candles and kerosene lamps that have a little thing on top. They're beautiful. People used those lamps a lot. I remember that I walked down the street holding a lamp. In that darkness people get together and there's no television. There's always someone who tells the little kids mystery stories, horror stories, scary stories. I remember then that I was panicked when it was time to go to sleep in my bed after the stories that an uncle would tell sometimes, and sometimes my father, my mother, somebody, an older cousin. Or sometimes you'd go to the farms and the overseer always had his stories and he'd tell you those stories, those scary stories. All that. A lot of that. That's why I say that Gabo's memory is important because he remembered many of the things he had been told. Things many people don't remember. He has the memory of an elephant.

IMPERIA DACONTE: They sent him to the Fergusson's Montessori, they lived close by.

EDUARDO MÁRCELES DACONTE: There was a teacher he had who was terrific. They've done a lot of interviews in that town because Gabo said he had learned a great deal with her. I also believe that Gabito saw his first film thanks to my grandfather. The only one who had a movie theater was my grandfather. He had his own electricity generator, an old thing, out back, so you wouldn't hear the noise. Later they set one up for the whole town.

IMPERIA DACONTE: The colonel was godfather to María, my sister. And María would say: "Papi, my godfather's house has been sad since he died." "That's how it will stay," my father would say. I was very little when he died. The colonel died first. His wife stayed because she had a lot of family.

EDUARDO MÁRCELES DACONTE: Gabito lived in Aracataca until he was eight. When his grandfather dies, he goes to Sucre because his father had been transferred there.

MARGOT GARCÍA MÁRQUEZ: I remember the funeral very well because I cried the whole blessed day, nothing could console me. Gabito wasn't with us because he had gone with my father and Luis Enrique to Sincé on another of the adventures that my father would undertake. Gabito returned to Aracataca several months after the death of Papá Lelo and perhaps for that reason I don't recall his reaction; it surely had to be deep sadness because they loved each other very much, they were inseparable. The two of us continued living a little while longer with my grandmother, Aunt Mama and Aunt Pa, whose name was Elvira Carrillo and who was the illegitimate daughter of my grandfather Nicolás, that is, my mother's half sister. Aunt Pa was a very good woman, she took care of my grandmother until she died with total dedication, as if she had been her own daughter.

We lived in my grandmother's house until the money began to run out and she had to live on what my uncle Juanito sent her; then they decided that Gabito and I would stay in our father's house, in Sucre. The family had moved there.

MARGARITA DE LA VEGA: For the first time he lives with his parents, who by now are in a better financial situation. By now his sister had been born, the one who later became a nun.

CARMELO MARTÍNEZ: Sucre was a very important town, but by the 1940s floods had caused a great deal of damage. It was a town with seven or eight thousand inhabitants. To get to Sucre you have to go to Magangué. In Magangué you take a boat with an outboard motor and go to Sucre. It depends, in a boat with two outboard motors of 100 or 150 horsepower each you get there in forty-five minutes.

Gabito lived in Sucre until he went to Barranquilla. Well, he was studying at the San José Academy, in Barranquilla, with the Jesuits. I met him in Sucre around 1940 (we were both thirteen) because his house, where his father, Dr. García, lived, was across from mine.

JUANCHO JINETE: As a boy he studied here in Barranquilla, at the Colegio San José.

MARGOT GARCÍA MÁRQUEZ: That's why when they sent Gabito to study for his diploma at the San José, in Barranquilla, I felt abandoned. I had always been very close to him, he was so loving, we seemed like twins. He finished primary school in Sucre, and when he was eleven or twelve, barely three months after we went to live in my parents' house, he went to Barranquilla and I was left all alone. The shock was tremendous. The calm and order I was used to disappeared, but what I missed most was my affection for my grandparents; I couldn't get close to my mother because she had no time, bringing up so many kids, and my father, even less so. He always seemed distant to me, so much so that all my brothers and sisters called him "*tú*" except for me; I called him "*usted.*"

CARMELO MARTÍNEZ: He always had a writer's calling because at the Colegio San José, in Barranquilla, he put out a little paper. I mean he basically was a writer, a journalist. He didn't talk about novels. That came later.

MARGOT GARCÍA MÁRQUEZ: He was a great student, he won prizes, medals for excellence, the best at the academy. Back then, the prizes they gave to the best students were little books about the Mass because, of course, it was a Jesuit academy; well, Gabito sent me the book they had given him, with a dedication to me; he sent me illustrated cards, medals, rosaries, everything they gave him he would send to me. I also wrote to him in Barranquilla, to the house of Uncle Eliécer García, the brother of our grandmother Argemira (my father's mother), where he was living. Ay! How happy I was when Gabito came home for vacation. Again the two of us were very close, I tried to get the best for him, I fixed him his little slices of fried plantains that he liked so much.

García Márquez at thirteen years old.

QUIQUE SCOPELL: I met him with Ricardo González Ripoll, my cousin, because they left here to study in Zipaquirá. We went up the Magdalena River in boats back when you had to go to Bogotá by boat and all that.

The three of us traveled by boat. I began to study in Bogotá, but I was in love and love was stronger than my studies, and since then I've been a drunkard all my life, that was when I began to drink rum. And then as a punishment they sent me to study in the United States.

FERNANDO RESTREPO: Gabo says that the National Academy of Zipaquirá was where he discovered his passion for literature and the novel, stimulated by a teacher who started him reading. I once asked him: "Hey, and how did you ever end up in Zipaquirá?" Then he tells me that his scholarship was for an academy in Bogotá but there was no more room and that finally they found him a place in the academy in Zipaquirá, and so he went there. I didn't know the school except that when he came to spend a weekend at my finca there, we passed by the school, and he looked at it and pointed out where he had been. It's an official academy that had a lot of boarders.

Only males. That is, it wasn't an important school. It wasn't known outside of local boundaries.

CARMELO MARTÍNEZ: He went to Zipaquirá to finish his baccalaureate, and then he went to law school.

MARGARITA DE LA VEGA: When they gave him the Nobel, his father gave an interview to the *Diario de la Costa* and mentioned all the towns where he had lived, saying that Gabo hadn't invented anything. That the story of Remedios, of course, was

Señora So-and-so, whose daughter or granddaughter had run away with some guy . . . She said that in fact the sheets had carried her away when she was hanging out the clothes, and she had disappeared. Divine. I kept that interview for a long time. Back then, remember, it was all newspaper clippings. In that interview, he said that the priests at San José had said that Gabo was schizophrenic and that he had cured him with some homeopathic drops. I imagine Gabo had an unusual imagination and had matured very quickly because he had grown up only with old people. And that happens when children grow up alone with old people or are very close to old people. He was like that back then.

JAIME ABELLO BANFI: Gabo was a clairvoyant. Or is a clairvoyant, excuse me. I mean, at that time he was clairvoyant in terms of his own culture. That is, a man very much of the Colombian Caribbean, who in one of his earliest articles is already talking about the problems of Colombian literature. He's a kid of twenty and he's already passing judgment on the Colombian novel. Incredible.

He talked about *vallenato* music when nobody paid any attention to the *vallenato*. He talked about a thousand things.

The thing is that, first of all, he's a genius. Don't be deceived. He has the intelligence of a genius. He's super-perceptive. And he also has the ability to get ahead of events. With a sixth sense. So he's a genius beyond any doubt. Second, he read a great deal from a very early age, so much so that they were afraid he'd lose his mind when he was young, he read so much. And third, his context. That context that's so well told in his family's memory, with all that traveling. That singular family. That condition of a kind of intermediate class. A person who had access to many people. That is, in financial terms they were poor but with access to all kinds. Trips through the entire region and the things with his grandfather. All of that is very interesting. All of that influenced his very special personality.

RAFAEL ULLOA: His mother always said that his novels were in code and she had the key. She would read the book and say: "This man he mentions here is So-and-so in Aracataca."

3

The Coast Gets Ready to Speak

*In which Gabito goes to Bogotá to study law and because of the Violence
returns to the coast and finds a job as a journalist*

CARMELO MARTÍNEZ: When I arrived in Bogotá in 1948, he was
in his second year of law school.

MIGUEL FALQUEZ-CERTAIN: At that time they publish his first
two stories in the literary supplement of *El Espectador*. The intellectuals in the capital begin to follow his progress.

CARMELO MARTÍNEZ: Then came what is known as the *Bogotazo*,*
the mass riots in Bogotá after the assassination of Luis Carlos Gaitán,
so he came to Cartagena and started working at *El Universal*.

NEREO LÓPEZ: I had to deal with the problem of the assassination
of Gaitán in Barrancabermeja. That murder was what started the
period of La Violencia when Liberals and Conservatives started
killing each other. I was the general manager of Cine Colombia
in Barrancabermeja. I managed not only the base theater but also

---

* The *Bogotazo* or *Gaitanazo* refers to the riots that followed the assassination of Liberal leader and presidential candidate Jorge Eliécer Gaitán on April 9, 1948. The riots left much
of downtown Bogotá destroyed. García Márquez writes in his memoirs that his typewriter
burnt down and he decided to take a plane to Cartagena where things were less turbulent.
The *Bogotazo* is also seen as the ignition of a period known as the Violence (La Violencia)
a bloody war between the Liberals and the Conservatives throughout the country. It ended
with a national pact between the two parties in 1958.

the theaters in nearby towns. And I'm talking now about 1948. Gaitán was assassinated April 9, 1948, and I was there until '52. That was where I contacted the people at *El Espectador* and that's how I arrived in Barranquilla as the graphic correspondent for *El Espectador*.

I lived right in the theater and at that time, after the death of Gaitán, came the Violence—Colombia still hasn't come out of that—which was the assault on the Liberals by the Conservatives. Luis Carlos Gaitán was the presidential candidate for the Liberals. People called the Conservatives "the *chulavitas*" [the boys from the hamlet of Chulavita] and in turn the Conservatives called the Liberals "*cachiporros*" [blackjacks]. I remember once a drunk, a Liberal, said to me: "I don't care that they call us *cachiporros*. What bothers me is the other name." "But what's the problem with the other name? What is it?" I asked him. "*Cachiporro* sonuvabitch." *Cachiporro* didn't bother him.

It was an absolute violence. I have two anecdotes about that. One is how at eleven at night—and there it was super late—some people came to the theater, knocked on the iron gates, and passed their revolvers over each iron bar, making the most grating ominous sound. "Nereo, we want you to come with us and take some photos." They were having an event glorifying a portrait of Laureano Gómez, the head of the Conservative Party at the time. I looked out and looked at them and said: "No way, man, it's very late." "Come on, man, come with us nicely." But banging his revolver nicely. So then, "nicely," in quotation marks, so I went to photograph the glorification event at the Hotel Pipatón. There the booze made the rounds, revolvers made the rounds. In short, a political orgy.

The abuse of power was so widespread that every government

employee wanted to go into the theater free of charge. Everybody, from the janitor at a jail to the police, and I opposed it and said no. What happened? They threatened me. And at that time they didn't kill you but they did beat you, they would put you in a dark room and fuck you up by beating you, and people came out of that sick or dead. They didn't kill you, but they turned you into nothing. They tortured you with blows. They didn't manage to get hold of me, though. I'm not much of a believer, but God is very great. It turned out that the army commandant, who was a religious fanatic, also loved photographs. When it was 100 degrees he would go to Mass wearing all his medals and his dress uniform, and he was the only one, and the priests said a Mass just for him. And I would develop his rolls of film. Colonel Acosta was his name, and I had access to him. If I had a problem, I'd come in and tell him and he solved the problem. Nobody messed with me anymore, but even so, the matter reached a point that although the business at the time was worth a million pesos, I sold it for 200,000 just to get out of Barrancabermeja. I came to New York to present my photography thesis, and from here I went to Baranquilla as a correspondent in '52.

MARGARITA DE LA VEGA: Gabo arrives in Cartagena after the Bogotazo. Bogotá was paralyzed, and he used that to get out of the commitment he had made to his father to study law, because at that time he was still struggling, and struggling a lot, in his father's shadow.

MARGOT GARCÍA MÁRQUEZ: We came to Cartagena in 1951 for several reasons: because Sucre began to decline, to lose its old prosperity, and my father's situation became tight and by then we were five students studying outside the home; and because Gabito said that only if we came there would he continue to study at the University of Cartagena. He didn't need much more to graduate as a lawyer, I think one more year.

MARGARITA DE LA VEGA: He arrives in Cartagena and enrolls in the Faculty of Law at Cartagena. Remember that Cartagena has a law school at the university. He's alone and had already written a little in Bogotá. They had published two or three things in *El Espectador*. Fiction.

In Cartagena we didn't feel the Violence. I arrived in Bogotá when Gabo arrived in Cartagena, more or less, and I discovered that the Violence did exist. That people were talking about it in the newspapers. In Cartagena it didn't exist. I remember April 9 because my uncle (actually, I have a lot of them) was the governor of the Department of Bolívar at the time. I remember that we went to my grandmother's house and my father went there and not to my house to eat, as he did every day, because my grandmother was distraught and frightened: she knew what had happened in Bogotá, that the city had been burned and Gaitán killed. That much was known but they were frightened that what was happening in Barranquilla would happen there, that people would go out and burn something in the Plaza de San Nicolás, on the Paseo Bolívar. And in Cartagena nothing happened. My uncle arrived late; instead of coming at seven in the evening he didn't come until eight thirty. And we didn't eat until he arrived because that was another of our families' customs.

HÉCTOR ROJAS HERAZO: Gabriel was already famous in the newspaper world. They had already written articles about him in *El Espectador* [because of his short stories]. Important ones. Zalamea Borda, the cousin of the other Zalamea Borda, wrote a beautiful piece about him. Gabriel must have been nineteen when this happened.

In fact nobody introduced us when he started to work at *El Universal* but we met and began to be friends. Of course, Maestro Zabala* played a part in this. Damn! He was another extraordinary character. Maestro Zabala. How I cried when he died. He was a very affectionate man . . . Well, the maestro was a great friend. An extraordinary person. And he was an individual who could smell out intelligence. When he smelled an intelligent person, whoever he was . . . And, of course, Gabo arrived. That's when they became linked . . .

MARGARITA DE LA VEGA: Clemente Zabala was the managing editor at *El Universal*. At the newspapers there was a managing director, who ran the operation, and another one who edited the articles. Another one took care of the political thing. There was an editing room and people met there. It wasn't the solitary work it is now. All the papers in Colombia were born as party papers. *El Universal* was Liberal and the *Diario de la Costa* was Conservative. When Gabo arrived it must have already belonged to the Escallón Villa family. People went broke owning newspapers. Now *El Universal* is the only one. Nothing has replaced the *Diario de la Costa*.

They had the same interests, so the ones who talked and the ones who didn't talk got together there. That's what you were

---

* Clemente Manuel Zabala was the editor of *El Universal* who hired García Márquez when he arrived in Cartagena, escaping law school and the Bogotazo. In his memoir, García Márquez remembers him as "peaceful," "confidential," "a wise man in the penumbra." He appears in a García Márquez story as Maestro Zabala and has a cameo as the reporter's editor in *Of Love and Other Demons*.

looking for. At that moment, they were the young intellectuals, the ones who wrote and all that. Remember that newspapers were also cultural instruments, and remember how important the literary supplements were. That's extremely important. They published poetry, did interviews, but they also published international figures. In a sense some of those were stolen because I'm not sure they were paying for the rights to what was published in Argentina, in Mexico, in the United States, in France, or in Italy. Those people were from different social backgrounds, middle class, upper class, even the *pueblo*, and nobody really knew how it was that everyone met on the same plane. Because they all had intellectual interests in literature, poetry, the theater; some more interested in some things than in others. And they met at the papers but also in the cafés, the squares . . . they were part of those conversations, many of them might have known El Tuerto López or others, you understand? They told stories and talked and conversed and read. Because there was a great love of reading. They lent one another books, but there was also a library, there was also a university. Being a humanist was thought to be an important thing. Humanist in the way of the Greek classics. Gustavo Ibarra Merlano would recite for you in Greek and in Latin.

HÉCTOR ROJAS HERAZO: Gabo was a very loved person. And he was always around the persons he loved. He talked about them, he used his column to speak in the best way he could about the things and people that interested him. That began to shake up Colombian journalism. All these things were being done at *El Universal* because *El Universal* was such a terrific place. They just had the lower part of a two-story building. It was the lower part and that's where the bubbling began . . .

The good thing is that we would talk about everything. Something that we always managed to talk about with him was the importance of Latin American letters. Because of something very simple: the different sectors that imposed their way of writing novels; that is, that had said what they had to say. English novelists, French novelists, Russian novelists . . . Afterward came the Faulkner thing, which was this thing . . . the narrative impulse in the United States. Then we said: "What the world needs now is what Latin America is going to say. Let's see." And we began to talk about Latin American things—that this was like this and that was like that—to see how we could achieve the most direct knowledge possible of the reality we were living and suffering. What happens is something: uncontrolled influence. We, the people who were being influenced at that moment—we had no control. We were influenced by the movies, by one thing and by another. Everything. A hunger for knowledge. But the fact is that each human being has to live ignorance, enjoy it, and transform it into creativity. It's like love. It always has to be suffered and admired and enjoyed individually.

Back then one really walked in a windstorm of influences of all kinds. Any great novelist, let's say Faulkner, Dostoyevsky, Tolstoy. The great ones. The great French novelist Balzac, who wrote close to a hundred books. I always kept in mind a thought of Tolstoy, the great Russian novelist. It says: "Look carefully at your village and you'll be universal." Then we kept that in mind. The village, the village, the village. Don't go beyond that.

MARGARITA DE LA VEGA: Rojas Herazo always had that poetic and metaphorical style of speaking. A little bit on the moon, let's say, very little in reality.

HÉCTOR ROJAS HERAZO: We talked about everything. The famous poet they murdered, García Lorca. About everything. Then we were all on the same track . . . Now *El Universal* in Cartagena is very good and has an imposing building, all those things. Now it's a different thing. But back then a great reporter, Gabriel "Gabo" Bazo, told us: "When you don't want anyone to know about a bad thing, publish it on the front page of a newspaper." The paper began as a thing worked on with much love because a number of us who had a desire to get somewhere were working on it . . .

MARGARITA DE LA VEGA: The poetry reunions in Cartagena were important, and the ones about film. Gabo's thing with the movies might come from the film clubs there. My father founded the one in Cartagena.

HÉCTOR ROJAS HERAZO: Besides, we people from the coast had a great advantage. We had no kind of vanity because we didn't have [a history of cultural greatness] . . . That is to say, the guards were silent until that moment. We'd had important people and achievements, but not on a grand scale. Then I remember one day, when I was in Cali, that I was interviewing the maestro [Pedro Nel Gómez], the painter from Antioquia who was very notable and so forth. As I was leaving, I began to tell him what we aspired to because he was a very pleasant, very affectionate man. And then he said to me: "Well, and what's going on with the coast that it hasn't produced anything until now?" And I: "Don't worry, maestro. We, the people from the coast, are now listening to the sound of the sea. When we are ready, let us stand up and speak and then you'll see what will happen."

MARGOT GARCÍA MÁRQUEZ: My father, as long as Gabito finished law school, went along, but what Gabito wanted was to write, and soon he told my father that he couldn't stand studying the law anymore; he left his studies and went to work at *El Universal*. At that time he lived in the house with us; I remember hearing him every night, *tack tack tack*, on the typewriter.

HÉCTOR ROJAS HERAZO: At least Gabo got somewhere . . . I knew he was going to make a difference. Yes, I always assumed he was going to be big but not colossal. There was already universal attention to what Latin America was writing. Then he arrived in time to catch the bus and he took off.

A Spanish writer, poet, and narrator came to Colombia and Gabriel was already working at *El Universal*. Then Maestro Zabala, Ibarra Merlano, and I went to hear him. Maestro Zabala invited us. He tells us: "Come on, we have to go there to meet this man." He was a famous poet and writer. One of the most important there in Spain at that time. He was a scholar of Luis de Góngora, the great poet of the singular period in Spain, and then we went to hear him. He talked and talked and talked. After his talk, when we were about to go, Maestro Zabala says: "No, no, no. We have to go and meet this gentleman. He's an important man who's come here and it's worth it." So we went. He's a charming person and asked us to bring him a sample of what we were doing in literature because he was delighted with us. He came with his wife. The writer I'm talking about is Dámaso Alonso, who was famous. Then the maestro, Gabo, and I decided to do this. So we decided not to take him anything of ours but for Gabo to represent us, though he was much younger, but he was already somewhat known. The maestro took Gabo's thing and then, much later, in

Spain, when the maestro was talking to this gentleman Dámaso Alonso, he said to him: "Maestro, do you know . . ." (They had already given Gabo the Nobel.) "Do you know the boy we introduced to you? He was Gabriel García Márquez." "What? Man, I remember!"

García Márquez surrounded by friends.

4

First and Last Friends

In which he arrives in Barranquilla and meets the "wise Catalonian" and the "four arguers" he immortalizes in the final chapter of One Hundred Years of Solitude *as "the last and first friends he ever had in his life"*

QUIQUE SCOPELL: He comes to live in Barranquilla when Alfonso Fuenmayor hired him at *El Heraldo*.

SANTIAGO MUTIS: When Gabo first goes to find work in Barranquilla, Alfonso says to him as a test: "Well, write tomorrow's editorial for me." Then he sits him down at his desk. Alfonso reads it and says: "Damn, this is very good!" And then he thinks: "This guy must have prepared the editorial ahead of time." Then he tells him: "Look, this is very good, but write me the one for the day after tomorrow." Gabo writes the one for the day after tomorrow. Then he takes it and goes to the editorial office and says: "You have to hire the boy." "Alfonso, we don't have the dough. There's no money for anybody," they tell him. "You have to do it," he insists. "We can't," they reply. "Then my next two-week salary check will be split in two. One for him, one for me," answered Alfonso. I mean, that was the quality of those people.

HÉCTOR ROJAS HERAZO: Cartagena and Barranquilla are very close, but they are different and it seems to me that he got on very well with that group in Barranquilla. They offered him a job. Because *El Heraldo* was there, which was more functional than *El Universal* from a financial point of view. It must have been that, don't you think?

MARGARITA DE LA VEGA: Cartagena is a very small provincial city that lives a great deal on its past glory. Even if it's not as traditional as they say. But there's no doubt that the contrast between Cartagena and Barranquilla was that Barranquilla was founded by people who didn't get ahead in Cartagena because no path was open to them. Many people from Cartagena went to Barranquilla because they were more dynamic, more modern. They had new ideas, and Barranquilla welcomed every immigrant with open arms. Jews, Turks, Russians, whatever.

JAIME ABELLO BANFI: García Márquez called me Barranquilloso, not Barranquillero. It's beyond demonym. It's like a state of mind and reminds me of the idea of dandyism. The Barranquilloso is a dandy but also something like a conqueror of the world.

MARGARITA DE LA VEGA: Cartagena had a series of immigrants and things went very well for some, and there are different kinds: Frenchmen, a few Jews; and there was no difference, it wasn't that people treated them badly, there weren't enough of them to form a colony. Then, new arrivals went directly to Barranquilla because Cartagena lost its port when they opened the Dique Canal and Bocas de Ceniza in Barranquilla. They tried to build a few projects that almost closed the bay of Cartagena because of the dredging and things like that.

JAIME ABELLO BANFI: Everybody in Barranquilla knew who

that reporter for *El Heraldo* was; that was the Barranquilla that García Márquez enjoyed. I remember that the poet Meira del Mar told me Gabo was famous when he was working at *El Heraldo*. And this man saw Barranquilla as a kind of metropolis. It was the metropolis of the Caribbean. A thriving city. People from other areas of the country lived there, it was the anchor city of the Caribbean. While Cartagena was colonial, historic, and so forth, Barranquilla was the modern city. The city with broad avenues, housing developments, public services, and an independent attitude among the people. The Barranquillero doesn't ask permission. A Barranquilloso doesn't ask permission. A Barranquilloso does whatever he has to do and Gabo fit right in . . . That's why he refers so often to the spirit of the Barranquilleros.

HÉCTOR ROJAS HERAZO: The first time I went to the Superior Normal School of Barranquilla, which had just opened and was very beautiful, I was sixteen years old. It was near the soccer stadium. When I went, I began to see things I didn't know about, like traffic lights turning off and on so the cars could go. I thought it was a really big city. I came from a tiny village, understand, and then I went there. And I also came from Cartagena, which was quieter. Cartagena didn't have wide streets, big department stores, cafés. Back then I thought Barranquilla was beautiful. My first impression. And the people really nice. Besides, the Barranquillero isn't fazed by anything. After the Nobel, this is how they greet Gabriel: "Hey, Mr. Prize?" as if it was impressive but maybe not so important. As I said one day: "There's no prestige here except in living." So that's something that takes tenacity away from people. No need to do more than just live. Barranquilleros are very good friends. Damn! Good friends. Great friends.

GERALD MARTIN: When I was talking to Cartageneros and Barranquilleros, the Cartageneros felt that Gabo hadn't given them enough credit, but it's also true that, with all the importance that Cartagena had in his formation, he wasn't as comfortable in Cartagena in the forties and fifties as he would be in Barranquilla.

JUANCHO JINETE: He began to show up here in '52. He came from Cartagena. I can tell you where he lived. He had no family here, and he lived in the Barrio Abajo, in a room. In Campana, I think it is, and he lived in a little house. Alfonso took me there several times. He had a room there and next to it was something called El Tokio. A shop that sold the most awful oatmeal.

He paid for room and board, because what they paid him I think was two pesos for each column. What happens is that when he worked at *El Heraldo* sometimes he did all the columns; and at *El Heraldo*, from the second or third floor they could look out and there was a brothel across from them. They would see a lady at the window taking care of her clients. And the poor old woman opened the window because it was so hot, and they got it into their heads to go to the brothel and see who she was. And since he liked writing those things, that's the story, then, of when he moved to the Skyscraper to live with those ladies . . .

QUIQUE SCOPELL: Yes, but then he moved over there near the Ley store, which is at Cuartel and 36th.

JUANCHO JINETE: Oh, of course. It had some stairs . . . *El Heraldo* paid fifteen pesos a month. It's what they paid. It was also the currency circulating at that time, but it wasn't a salary you could live on decently; Alfonso couldn't live decently then. And Gabito was less than Alfonso at *El Heraldo*, so he must have earned twelve pesos a month.

QUIQUE SCOPELL: We were all broke. Álvaro Cepeda had money because he inherited the money when his father died. He was born with money. And I lived well because my father supported me and I was a pauper during secondary school. We were the only ones that had some dough there, because Alfonso was broke. Germán Vargas, broke. Gabito, broke. Alejandro wasn't here.

JUANCHO JINETE: He was in Albany.

QUIQUE SCOPELL: Is that tape recorder on or off? Leave it on! Then Alfonso had the idea of starting a newspaper to support himself. It was called *Crónica*, a tabloid. You can get the issues at *El Heraldo*. They must be in the files there because Alfonso printed them at *El Heraldo* to earn a few more pesos. Even when the masthead of that paper said "Executive Manager: Julio Mario Santo Domingo,"* Julio never

---

* Julio Mario Santo Domingo, born in Barranquilla in 1923, was Colombia's first jet-setting billionaire. His father, Don Mario Santo Domingo, built what is today one of the world's largest brewery fortunes, still in the hands of Julio Mario's immediate family.

When García Márquez arrived in Barranquilla penniless and started befriending the local bohemians, Julio Mario was the rich dandy of the group living abroad. When in Barranquilla for short visits, he enjoyed hanging out with his buddy Álvaro Cepeda Samudio, who was part of the group of journalists, painters, and wannabe writers like García Márquez. Thanks to Santo Domingo's friendship with Cepeda, the group had nice access to the coffers of his family's brewery when Cepeda became the head of public relations for Cervecería Águila (Águila Brewery). Julio Mario Santo Domingo, in many ways, may be the benefactor of the posse that became the "arguers" García Márquez names in *One Hundred Years of Solitude* and calls "the first and last friends that he ever had in his life."

They were: Alfonso Fuenmayor, the eldest of the group, a journalist and columnist; Álvaro Cepeda Samudio, the charismatic playboy with a huge library and literary sensibilities; and Germán Vargas, the quiet one of the set, a radio commentator and literary critic. Gabo doesn't mention an important member of the group: Alejandro Obregón, the eccentric painter who liked to pick a bar fight and whose family, like Santo Domingo's, was part of the city's elite. The group first appears as "the pranksters of La Cueva" in *Big Mama's Funeral*.

wrote a goddamn article. As they say, the paper can stand anything. All he can do is multiply by eight. He knows how to multiply because he knows how to make money. He knows how to do that. Make money. But I don't think he knows how to write. Back then our paper was: a guy named Álvaro Cepeda; a guy named Alfonso Fuenmayor, who was the editor; Germán Vargas, who's better educated than any of them; Gabito. Álvaro translated an American story, Germán Vargas wrote something for it. A guy named Alejandro Obregón did the illustrations and a guy named Figurita Orlando Rivera did the smaller ones. Aha! What a list! Nowadays in Colombia, with those five guys, you'd be publishing *Cromos* or *Semana*. And I took the photographs. I'm a photographer, and then I'm a drunkard. I was raised with photographs. Then a guy named Gabito wrote a column that was called "The Giraffe." Nobody read the goddamn column in that thing. Afterward they said the thing was genius . . . Because after Gabito became a Nobel laureate, they discovered all his virtues: before that, he was nothing but an asshole. And we'd go out on Saturdays to sell *Crónica*. And do you know what we did to sell that thing? We traded it for beer, because the store guy said to us: "Oh, man, that thing won't sell." A real disappointment. Two thousand copies were printed and 1,990 were left over. They gave away 1,990 copies. They were printed at *El Heraldo*. And Gabito was the only one Alfonso paid for the losses. Alfonso paid Gabito two pesos a week to put together that magazine.

Afterward they invented something that was the thing that sold the paper most. It was a weekly magazine. What sold most was their switching from literature to soccer, because at that time those Argentine soccer players who came got all the girls in Barranquilla. They came to play for the two teams, Junior and the Sporting, but all the ones who came to the Sporting were for export. Some good-looking sonsofbitches. Italian Argentines, you know that those Argentines . . .

JUANCHO JINETE: Yes, they were handsome.

QUIQUE SCOPELL: Alfonso called me the Philosopher. He would say to me: "And you, why don't you write a book?" Because I don't know. What I know is how to talk shit. I don't know how to write. Talking, yes, but I don't know how to write. I don't even know how to write the Our Father. Ask me to write the Our Father and you'll see . . . "Our Father . . ." that's as far as I get. And Alfonso said to me: "Don't fuck around, Philosopher, why don't you write yourself a novel?" No, man, don't be a faggot. I don't have the head to write a novel. To talk shit, yes.

MIGUEL FALQUEZ-CERTAIN: And it's supposed that in those meetings, those get-togethers in the 1950s, when García Márquez arrives in Barranquilla after having studied I think a year of law in Cartagena and having worked at *El Universal*, he met mainly Alfonso Fuenmayor and Germán Vargas, the literary types. They would meet in a bookstore presided over by the Catalan wise man Don Ramón Vinyes, who spoke Spanish and was Catalan. He spoke Catalan, he had books in Catalan, he read English, and he also translated I think from French. He was a very erudite man. He died in Spain during the 1950s. People say he missed Barranquilla and had bought a boat ticket to return. But he died in Barcelona a few days before he was supposed to leave. Ramón Bacca visited his grave.

GUILLERMO ANGULO: Originally Gabo tries to write *One Hundred Years of Solitude*. It was something he didn't talk about, that he called the 'monster,' and he couldn't do it. He realizes it. Then he knew that the novel needed a much more experienced writer, which he wasn't, and he had the patience to wait until he was the writer capable of writing *One Hundred Years of Solitude*.

QUIQUE SCOPELL: That's where I was going. And you can publish that because it's the truth. Even as I'm drinking, but I wouldn't like to say something and then have them say that I said that Gabito is a sonuvabitch. Of course he's a sonuvabitch, but I also can't say it publicly because he's a man who, first of all, is already distinguished by his merits. For me, he has the great merit of obstinacy. An obstinate man, obstinate, who insists, insists and keeps at it and keeps at the sonuvabitch novel, and keeps at it and keeps at it. He'd come with rolls of newsprint under his arm, which is what he used to write on. Because he worked at *El Heraldo* and Alfonso worked at *El Heraldo*. And I repeat, Alfonso from the very beginning, Alfonso saw into Gabito . . . For me, the only one who saw into Gabito is named Alfonso Fuenmayor. And Alfonso believed in Gabito his whole life. The ones who influenced Gabito are named Álvaro Cepeda and José Félix Fuenmayor, Alfonso's father, who was a literary genius. The old man knew the literature of the time. Because sixty, seventy years ago, literature wasn't the way it is today.

JUANCHO JINETE: Don Ramón Vinyes was an old man, a Spaniard who came here during the time of Franco. He came to the bookstore. They always came looking for Fuenmayor because Fuenmayor wrote and they published his things in foreign newspapers, literary ones. And then Gabo also became a very good friend, he would go there to see Fuenmayor and also this Spaniard.

QUIQUE SCOPELL: The man who oriented him was Don José Félix Fuenmayor. Because we would go there to the house Don José Félix Fuenmayor had in Galapa. Álvaro and I would go with Gabito so that Don José Félix Fuenmayor could give Gabito lectures on literature.

MIGUEL FALQUEZ-CERTAIN: Alfonso Fuenmayor was the bridge between the newspaper *El Heraldo* and the wise man Don Ramón because the Spaniard lived in a place, which I got to know, that was a den where there were whores and everything. It was just across from *El Heraldo*. Later on I went there a good deal, in the sixties, with a friend. We went to see *Midnight Cowboy* at the Rex Cinema. It was nearby and we went to smoke there in that place, and some prostitutes had a room there. Alfredo de la Espriella, the founder of the city's Romantic Museum, was the one who told me: "Gabo lived there, in that place. Because the Catalan wise man lived there too." It was just opposite *El Heraldo* there on the Calle del Crimen, near the Church of San Nicolás. A two-story Republican-style building. But it was very run-down and it had a kind of staircase. Since the rooms faced the street, you could go up. And Alfredo told me: "Gabo lived with the Catalan wise man because he didn't have five cents."

Alfredo has the typewriter that García Márquez wrote on at *El Heraldo*. I think that place where I visited, which was decrepit, that's the place García Márquez refers to. And the old man must be the Catalan wise man because he lived there and they say it's the place that appears in his last book, the one about my whores and some damn thing. *Memories of My Melancholy Whores*.

JUANCHO JINETE: He's the wise Catalonian that he puts in *One Hundred Years*. And we did know the other one. Germán Vargas was working with him. The one from the Bogotá bookstore. Not the Buchholz but the other one. The one in the film *The Blue Lobster*.

NEREO LÓPEZ: Luis Vicens. The original story about *The Blue Lobster* is by Álvaro Cepeda. And Vicens, who was a movie fan, wrote a script with the painter Enrique Grau. And they sent that script to Gabito, and Gabito read it to see whether he would join them. They brought it to him so that he'd take a good look at the script, or so that he'd write the script. They filmed it in '55 or '56. And now the credits say that the script is by Gabito, but all he did was read it in a hurry and that's all.

QUIQUE SCOPELL: Alfonso was the one who corrected his syntax and spelling . . . Alfonso would show up with Gabo's manuscripts. At the brothel owned by Black Eufemia, the house across from the police station . . . What was it called again? White Sea. That's where Alfonso was correcting those things.

RAFAEL ULLOA: When I came here to Barranquilla, when I was studying at the Universidad del Atlántico, I saw him. Gabito was working then at *El Heraldo* and I lived on Road Forty-Nine at Sixty-Seventh, with people who were my family and his. And he would come there to write articles around the Hotel El Prado. He would start to drink beer with the older sons of the family. Well, I was younger. I would go to buy the beer there in the store. He never wore socks. Always without socks and in a guayabera, blue or green. The people here called him Crazy Rags, and he went around with the cab drivers and went whoring more than goddamn anybody else. He would go into the bars there on Crime Street to have drinks with the women and then he didn't have money to pay. Then he would leave the manuscripts of *Leaf Storm* there as pledges. All his early books . . .The first book of his that was well known was *Leaf Storm*. Then came *Big Mama's Funeral* . . . Of course, I went out to buy them.

CARMEN BALCELLS: It was sometime in the sixties. José Manuel Caballero Bonald, a Spanish poet, was in Colombia at the time and recommended that I read a new writer named Gabriel García Márquez. Then that young man named Gabriel García Márquez sent me—or I don't know if it was him or Caballero, it's all the same—his two books, which were *Big Mama's Funeral* and *Leaf Storm*. I have no idea right now. What I do remember very clearly is the great pleasure it was to read him. After that we corresponded, and I confirmed that I would represent him, be his agent, and sold them and other short narratives not only in Italy but in the United States too, in 1965.

RAFAEL ULLOA: I'm a García Márquez fanatic. I have his photo. Not a photograph but a clipping from a magazine. On the doors to the library. That's where I have it. Then when people come to the house and ask, "And who the hell is this?" I say: "Shit, that's a relative of mine."

5

The Citation of *One Hundred Years of Solitude*

In which the lives and deeds of the arguers and the others who remained outside are explained

That encyclopedic coincidence was the beginning of a great friendship. Aureliano continued getting together in the afternoon with the four arguers, whose names were Álvaro, Germán, Alfonso, and Gabriel, the first and last friends that he ever had in his life. For a man like him, holed up in written reality, those stormy sessions that began in the bookstore and ended at dawn in the brothels were a revelation. It had never occurred to him until then to think that literature was the best plaything that had ever been invented to make fun of people, as Álvaro demonstrated during one night of revels.

—from *One Hundred Years of Solitude*

MIGUEL FALQUEZ-CERTAIN: In '68 I went to a lecture Plinio Apuleyo Mendoza gave at the Colegio Americano. He was the first to speak about the book, in a masterly lecture, when *One Hundred Years* came out. He mentioned that García Márquez was obsessed with Carlos Fuentes, and for that reason he put in General Artemio Cruz and he explained "Mambrú Went to

War," the children's song we all know. Mambrú was the Duke of Marlborough. He also said Gabo admired Julio Cortázar and that's why he mentioned Rocamadour, the child character from *Hopscotch*. All the critics understood that García Márquez arbitrarily includes these people as a private homage. They also discovered that the names at the end of the book were genuine and began to find out who they were. There were four: Alfonso, Álvaro Cepeda, Germán, and Gabriel.* Alfonso is his Maecenas. Germán as well. There was literary rivalry with Álvaro, but at the same time they were keys. The Catalan wise man was named Ramón Vinyes. He doesn't mention Alejandro Obregón, though he was part of the group, and he was Gabriel. He puts in himself. He also leaves out Julio Mario Santo Domingo, the dandy who was heir to the most important fortune in Barranquilla, the owners of Águila Brewery.

JAIME ABELLO BANFI: They were keys, as we say in the Caribbean. That is, solidarity.

---

* When García Márquez wrote *Big Mama's Funeral*, he mentions the "pranksters of La Cueva." He is referring to his wild friends from Barranquilla. *Mamagallista*, a prankster or jokester, is a word used in the city's slang that García Márquez used in his writing and entered the country's lexicon. La Cueva (the Cave) is the name of their favorite watering hole. He mentions them again in *One Hundred Years of Solitude*. Alfonso, Álvaro, and Germán appear by name. Gabriel is himself.

ALFONSO FUENMAYOR

JUANCHO JINETE: Alfonso Fuenmayor was the oldest. He's from 1922 or '23.

QUIQUE SCOPELL: Alfonso was the most cultivated. Then, in their culture, are Alfonso and Alejandro Obregón; then comes Álvaro Cepeda, and then Germán Vargas. Gabito was learning.

HÉCTOR ROJAS HERAZO: Alfonso Fuenmayor was a very cordial person. Very lively. Very cultivated.

JUANCHO JINETE: Alfonso Fuenmayor wrote the editorials, things like that. The old Juan B. [Fernández], the father, managed the paper. At that time Gabriel García Márquez contributed a column called "The Giraffe."

JAIME ABELLO BANFI: Well, Alfonso is divine. I'll never forget Alfonso. With my Carnival group, every Carnival Monday we had a party, and for years Alfonso Fuenmayor would drop in at that party. And Alfonso had half a stammer. Always stammering. Always with a glass of whiskey in his hand. Plump, congenial, brilliant. He was like Gabo's older brother. Gabo would call him "maestro" because Fuenmayor was always concerned about him. Fuenmayor took care of him a little. He tried to find him work. At the same time his father had been a reference for all of them, Don José Félix. It was a relationship with a good deal of friendship, affection, and respect. Fuenmayor was like an older brother then. Exactly like that.

GERMÁN VARGAS

MIGUEL FALQUEZ-CERTAIN: Germán Vargas was a journalist and one of those who would meet at the Mundo Bookstore, which I never knew. It was in Calle San Blas. They would meet there and that was where the Catalan wise man would preside.

JAIME ABELLO BANFI: Germán. Germán was, above all, a man of culture. And Germán was a man of great sweetness, very serious and a very good friend, very affectionate. Very serene.

MARGARITA DE LA VEGA: Germán was the most timid, the most silent, or the most reserved of the group. But he was one of the intimate friends. After Barranquilla he went to Bogotá, a little like Ibarra

Merlano, who was a lawyer. I don't know what else he did, but he worked at Radio Nacional and at HJCK. On the radio he did many things that helped culture, like programs with poets, and interviews.

He was an upright guy, already graying when I met him. Supremely amiable, but he almost didn't seem like someone from the coast. He was reserved but also a good conversationalist.

MIGUEL FALQUEZ-CERTAIN: In the late fifties or early sixties, Germán went to Bogotá. He had a column there. After he came back to Barranquilla, he had a column in *El Heraldo*. He reviewed books. The Vargases were originally from Santander, I think. I don't believe he was born in Barranquilla. He was a critic and did things like that, but he couldn't live on that and for many years he worked for an organization that specializes in Colombian statistics. He was an official in that company and went with them to Bogotá. I believe he was serious. Not such a prankster.

ÁLVARO CEPEDA SAMUDIO

JUANCHO JINETE: I was born on Calle Obando and Álvaro Cepeda lived on Calle Medellín. We went to the Colegio Americano for boys, which back then was run by gringos, very

American but Protestant. We celebrated every American holiday at the Colegio. Álvaro Cepeda was already something of an intellectual and like that. Damn . . . I don't remember whole years. I must have been eighteen and now I'm seventy-two. Now I'm not even good with numbers. Álvaro was older than me. In '46 Álvaro founded a literary center during the school year and got me into those things. In his house he had a kind of office where he typed a newspaper, I don't remember what it was called. Álvaro had lots of things like that. He was very restless.

MIGUEL FALQUEZ-CERTAIN: The Kid, as they called him, was originally from Ciénaga, but his family has lived in Barranquilla for a hundred years. I saw him in the airport once when I happened to fly to New York on the same plane and he was with Julio Mario Santo Domingo. Julio Mario was dressed very well, in a jacket and tie, carrying a briefcase, and Álvaro had his shirt open and you could see the hair on his chest. He was wearing sandals. He was a *camaján*, a word they used in Barranquilla. It's a kind of gigolo who also dresses in two-tone shoes and makes his living from women. Usually they didn't work, but they had money, and if they didn't have it, they would find it. He had the gift of gab. He was a hustler. Back then Kid Cepeda and Obregón were very similar in that regard. They didn't respect the rules of society.

HÉCTOR ROJAS HERAZO: Kid had a hoarse voice: "Keep on moving" and such. Like "Yo, wassup." What was the name of the place where they would get together? La Cueva. Cepeda was also trying to create. He had a will . . . But no, he never had the tenacity; he isn't the same as Gabo. It's a calmer thing. But more than anything else his temperament is what mattered. He was an extraordinary boy. A great friend to Gabo. And laughter and things. No, and stories. *We Were All Waiting.* I said he was the best short story writer in Colombia. He was a guy with talent. But insistent creativity, like Gabo's, that's something else.

QUIQUE SCOPELL: Álvaro Cepeda is more of a natural writer than Gabito. What happens is that an angel appeared to Álvaro. His name was Julio Mario Santo Domingo, and he said to him: "Come and work with me. Salary? No, what salary! You take some whenever you want. There's money."

HÉCTOR ROJAS HERAZO: Because he was one of Faulkner's great admirers. So he resolved to meet him. Faulkner lived in the Deep South. He got there and saw Faulkner who sat at that hour in the doorway of his house to drink. Then he stopped the car and began to watch Faulkner drinking. Each time Faulkner took a drink, so did he. He wanted to have a dialogue with him . . . and he was getting drunk. And suddenly he said to himself: "What the hell am I going to say to Faulkner? That I'm a jerk. You're an asshole. What am I going to say to him? Let's go, then. See you later, Faulkner!" He was a man with a sense of irony.

QUIQUE SCOPELL: Gabito picked up a lot of culture when he got old. But Cepeda had more culture. First, he had money to read books and Gabito didn't. Álvaro read Faulkner, who at that time was popular, and afterward he lent his books to Gabito. Gabito had no money. He was fucked. He worked at *El Heraldo*, where they paid him three pesos a week. That shit Juan B., paying him three pesos. Gabito was up the creek, getting fifty-cent whores because he couldn't afford any better. Don't fuck around . . .

Like I'm telling you, their friendship was literature. Álvaro as a young man was better read than when he got older. Because at first he was more drawn to literature but he ran across a guy named Julio Mario Santo Domingo. Julio Mario was the ship that comes into port. You have to have a will of iron to say no to all that dough.

MIGUEL FALQUEZ-CERTAIN: They called Cepeda "Shaggy" because his hair was wild then, in the forties, when it wasn't fashionable. He was ahead of his time. I have a photo of him wearing a baseball cap backwards. Back then nobody did that.

QUIQUE SCOPELL: Don't fuck around! Álvaro was eccentric . . . He never wore shoes. Spanish alpargatas, that's what he wore. And he never wore a business shirt or anything, he was always badly dressed.

JUANCHO JINETE: He went around like a hippie. A prankster. Cecilia Porras's husband called him the Anthony Quinn of America.

QUIQUE SCOPELL: Well, look: Álvaro and I went to study in the United States. I think I went to the university three times to matriculate, and Álvaro twice. We were going to Baton Rouge, in Louisiana, but my grandmother lived in Havana. Then Álvaro said to me: "Don't be a faggot. Before we go to the university, let's spend a week in Havana and stay with your grandmother." Well, my grandmother was delighted to have me there in Havana. And there we met two penniless Venezuelan girls and we began to go around with the Venezuelans. They told us they were going to study in Ann Arbor, Michigan. Look, from Louisiana to Ann

Arbor, from Baton Rouge to Michigan is all of the United States. Then Álvaro said: "Listen and if now . . . what will we do starving in Baton Rouge? Let's go with those lunatics to Ann Arbor." That's why we went to Ann Arbor. And now I'll tell you: I went to the university like three times; Álvaro must have gone twice. Then he became "Dr. Álvaro Cepeda." He studied journalism. What journalism! In his book of short stories, *Juana's Stories*, there's the story of that black girl who lived with Álvaro in New York. Afterward he came up with a diploma in journalism from Columbia. A lie! It never happened. Nothing ever happened. You have to tell things the way they are because people invent stories. People who don't know people and begin to make up stories.

ALEJANDRO OBREGÓN

SANTIAGO MUTIS: Art critic Marta Traba said that young painters should pass before Alejandro Obregón like Ulysses before the Sirens, but in this case with their eyes blindfolded.

MIGUEL FALQUEZ-CERTAIN: He came from a distinguished family. His sister, Beatriz Elena, an intimate friend of my aunt La Nena, was a super distinguished lady. I put on magic shows for her. All those Obregóns were from a family from the highest Barranquilla society.

He always wore khakis, with his hair uncombed, and he didn't bathe. Or he did bathe, I don't know, but he didn't use deodorant, like the French. He had that strong, concentrated odor. And Mona Falquez, who was the tidiest, neatest woman in the world, when he would show up—he adored my Aunt Mona—and kiss her, then Mona would give him a kiss and all and say: "Ay, but what an odor Alejandro has!"

JUANCHO JINETE: There's a story about Maestro Obregón. La Cueva, which was a house and a bar, also had a living room and a dining room, rented to old Movilla. So the old man lived there. And there was a refrigerator, and that old man was bizarre; he made up that he was a cook and presented himself as one. Sometimes Álvaro cooked at La Cueva. One day he made rice with iguana eggs . . . the least of the stupidities that crazy old man did. He had a pet cricket. Listen, this is true! He had a cricket that he called Fifififi. He put out food and things like that for him. And then one day that little cricket came out and he said: "Maestro, maestro, I prepared something there for you today." The maestro sees the cricket and thinks . . . the little cricket. We were fixing some things with sausage when the maestro takes two pieces of bread and he took the cricket and *wham!* gobbled him.

NEREO LÓPEZ: And Alejandro loved to fight, he would get drunk and look for a fight. I made the best portraits of Alejandro Obregón. Spectacular photographs. Even to take one I had to fight with him. I remember that I said to him: "Pick up brushes, open them and put them up to your eye." And he: "No, because . . ."

JULIO MARIO SANTO DOMINGO

MIGUEL FALQUEZ-CERTAIN: The story I had heard since I was a boy is that the old man, Don Mario, his father (later on I learned he was also named Julio Mario, though nobody called him that) came on foot from Panama to Barranquilla. He had money but he wasn't a millionaire. He had money put away from his business there in Panama. He was an ordinary person. This Señor Mario Santo Domingo came to Barranquilla with money in his pocket and he became connected to the Barranquilla society of that time, which must have been very small, and he became related by marriage to the Pumarejo family. The Pumarejos originally came from La Guajira, from Valledupar, around there. My mother's family would go there sometimes because they had parties there on the farm in Dibulla. It belonged to the Pumarejos and people went there for a rest. They were there for a week and there were parties; people came from Bogotá and paid attention to them.

Don Mario married the sister of Alberto Pumarejo and began a brilliant career. When I was a boy, the richest family in Barranquilla wasn't Mario Santo Domingo's. The famous ones were the Mancinis. The Mancinis were the richest.

When I was studying economics in '70, my teacher used Julio Mario's surprise as an example. Julio Mario was a dandy for a time, a playboy. He didn't settle down until the seventies because he had a brother, Pipe Santo Domingo, who was killed in a car accident in Puerto Colombia. He was with Diana Limnander de Nieuwenhove. Diana survived and Pipe was killed, and that was a tragedy for the old man. And Julio Mario, who had spent his time traveling and living the good life, had to make himself respectable because Pipe died. The same thing that happened to John F. Kennedy with his brother who died (his older brother Joseph): he had to pick up the reins.

Julio Mario took advantage of the fact that his father was cautiously buying stocks in various companies. My grandfather had one hundred, two hundred. But old Mario was methodical and bought shares and shares and kept them. At the time of the conflict between the Germania Brewery and Águila, he created the Santo Domingo Group. He formed the Santo Domingo Group with people from Barranquilla who also had shares, among them Pacho Posada and a number of men, and with my father's block and those shares he appeared before the general assembly of stockholders. Those guys had no damn idea. They were going to have their general assembly, they were going to name a new board of directors, and when they counted those shares, Julio Mario's amounted to 51 percent. So they seized the reins of Germania and that was Julio Mario's brilliant coup of '69, around then. He became the lord and master of Colombia.

QUIQUE SCOPELL: It isn't that Julio Mario was arrogant but he had different habits. He was a club type.

MIGUEL FALQUEZ-CERTAIN: Julio studied at Columbia University, I think. This must have been in '46. And he paid for the Kid's studies at Columbia University. The Kid studied journalism and there's where he wrote the stories in *We Were All Waiting*. People supposed that he read William Saroyan and wrote the stories while he was living in New York. When he returned to Barranquilla he didn't have a job, and since Julio Mario had money and wanted to invest it, he started the *Diario del Caribe* in order to give it to the Kid Cepeda. That's the story I know. And he made the Kid Cepeda the editor in chief. The *Diario del Caribe* was originally a Liberal paper because Julio Mario was from a Liberal family, of course. His mother was Alberto Pumarejo's sister. Later, because of Pacho Posada, he became Conservative.

THE PRANKSTERS OF LA CUEVA

CARMEN BALCELLS: Starting in the year 1965, I made quite a few trips to Colombia as well as to Mexico. On one of those trips I was in La Cueva and I met the individuals whose names at this moment I can't recall. I was accompanied by Álvaro Cepeda Samudio, who introduced me in depth to the world of Barranquilla: La Cueva, the bookstores, Vinyes, and everything that now forms part of the mythic life of the author of *One Hundred Years*.

SANTIAGO MUTIS: It's all there. They're all friends with one another because they were all very great. Because Obregón was no fool. I mean, Obregón was a prodigious personality. Alejandro's presence was like an animal's. Alejandro disturbed. One felt a hope. A beautiful thing. And Alfonso was like being in a place, like saying: "We've arrived, something good is going to happen here." With Rojas Herazo too, because they were people capable of responding to life, capable of giving life. Strong internally. Beautiful. So a number of very beautiful things converged there.

They were all special people. It wasn't friendship alone, it was just good-natured and easygoing. They were united by love for humanity and for literature, and that's the same thing.

La Cueva in its heyday.

6

To Be a Prankster or a Writer

In which what is required to be a mamagallista *is explained, the term being an expression totally unknown before the publication of* One Hundred Years of Solitude, *or How only a writer could make the pranksters famous*

HERIBERTO FIORILLO: In La Cueva there were four principal actors; three of them appear later in the last chapter of *One Hundred Years of Solitude*. They are Alfonso, Germán, Álvaro, and Alejandro. The Vaivén was a store that was at Victoria and Veinte de Julio, and it became La Cueva. The owner, Eduardo Vilá, was Alfonso's cousin and it humiliated him to have to sell groceries. He only wanted to wait on his hunter friends. Alfonso called Álvaro who transformed the store into the bar La Cueva. The urinals were very close to the bar, as proposed by Obregón. In the late fifties I lived two blocks from there, and would walk past with my father on our way to the nearby movie theaters. One day he said to me: "This is where some gentlemen who are artists get together and drink beer and come to blows and then they argue and drink and come to blows again and . . ." He also told me this as a warning, and that awakened a great curiosity in me. Later, when I began to read Colombian literature, you know, Cepeda Samudio, Rojas Herazo, García Márquez, I realized they were those same friends. And from Tarzan and Batman, my heroes at the time, I passed on to my new heroes, the madmen in La Cueva.

MIGUEL FALQUEZ-CERTAIN: When *One Hundred Years of Solitude* came out, he referred to the jokers of La Cueva, and called them the "four arguers." He used a number of regional words that weren't known in the rest of the country. People began to ask themselves what he meant by them. For example, the term "male swallow," which they thought was a bird, and everybody knows that the male swallow in Barranquilla is when the pores in your armpits become clogged and you get boils.

Like the term "prankster," or "*mamar gallo*," also appeared. They began to speculate in *El Tiempo*, in *El Espectador*, about what García Márquez meant by that, and they asked questions and such. That was the origin of that theory, which is the one I remember. It comes from cockfights. I never went to a cockfight in Barranquilla in my life. That wasn't common. I never saw a cockfight until I went to La Guajira. It's a ritual there; like drinking contraband whiskey and listening to *vallenatos*, being in the group that went from house to house with the trio, going to cockfights too. In the cockpits people were very belligerent but also great jokers; then it was between making jokes and being aggressive. The comic thing could change and the man would take a revolver and kill you because you were mocking him. Then the etymological origin is that the rooster has a natural spur. But roosters never fight with their own spurs but they put things on them that are made of copper. Then, to put the copper on, as an imitation of a spur, they put wax inside and then set that wax on a candle, put it in fire. When the wax has melted they put it on the rooster's spur and set it in place so that it stays on the natural spur. And then, to cement it, they put it in their mouth and suck the spur. That's why they say "nurse," or *mamar*, to nurse is to suck.

So that's the etymological origin and meaning. It's very difficult to translate, not only to another language but to other cultures too. The phenomenon most similar to being a *mamagallista* or to *mamar gallo* is the teller of the tall tale. The Irish tell unbelievable stories with a serious expression on their face.

I'll give you an example: I would tell my friend Joaquín the most absurd lies. That I did this and I did that and I swore it was true. Then he would keep looking at me and I would tell him: "No, man, no, that's a lie." And he would say: "But why do you tell me that stuff? You swore it was true and all this time I thought it was true." That's when you're "nursing on a rooster." That is what makes you a prankster of La Cueva. You're making situations that are completely false and you're making another person believe them.

MARGARITA DE LA VEGA: That's what *mamagallismo* is: constructing a tiresome joke.

As for Gabo being one, he was. And he loved to tell stories that can be truth or fiction. It's using hyperbole, to use an elegant term. Exaggeration. It's telling a story where there's some silly thing. When they tell you on the coast that there was a lunch that lasted until the next day, well, in Valledupar there really are lunches like that. Gabo certainly was a *mamador de gallo*. He liked to play jokes. That's where certain things in the novels come from. That comes from the culture. That's what he was living.

RAFAEL ULLOA: You couldn't have a serious conversation with Gabito without its being a joke. Later on he must have changed, but when he was here he was a full-fledged *mamadera de gallo*. And he's a guy who . . . how shall I say it? Popular. He talked to everybody and said fuck you to life. So one day Gabito said to me: "Listen, Rafa, have you already smoked the tobacco?" "What tobacco?" "The grass your cousin gave you." Doña Victoria, who was a relative of mine, would say, "Just be patient, my son Alfonso smokes marijuana." So when he sees me, Gabo says to me: "Aha, burro." You know that here [in Barranquilla] they call people who smoke marijuana burros. And I come from a town where burros are the ones that fuck burras. And he was asking me if I was a burro . . .

JUANCHO JINETE: Gabito was another *mamador de gallo*.

JAIME ABELLO BANFI: The pranksters of La Cueva were basically a group of friends who had a central nucleus. The people who were part of the central nucleus were people dedicated to literature, to journalism, to art. Very cultivated people who always preferred a sense of humor and laughter and the ability to mock everything to pretensions of seriousness or even to leaving a legacy or a very clear body of work. I believe they valued being alive, having a good time, sharing. And they valued their surroundings very much. Gabo said to me: "Barranquilla is Macondo when it became a city."

7

Another Whiskey

In which Quique and Juancho, the only survivors of the group of mamagallistas at La Cueva, take us on a stroll around the Barranquilla of the 1950s, when García Márquez arrived and they saw him as a total hick

JUANCHO JINETE: Here it's all Gabo, Gabo up and Gabo down. That's now.

QUIQUE SCOPELL: I'm telling you, people divide it all in two. It's Gabito before the Nobel and after the Nobel. Before the Nobel, nobody paid any attention to Gabito. They called him the lizard. "Let's get out of here, here comes Gabito." People hid from him.

MIGUEL FALQUEZ-CERTAIN: A lizard is a busybody who goes where he doesn't fit in, who isn't part of the group, who pushes in, somebody who approaches a group and is seen as beneath them. A lizard is somebody who becomes unbearable, who wants help, who pushes in everywhere. What they mean is that Obregón and Cepeda didn't appreciate García Márquez.

QUIQUE SCOPELL: The Nobel Prize fucking hurt Colombian literature with García Márquez. Because now everybody wants to be García Márquez. So "Ah noooo! If García Márquez didn't say it then it isn't literature!" It's a very large shadow. A ceiba tree.

It fucked up literature. "Ah, if Gabito didn't say it . . . !" Even the president, Alfonso López, says: "Because, as Gabito said . . ." You tell me, Alfonso López, when the hell did you ever meet Gabito? You met him after the boom of the Nobel Prize. Before that Gabito was an outsider . . . He went around with those manuscripts under his arm and he received a letter that said: "Señor García Márquez, dedicate yourself to something else because you're no good as a writer."

GUILLERMO ANGULO: He tried to write *One Hundred Years of Solitude* in Barranquilla, but he realized it was too big for him. It ended up as *Leaf Storm*, his first book, published in 1955.

GUSTAVO GARCÍA MÁRQUEZ: Once he had finished *Leaf Storm,* he took it to the guy from Losada. And this was the answer he got: "Look, Señor García, take up something else, because this isn't right for you."

JUANCHO JINETE: It seems to me the Mundo Bookstore is where everything is born . . . It was there in the center of town, near the Colombia movie theater. So there on the corner was the Mundo Bookstore and then that Café Colombia on the corner. So there in the café is where that bunch of . . . all of them . . . Then Alfonso took Gabo there and introduced him, and after that he began to go there. I knew him. I saw him when he began to sing *vallenatos** and we hadn't heard that here. The *vallenato* was something that was not liked

---

* *Vallenato* is northern Colombia's country music. Accordion-heavy and troubadour-like, it tells of the travails, friendships, and love stories of the men of the Valley of Upar, located between the Sierra Nevada de Santa Marta and the Serranía de Perijá in northeast Colombia. In the times of García Márquez, it was frowned upon as music of the lower classes and farmers. Today, it is a proud export to the world; there is even a *vallenato* category in the Latin Grammys. García Márquez, always a lover and promoter of the genre, has said that *One Hundred Years of Solitude* is a 360-page *vallenato* song.

here . . . When we would get together there and have a few beers, then he would sing. No, of course not! Not a good voice at all. But he liked it. He didn't play anything. That's how the thing happened.

I wasn't literary or anything like that. I was a listener. But I went around with them. A café already existed here, a bookstore called Mundo Bookstore, it belonged to a Señor Rendón, one of the brothers . . .

HÉCTOR ROJAS HERAZO: Books came in, especially to Barranquilla. You'd say such-and-such a book, and generally they had it, but in case they didn't they'd say to you: "Okay, come on such-and-such a day," and they'd have the book for you.

QUIQUE SCOPELL: That no longer exists because they knocked it down and now they put up something that's called . . . What's the name of that man who shows up? Alladin.

Álvaro, since he had money, bought books at the Mundo Bookstore. Gabo would go to the bookstore to read. Don Jorge Rendón was very . . . You can't research that because he is up there in heaven with his memories, but he was a wonderful man and helped Gabito a lot.

Because he would say: "Oh man, poor boy, he's fucked." He would lend him books. He said: "This boy is worth it because he's a thoughtful boy and he's curious, studious. The kid's worth it." Like Alfonso Fuenmayor always believed in Gabito a lot. He bears a lot of the blame for Gabito being . . . Because that business with Gabito is a sickness.

Listen. Álvaro was studying at the Colegio Americano. And I was at the Colegio San José. So we'd meet there. We got out of school at two or three in the afternoon, at four or five we'd meet there.

JUANCHO JINETE: Because there was an entrance there, and the Café Colombia was close by.

QUIQUE SCOPELL: The Colombia Theater was there. They knocked that down and made a commercial center. At the back was the Colombia Theater. Here to the side was a bar, and there was the Mundo Bookstore. We would meet there in the afternoon. Especially in the afternoon, that's where we would meet. Álvaro was studying at the Colegio Americano.

JUANCHO JINETE: With me.

QUIQUE SCOPELL: Everybody would say: "How much dough do you have?" Wow, I had thirty-five cents. Álvaro had fifty cents. Alfonso had twenty, and Gabito didn't have shit. He was flat broke. Germán worked at the comptroller's office, and Germán had fifteen cents. Then we'd leave, leave the Mundo Bookstore, for the Japi, which is at San Juan and Veinte de Julio, but just after the bookstore, now where the electric company is. Next to it was the Japi Bar. Then we would order a bottle of white rum and a bottle of tamarind. A bottle of white rum with a bottle of tamarind cost twenty-five cents. And they added slices of lemon. Germán was the one who mixed it: he'd add the lemon, and with the sixty or seventy cents that we had we could drink three bottles of white rum. We must have been seventeen, eighteen years old. And then each of us went home. There was no money for anything else. He would sit with us there in the Japi because, I repeat, he didn't drink. He drank very little.

RAFAEL ULLOA: At that time Gabito must have been twenty-three years old. He was already writing here. No, no, no . . . Initially he was a guy nobody paid any attention to. Besides, they thought he was crazy. His clothes were sloppy. People, I'm not kidding, saw him . . . as a lost cause.

EDUARDO MÁRCELES DACONTE: But we can't forget that at the age of twenty-three he was already writing *Leaf Storm*.

QUIQUE SCOPELL: Gabito isn't much of a drinker and he doesn't chase women. He doesn't chase women and he's not a drinker, my girl, and that's why I'm telling you that Alejandro and Álvaro would say: "Here comes that damn lizard to talk about literature." "And look, now Doña Manuela is going to marry . . ." Man, don't be a faggot. I've already read that novel two hundred thousand times in the Japi. Every day he read a goddamn chapter of that thing and everybody told him it wasn't worth a damn.

"Maestro, look," he would say to Alfonso Fuenmayor. "Maestro, I sent it to Argentina. And no joke, you'll see how contracts for that thing are going to come in." The Mexican and the Spaniard publishers told him they didn't want the novel, but the Argentine was the one who said: "Señor García, try something else, because you're no good at this."

GERALD MARTIN: Gabo doesn't like to be helped by other people. He had no money and I'm sure that was the reason he didn't drink a lot at that table; and not drinking very much was a diplomatic disaster in the Barranquilla of that time.

RAFAEL ULLOA: His father had a lot of faith in him, understand? His father would tell the relatives that Gabito was the very best and like that, but, of course, people didn't believe him because appearances are deceiving and so they didn't believe him. He says Gabito is two-headed, that he had two brains. That's the old man's fiction. The fact is the old man's a storyteller too. The fact is we have a goddamn strain of first-class liars. It's a family thing.

JUANCHO JINETE: He lived here, but he would always disappear.

MIGUEL FALQUEZ-CERTAIN: Later, when *One Hundred Years of Solitude* comes out, this is what Jacques Gilard, the French academic who comes to Colombia in '76 to decipher Macondo, baptizes as the Barranquilla Group.

QUIQUE SCOPELL: But you have to understand that the Barranquilla Group never existed. Never. That was something that intellectuals made up.

García Márquez walking with a friend in Bogotá.

8

La Cueva

Concerning the emergence of La Cueva, the bar that Gabo apparently did not frequent very often, and that thanks to him is today a national treasure

MIGUEL FALQUEZ-CERTAIN: I'm going to tell you how we drank in Barranquilla. In Barranquilla there really were very few elegant bars. At that time only the important hotels had them. The Patio Andaluz was the most elegant, it was in the Hotel El Prado, but there they kept it dim and so married men took their girlfriends there to dance. The Patio Andaluz was dangerous because that was in El Prado and they could tell your wife. And there were what they called "grills." These were in second-rate hotels in other parts of Barranquilla, in the center of town, and such. They became famous. And you went in and couldn't see anybody. Back then they had chairs and armchairs and you sat down, and they brought you your drink. You would bring the current girlfriend, dance very close, and then go to a hotel to fuck. There was a very famous one called the Sitting Bull. And there was the grill of the Hotel Génova and the grill of another hotel that was divine, like a European hotel, and that was the Hotel Astoria. Those were the grills that the rich men in Barranquilla used, where they took women who were their lovers. Then there was a form I didn't like, but there was another alternative, and that was to drink in shops.

There was a shop on every corner, in every neighborhood in

Barranquilla, before supermarkets existed. In Barranquilla there was just one market, the Grain Market. Back then you had to go downtown. Then, for the people who lived in the Boston and El Prado districts, they opened the Boston Market, and it was cleaner, nice for society ladies. And the ladies would go with their maids. If they needed something, they would send to the corner and on the corner there was always a shop and it usually belonged to people from the capital. Some were in the garages of houses and others were local. They sold beer and sometimes there were tables at the door. People would sit there and talk. The table would be covered with bottles, and only men would go there.

That's what La Cueva was. A shop.

QUIQUE SCOPELL: You have to separate La Cueva from what's called the Barranquilla Group. They're two different things. It's the same thing, but they're two different things. At La Cueva we never talked about literature . . . La Cueva began with Alfonso Fuenmayor, who was the one who set up the shops for Álvaro, because Álvaro was the head of publicity for the Águila Brewery owned by Santo Domingo. He set up the shops to sell beer. That was his job. Then one afternoon Alfonso said to him: "Don't fuck around Álvaro. Come over here, to Veinte de Julio and Sesenta y nueve." (Friend, do me a favor and pour me a whiskey over here, please.)

JUANCHO JINETE: Another one over here, too. I'll read to you from this old newspaper: "The place speaks now of afternoons of conversation, beer, and boleros, of photos of fishermen. A place enlivened by the presence of Fuenmayor, Gabriel García Márquez, Alejandro Obregón, Germán Vargas Cantillo, Álvaro

Cepeda Samudio, and others like the painter Noé León, Enrique
Scopell, Juancho Jinete, Abel Valle, and the figure of the Spaniard
Ramón Vinyes, better known as the wise Catalonian." But, as I
was saying, it began to have a certain air, we could even name
governors, that's when they were appointed, not elected like now.
And La Cueva had that. Old man President López came to Barranquilla and he went to the La Cueva. All those characters . . .

The story is that Alfonso Fuenmayor had a cousin, Eduardo
Vilá, who had a shop and put in stereo equipment. We would go
there to listen to music, and in the end, the shop became a bar. It's
there in the Boston district.

QUIQUE SCOPELL: Look, Alfonso Fuenmayor is a shop drinker.
So he calls Álvaro and says: "Álvaro, I have a damn fine corner
here for you." Álvaro knew the corners because he lived in Barranquilla his whole life. It was at Veinte de Julio and Setenta y cinco.
"Come here so you can see what kind of thing it is." So he goes
and there they have a shop called the Fluctuation. The shop was
called Fluctuation, like his wife, who fluctuated in her faithfulness
as well. And the fact is it's true . . . So it turns out that Vilá turned
out to be Alfonso's cousin because he's a Vilá Fuenmayor. Alfonso
asks him:

"And what's your name?"

"Eduardo Vilá Fuenmayor."

"What? And who's your father? And your mother, who is she?"

"A Fuenmayor."

"Wow! She's my father's sister."

They were cousins and didn't know each other. Then, when
he saw the shop, Álvaro immediately said to him: "Don't fuck
around, maestro, really! This is good!" Because it's right on the

corner, as soon as you come to the end of Veinte de Julio you run into that house . . . Then Álvaro says to him: "Would you sell this, this business here, and put up something from the brewery?" And Vilá said to him: "Well, that depends. Wait and tell me how that idea of yours goes." "Well, I'll call the brewery. And you tell me how much are all the plantains and bananas that you have here worth?" And he bought the place.

"This thing is mine."

"So how much is this thing worth?"

"It's worth about ten thousand pesos. Give me about ten thousand pesos."

"Well, I'll buy the whole thing from you and throw it all out at once. And I'll call the painters and set up this thing for you. We'll make a bar here. No store, no nothing. No rice and plantains. A bar. And what will we call it? We'll call it La Cueva."

I don't know who said they should call it La Cueva. If it was Alfonso, or Germán, or . . . Then, Álvaro said: "Agreed?" "Well, yes, agreed," said the other one. "All right, then."

EDUARDO MÁRCELES DACONTE: It was like a house and there was like a little terrace. You went in and then there was a bar, a folkloric bar, I mean, with all kinds of hats, and then there were some armchairs and some little tables, and this was a meeting place for hunters and the reporters who were working then and painters. But at that moment there were more reporters. The literary question was just starting and it was their meeting place. We went a couple of times to have some beers there and see the place.

NEREO LÓPEZ: Vilá was a frustrated dentist.

JUANCHO JINETE: Vilá was a hunter and he went around with those pricks, those hunters . . .

QUIQUE SCOPELL: Yes, but when he had a shop the hunters didn't go there. Later on the hunters went to La Cueva. Not to the shop. Alfonso found that shop, and Álvaro said to him: "All right, what's all the rice that you have here worth? Put it in the doorway so everybody, every pauper who goes by, can take what he wants from here." He called the brewery: "Once and for all, send me the truck with this stuff. With four refrigerators, ten gallons of beer, and two hundred bottles." And I don't know what else. Called painters who wrote *La Cueva* up high. And I don't know what else. In half an hour the Fluctuation was transformed into La Cueva because this madman brought him three coolers. Two freezers. Two refrigerators. Two syphon barrels. They're still there.

JOSÉ ANTONIO PATERNOSTRO: A group of us, friends, would go after leaving the office on Saturday to have a beer from the tap and talk about politics and the economy. See what we could do for Barranquilla. We would go to La Cueva in a jacket and tie and Cepeda was there in rags. The Kid, an irreverent madman, called us "the clowns." We were clowns because we belonged to the business sector. Kid Cepeda was already at a table having a drink and would say: "Here come the clowns." Scopell was with him. Jinete was there.

QUIQUE SCOPELL: We would sit at the bar. Álvaro's office was there. He moved the office from the brewery, he moved it there. Then Álvaro, Alfonso, Alejandro, and I would go. Then, since Álvaro's office was there, everybody went to get him to buy ads from them. You know that the brewery is the principal producer of advertisements in Colombia. All the radio broadcasters would go to ask Álvaro for publicity ads, to haggle with Álvaro.

NEREO LÓPEZ: It was a team of drunkards. There were no women. The only woman I saw there was Cecilia Porras. She was a painter, the wife of Jorge Child. Nobody took women there.

MARGARITA DE LA VEGA: Cecilia was a Cartagena painter but she lived in Bogotá. She was one of the few women they treated as an equal, which was not very frequent. She was very pretty. The coastal type: black hair, white skin, pretty eyes, a great body. Very charming. If you saw her in *The Blue Lobster* you'd see the charm she had. She lived in Bogotá. She would go to cafés with men when women didn't go to cafés. Let's say she was a bold woman, unconventional. She was as good a painter as Obregón and Grau but was never recognized because she was a woman, and there one is always somebody's wife or somebody's daughter, and she couldn't break with that. Her husband was the founder of the magazine *Mito*. She died when she was relatively young, of cancer, I think. In a sense she's a tragic figure. She would get drunk with them.

NEREO LÓPEZ: Everybody went there to drink. Especially on tap, which was what there was. Beer on tap. If you ate, it was snacks. It was a tavern. Alfonso Fuenmayor would go. Germán Vargas would go. The crocodile hunters would go. People who were his clients would go, they went to drink beer on tap. When I came to Barranquilla, La Cueva was already there. You'd go there, order from the demijohn. I came as a graphic reporter for *El Espectador*.

I was a friend of all of them. Álvaro and Alejandro and Fuenmayor and Gabito. But there was never a separation of talents. Scopell would come in and order a beer. Álvaro came in and ordered a beer. Alejandro came in and so forth. They came in. The hunters arrived and drank. A mix of people drinking beer at a bar.

JUANCHO JINETE: Well, it was all a flood of rum and of . . . but people believe that's how La Cueva was, and that we were there talking about literature and things like that. Then one day some kids from the universities showed up so we would talk to them about La Cueva, and Quique already had the drinks because that's how it's always done. And suddenly Quique says: "I'm sick to death of this shit. There in La Cueva, nobody ever talked about literature there. What happened is that the literary types were Alfonso Fuenmayor, Germán Vargas, Álvaro Cepeda, Alejandro Obregón, and Señor García Márquez, when he came here. That was all. Because of us, all the rest of our friends would meet there too, and what we talked about was rum and things, and from there we would go to the whores." "Man, Quique, no, no." "No! I'm sick of this shit. Don't make me keep repeating the same shit about this being a temple of literature. What literature, damn it! What philosophy!"

9

"The Guy Has the Persistence of That Business"

In which the reader understands that Gabito, although a prankster, never stopped writing

QUIQUE SCOPELL: What else shall I tell you about Gabito? Let's have another to keep talking about this. (*He realizes that the bottle of whiskey is empty. Holding up his glass, he calls to a waiter who is passing.*) Hey, hey! The same again. I drink whiskey on the rocks but with ice and a little water on the side . . . When Gabito wasn't yet . . .

JUANCHO JINETE: He'd show up here at different times.

QUIQUE SCOPELL: The guy has the persistence of that business. He drank with us every day with a notebook under his arm . . . and he sent his manuscript to Argentina, to Mexico, to Spain, and from Argentina they wrote back: "Señor García Márquez, do something else because you're no good as a writer. This is a terrible novel. This isn't worth a damn." And the only one who said the novel was good was Alfonso Fuenmayor. Among other things, Álvaro said: "This is shit. This . . . don't fuck around."

JUANCHO JINETE: Gabito would send the originals of the stories to Fuenmayor.

Alfonso was a scholar in syntax and things like that . . . He'd come with his big notebook, and since Alfonso would come wearing a jacket, he'd put the papers in his pockets. I don't know how he didn't lose them.

QUIQUE SCOPELL: Every day he'd write a new chapter and then he'd say to us: "Read this." Álvaro would say: "Don't fuck around, you have a lot of balls, this is shit!" I didn't read *One Hundred Years of Solitude* after it was published, but I read it two hundred thousand times because every day that madman would read it to us; he'd read the damn chapter he had written the night before. It wasn't called *One Hundred Years* yet. He'd bring it, along with the same damn fifty centavos he'd gone to bed with. He has a persistence . . . because he insisted, insisted, and insisted until a madwoman showed up, that woman . . . What was the name of that Spanish woman?

CARMEN BALCELLS: Who was Carmen Balcells? I was the same as I am today but less known or not known at all. I was an unassuming girl from a working-class family, educated in a nuns' school, who wanted to be emancipated and earn her living before anything else. And a friend of mine named Joaquín Sabria recommended a job that he said was called literary agent and he brought me some books and a roll of paper. And I began this job before receiving that mandate from Caballero Bonald with the recommendation of García Márquez.

JAIME ABELLO BANFI: Those years in Barranquilla always loomed large in his life. In 1994, he decides to return so he buys an apartment, and decides to come stay in it for a few weeks. And then he dedicated himself to playing tennis at the Hotel El Prado with my brother Mauricio the doctor, who was his tennis buddy. It was in '94. A key year in García Márquez's life. It's the year when he's ready to come back to the country. And then sometimes we went out to look around the city. He told me a few things there. We went with his driver. At that time he had a kind of air-conditioned van, sort of silver-colored. The two of us would go. He was taking notes for his memoirs. He went around with a mixture of memories and writing, I think. At one time he talked about writing three short novels, one of them turned out to be *Memories of My Melancholy Whores*. At that time he had even asked me to make a few inquiries, which I did. He sent me a questionnaire and I went into the periodical archive.

QUIQUE SCOPELL: He always sent questionnaires to me. To Alfonso. Things he wanted to clarify.

JAIME ABELLO BANFI: A questionnaire that asked about when the first ship entered Bocas de Cenizas; like what was the ship's name; when was the Atomic Match played, which was a soccer game; which people were on the field; what was the name of the then manager of the Junior, the city's team, and how . . . Very amusing. There was a question about whorehouses in Barranquilla. I was personally checking the periodicals in the Nieto Arteta Archive. And, among other things, I found a number of amusing items that I also sent to him. References to the Diva Sagibi, who was a famous occultist in Barranquilla during the 1950s. I looked at the newspaper *La Prensa* at that time, and I looked at the other papers, and so I passed information on to him. And then he comes to Barranquilla to take possession of his new apartment. He stays there for quite a few days. I think it was two weeks, something like that, and among other things it was my job to accompany him on that tour around the center of town. And the tour was looking for things (here's such and such, so-and-so building, the bookstore was here, this was here, the other was here), and taking notes. It was one day. A Saturday.

Saturday at eleven in the morning. From time to time he lowered the window and the people saw him and yelled: "Aha, Gabo. García Márquez!" And he joked back in turn.

ALLIANCE PINZÓN: I am working here at the Romantic Museum in Barranquilla as part of my military service. I give the tours. Here, we house all the important things about the history of Barranquilla since 1620, when it was called Sabanita de Camacho. It consists of twenty-six rooms. The material about García Márquez is down below. We have some things from García Márquez but they are taken out only when there's a García Márquez event. Then they take out all the paintings of García Márquez and place them there, outside. We have a García Márquez typewriter. The fact is that while giving you this tour I didn't attribute much importance to him, but there it is. His typewriter. It was his. He wrote *Leaf Storm* on that typewriter. (*The lights go out all over the museum.*) Ah, that happens almost every day. Don't worry. They'll come back on right away.

10

Slickers and Hicks

In which Gabito, the ugly duckling, the hick from the coast, moves to the
cold, slick capital to work as a reporter for
El Espectador

JUANCHO JINETE: One day he left for Bogotá and went to work at *El Espectador*. And he would show up here from time to time.

JOSÉ SALGAR: Gabo came to *El Espectador* with a little bit of fame that *El Espectador* itself had given him without knowing him. He already had fame as a writer because of Eduardo Zalamea and the short story of Gabo's that was published in *El Espectador*. But when he came and they gave him to me, he was an ordinary run-of-the-mill reporter. Besides, he was from the coast. Common. Vulgar. They have a very good word there: a hick. Very shy then . . . And I was the editor in chief, I was the veteran.

MIGUEL FALQUEZ-CERTAIN: And we know very well that being from the coast is not the same as being vulgar. On the contrary. Barranquilla was a village in the 1940s. In '48 they killed Gaitán, then the Violence began for ten years and a lot of people, especially from the interior, not only from Bogotá but from Santander, too, began to come down the Magdalena River. All those people displaced by the first violence (from '48 to '58), who began to come down the river . . . Hicks were the ones that came from small towns to Barranquilla and stayed.

Barranquilla was a family in those days. Everybody knew everybody else in the thirties and forties. When the diaspora begins because of the Violence, they begin to come first from the towns along the Magdalena River and then from Tunja, from Popayán and Tuluá, where the slaughter was going on between Conservatives and Liberals. Then that entire generation was called hicks, *corronchos*, because they didn't have the manners of the quote-unquote decent people of Barranquilla. Before then, when I was a boy, they didn't say "hick." My father didn't say "hick," he would say "uncouth." People who weren't in society were uncouth and had bad taste. They had no manners. That word exists in every culture. In Spain they call them *paletos*, the village people who go to Madrid. In Cuba they call them *guajiros*, who are the peasants. In Puerto Rico they're called *jíbaros*. Every place has a nasty word for the rustic who comes to the city and doesn't know how to behave. Who doesn't know how to handle the silverware. Who embarrasses himself.

PLINIO APULEYO MENDOZA: I met him in a café. He was badly dressed and was a chain smoker . . .

SANTIAGO MUTIS: The fact is, look, let's say that in Bogotá they were nurturing a great contempt for Colombia: a great contempt for the provinces, a great contempt for poverty. It's lamentable, but it's also a force that the country still maintains. At that time everything comes from England, it comes from France, from Mexico, from the United States. All the painters went to study in Mexico because the muralists were there. It wasn't coming from Cézanne anymore. Now it was coming from Mexico. It's always going to come from the outside. And then there are the ones who come along who say: "Nowhere else. It's here."

HÉCTOR ROJAS HERAZO: We had to have confidence in ourselves because there was no generosity then. People were very pretentious. Yes . . . Humph! What does one have to be vain about? You have to enjoy your ignorance and use it as a creative element. Ah, no! You came to Bogotá and then they showed you: "He's the poet so-and-so . . ." They had so much vanity . . .

MARGARITA DE LA VEGA: They used "slicker" in Bogotá and it means a very elegant gentleman. A *cachaco*. Let's say Arturo Abella, who was incredible—I worked a great deal with him—he was very much a slicker, very much a Bogotano. Arturo always said: "For us, a slicker is a refined, elegant person who knows how to dress, who knows how to eat, who does the appropriate thing, and you people from the coast call us slickers as a put-down."

MIGUEL FALQUEZ-CERTAIN: In Barranquilla they have the bad habit of calling any person who's not from the coast a slicker. A Barranquillan friend of mine, Campo Elías Romero, used to say that everything that comes after Gamarra is slick. Gamarra is a village on the Magdalena. Everything that comes after halfway down the Magdalena is slick. But in reality, I never used it as an insult because my godfather is from Bogotá. In my house it was used the way Bogotans use it (meaning that he's elegant). It's a word that even the Bogotans use when they say "Hey, how slick you look!" And it means: "How well-dressed you are, how elegant."

Colombia has always been a very divided country, there's always been this rivalry. Even along the coast, the Barranquillans and the Cartagenans have always taken potshots at one another. In Santa Marta, when the Junior played, they threw rocks. In Cartagena they always say that Cartagena is the one that has a history. When

[Gustavo] Bell said in his CV when he was running for vice president that he had studied history in London and had written a book on the history of Barranquilla, the Cartagenans held their noses and said: "What history!"

JOSÉ SALGAR: Gabo exaggerates when he says it was a writing staff of wise men and that it was marvelous. That's from the coastal point of view. The environment along the coast saw the people at *El Tiempo* and *El Espectador* as the elite of national journalism. At *El Espectador* there were very brilliant figures: Zalamea, de Greiff, Villegas.

HÉCTOR ROJAS HERAZO: I love Bogotá in spite of that whole thing of their thinking they're superior. They thought they were wise men and like that.

What was it I said in an article I wrote when they assassinated Gaitán? That in Bogotá they said hello, damn it!, in Latin . . . convinced they were extremely refined . . . and they called it . . . What did they call it? They said it was the Athens of South America. And they believed it. Something so comical, and of course when the thing happened, the impetus that brought the death of Gaitán . . . If it hadn't rained as hard as it rained that day, they would have finished off Bogotá. They would have burned it. Fortunately, damn it!, Jesus Christ came out and sent the downpour . . . But Bogotá had something . . . It had a silent thing deep down. Some beautiful parks. It had tranquillity. It was a peaceful capital. It looked like a terminal . . . Melancholy . . . Like all endured joy that turns into melancholy. It's muffled. It's peaceful. That's why the horror of assassinations frightened people so much here. It has always been a very sweet city. Very peaceful. You arrived, let's say, there were some places where you went to eat or to think. A few places where the food was cheap. We would go there every day and we had friends. That was where you made friends because the other places were too haughty. But Bogotá is certainly very loved . . .

SANTIAGO MUTIS: Now, Bogotá, what does it have to offer Gabo? Writers. That's it.

JOSÉ SALGAR: And there's a name that belongs to that moment, which is our friend. Eduardo Zalamea Borda. He was also a novelist. He wrote a famous novel: *Four Years Aboard Myself.* He was also a great journalist, but he embellished his literature a great deal with the atmosphere of La Guajira. *Four Years Aboard Myself* is the adventures of a Bogotan along the coast. It also had a great influence on that magic moment that presented itself to Gabo. He says: "Well, I can stop making literature, the literature that obsesses me, and then I'll devote myself exclusively to journalism. But journalism and reality are very cold, even ugly. You have to bring imagination to that."

SANTIAGO MUTIS: What Gabo's doing is confirming a possibility. It's a road they're opening. Opening it in a newspaper, an editorial, a circle of friends, making their own lives. When those things stop being that way, the truth begins to appear and they're the ones who begin to make that truth. There are many things against them. But they can't do anything against Gabo. One sentence of Gabo's undoes everything; nobody has a greater talent for contradicting; they couldn't do anything with him.

HÉCTOR ROJAS HERAZO: Besides, what one had to do in life, Gabo did. One thing is for sure, our desire to accomplish was the right desire.

II

The Neck of the Swan

*In which the lost cause is transformed into a great journalist by day and
a short story writer by night*

JOSÉ SALGAR: Of course Gabo was good, but at that time I also had magnificent reporters, more brilliant and more skillful in reporting. The editorial board of the newspaper would meet to deal with the day's topics, and say: "Today you go there and cover this," and give some instructions. But there's also personal initiative by which it occurs to the reporter: "I'm going to write on this subject," he proposes it, and you tell him to do it or not to do it. He? Initiative? Not much. Not much. Gabo had initiative for his novels and for the worm of magical realism and literature, but at the newspaper as a journalist he had to march in time with everybody else . . .

At that moment he resisted, but afterward, almost as soon as he started reporting, he grew fond of it. And he grew even fonder when he started writing. It was certainly fast. The paper had to get out, and often I would pull the text out of his typewriter, pass it along to a copy editor for fast correction, and it went out, though a little rough. One of Gabo's characteristics is not turning in originals with errors. If he has something he has to correct, he tears it up and begins again. His wastebasket was always full of crumpled drafts. He'd repeat the process until he had an original as perfect as possible. Except for some things. Somewhere I have an original that he declared finished but only because he was in a hurry.

MARGARITA DE LA VEGA: He wrote movie reviews. You can look at the articles. Film was a part of the culture. Film clubs were a very important element in the cultural life of the entire country, and that was an inheritance from the French. My father, who studied medicine in Paris and married a Frenchwoman, started the first film club in Cartagena with Eduardo Lemaitre. There were also poetry get-togethers where, for example, Meira del Mar, the Barranquillan poet who died a little while ago, got her start. People met to recite poetry. In Bogotá too, but the idea that Bogotá was Athens and we were idiots is a lie.

JOSÉ SALGAR: Gabo loved articles about film and had written them at *El Heraldo.* Then he came to *El Espectador.* What he liked best was writing, and what ended up being a mission for him were the "From Day to Day" notes and movie reviews. Then he discovered something different. It was giving his opinion about something in the arts through his movie reviews. And he also wrote book reviews. He emulated very famous writers like Eduardo Zalamea, Abelardo Forero Benavides, very distinguished men, and at that time those "From Day to Day" notes had considerable importance and allowed him to make a little literature and write well.

I knew what he was doing: I had read his stories and thought he was an excellent writer. The only concrete thing, the impression I always had of him at that time, was that he turned in the best originals I've ever received.

First, immensely neat, very hardworking, because he tossed everything he didn't like into the wastebasket until he came up with a perfect original. I thought that was terrific, but that he needed to apply himself more to the reality of journalism . . . The fact is he had two totally distinct faces. One was his obsession with literature. He was discovering literature; he discovered it with his literature teachers at the secondary school in Zipaquirá. He turned to them for his memoirs. They were obsessed with literature and he was discovering Joyce, all the great writers of the time. Then, at night, he would think of literature as fiction and as beautiful language. He was writing stories.

JUANCHO JINETE: "The Handsomest Drowned Man in the World" was Álvaro Cepeda's and Álvaro says I was the one who told the story to Gabito. "Sonuvabitch, why did you tell him that?" And I say: "Come on, he got it out first."

Man, that happened in Santa Marta. Do you know the Santa Marta Bay? In Tasajera, it's fishermen. The guys there, they go out to fish. Then this guy went out to fish and didn't come back the next day. On the third day they went out to look for him. Then they began to get together for the wake, and you know you have a wake with rum. Then after five days . . . You know that in those houses the courtyard is right next to the swamp, and out of the swamp, ay, comes the handsomest drowned man in the world. They told it to us there, and then one day Álvaro says: "Aha, Gabo, that's a great story about the drowned man." And he says: "Which one is that?" I tell it to him, and *wham!* he brought it out first. Afterward Álvaro wrote it, but in another form.

Then there's the story "The Night of the Curlews." So there in the brothel of Black Eufemia we woke up one morning: Álvaro, Gabito, Alfonso, and I. And since it was like our house because Alfonso's father was the owner and rented it out, they treated us well. At night they turned the curlews loose.

QUIQUE SCOPELL: It's a bird like a heron that sings a lot at dawn. Then Black Eufemia, since she ran the brothel, had her twenty women in their rooms. And at night, at two or three in the morning, when the women were going to bed, she would bring out the curlews . . .

JUANCHO JINETE: Into the garden.

QUIQUE SCOPELL: Black Eufemia died. And one of her clients put the whores to work in his factory . . . and this guy, who was a client, said to the twenty whores: "You don't have to work at this business, you can have a decent life. I'll take you to my factory to work. You can all be working in my factory." And he took them. He had a paper bag factory. The man was one of those Christians, full of charity. He had the most altruistic idea in the world. He took them to work and the whores, after twenty days, said: "No, this is as far as we go."

JOSÉ SALGAR: But in the daytime, when he came and the paper hired him to be a reporter, he had to put all that aside, tell the truth exactly, and have some journalistic parameters that he didn't have. First, to tell things the right way. Second, to turn things in on time. And devote all his efforts to the paper that was paying his salary. Then I ran into a problem. He would come in with his hair uncombed and bags under his eyes, and then I said to him: "We just can't work this way, no . . ." The story is that as head of the editorial staff I demanded that he walk the line and come in early, and Gabo said that he came in late because he was writing something or other. "You're dedicated to something else," I said to him. "Why don't you wring the neck of the swan and dedicate yourself to writing journalism? Journalism lets you use literature as a tool." Then this is what happened. He said: "Well, then I'll give up literature." He meant that he heard me and was dedicating himself to journalism. And he began to write very good journalism, but in time I realized he wasn't.

Here it is, this was in '55: "For the great José Salgar, let's see if I wring the neck of the swan. With my friendship, Gabo." First edition of *Leaf Storm*, which was a little clandestine.

GUILLERMO ANGULO: I was working in Mexico. I was a photographer. One day Gabo published something very false about me, but very beautiful, saying: "Colombian makes neorealist films in Mexico." I wasn't making films. I took some photos of a popular Holy Week, like the one they do here; it was in Reyes, in Ixtapalapa. And he liked it very much. He published a commentary in *El Espectador*. And I wrote to him, thanking him: "I'd like to meet you." I was returning to the country, I don't know, it must have been in '55. He said: "Yes, I'm at *El Espectador*."

JOSÉ SALGAR: Gabo was sent to cover the Vuelta a Colombia, the bicycle tour, and to talk to Cochise Rodríguez, who was the champion but still quite dull. "Talk about the life of Cochise Rodríguez." Any reporter would say, "What a boring assignment to send me to interview Cochise Rodríguez." Gabo did it. Damn! He sharpened his pencil and went. As soon as he was given a topic, the man warmed up, would start finding the details and then began to verify things. And once he was writing he remembered more things . . . The thing was very well done even if it was a boring thing like a bicycle tour.

He specialized in writing newspaper series. There's also that very long story about the department of El Choco. When Rojas Pinilla, president at the time, announced he was going to dissolve it, our reporter there sends a story about a huge protest. But when Gabo arrives, he realizes that the guy had made it up. Gabo actually had to make it happen. The news existed, but no one wanted to talk about it and tell the story about the poverty that existed in that region. He did that.

QUIQUE SCOPELL: Gabo was a normal guy. I think he has a great virtue, which is tenacity. The man is tenacious, tenacious, and for his whole life he wanted to be what he was. A journalist. He's a great journalist. No, I don't think I thought so before. But he is.

JOSÉ SALGAR: We sent Gabo with General Rojas Pinilla to cover something in Melgar. When he arrived at the Melgar airport he saw that another plane was flying somewhere else and he said: "Where's it going?" They told him: "They discovered guerrillas in Villa Rica, in El Tolima." So he went to Villa Rica and not to Melgar. And he arrived with the photographer and there was nothing there. But suddenly somebody told him: "The guerrillas are there." And he went and he found the thing and saw that the guerrillas had killed four soldiers. And they were present at the thing. And surely, they brought down the soldiers, but the government, which was Rojas, completely denied it. He couldn't publish anything. We lived with censorship at the time. Then he was left with the four dead men covered up, and now, fifty years afterward, he's reliving all that but in detail for his memoirs. He called to ask me facts about it . . . With him, it has to be perfect. A month ago he called me from Mexico to ask me the name of the photographer who had gone with him to something. And on the basis of that we talked about other similar news items. We talked for an hour and a quarter.

JUANCHO JINETE: He stood out because of that time he reported on the sailors they threw into the water at the naval base. That's when . . .

JOSÉ SALGAR: There's the *Story of a Shipwrecked Sailor*. That was an ordinary, run-of-the-mill piece of news. Big and all that, but the news item was already dead. And the anecdote is very curious. Gabo and Velasco, the shipwrecked sailor, met, and Velasco had already told everything to other journalists, but they met because we told Gabo that it was a question of getting a few things out of him. They met in a café and the guy began to tell him his story and become excited: he suddenly realizes what he's saying . . . That was the spark that gave rise to the story. That happened with Gabo's things. But what is it? It's meticulousness. The journalistic responsibility to find out.

JUANCHO JINETE: There was a shipwreck but no one had figured out that the navy ship was carrying contraband, refrigerators and things like that, and they threw a boy overboard, one of the sailors . . . And that was his scoop. He wrote a feature article and nobody here dared to write a feature about that. Well, first because it had to do with the navy. That boy's calamity and how he was saved.

JOSÉ SALGAR: The famous *Story of a Shipwrecked Sailor . . .* He never realized the importance it finally had. It was one of the reasons for the fall of Rojas Pinilla. Because he was writing under press censorship when he went to see the hero, who said some things about his ship tilting when it came in. But Gabo finds out that it wasn't a storm but the weight of the contraband refrigerators it was carrying. The sailor said it naively, Gabo confirmed it, and published it with the title *The Story of a Shipwrecked Sailor*

Who Spent Ten Days Adrift on a Raft with Nothing to Eat or Drink Who Was Proclaimed a Hero of the Nation, Kissed by Beauty Queens and Made Rich by Publicity, and Then Abandoned by the Government and Forgotten Forever.

RAFAEL ULLOA: *The Story of a Shipwrecked Sailor* made him famous. Rojas Pinilla was going to have him arrested.

GUILLERMO ANGULO: The fact is there's nothing like dictatorship. Look, Rojas Pinilla called Fernando Gómez Agudelo because Fernando's father was a great jurist. They called him "Toad Gómez" and he was the one who resolved Rojas Pinilla's legal problems. Then, as a gift, they allowed his boy, who was twenty-two, twenty-three years old, to introduce television in Colombia. Rojas said to him: "You're going to set up television, but it has to be ready within a year, when it's the anniversary of my government." Then he went to the United States and told them about the problem of television in Colombia. They told him: "That's impossible, in a place with so many mountains, you can't have television." Then he went to Germany. In Germany they told him yes, but it was very expensive. "You have to have booster antennas on each mountain and you can bring television wherever you like as long as you have money for booster antennas." And he said: "Let's go."

There were just a few days to go and the sets arrived, the last ones they needed, from Germany on a KLM plane. And the director of Civil Aeronautics said: "That plane can't land." "Why?" "Because we don't have an aviation agreement with Holland." Then they call Fernando and tell him: "No, the plane is going back." And he says: "Just a moment. Tell the plane to fly around and I'll settle this in ten minutes." He calls Rojas Pinilla and Rojas Pinilla tells him: "Listen, I am too busy to deal with this. You call the director of Civil Aeronautics. Tell him that if that plane isn't on land in five minutes, he's fired and you'll become the director of Civil Aeronautics and you settle this." And that's what happened. There really isn't anything like dictatorship.

HÉCTOR ROJAS HERAZO: And then came his desire to leave for Europe. *El Espectador* sends him.

In Paris with an open hand, taken in 1954.

12

SOFTAG: Society of Friends to Aid Gabito

In which García Márquez, thanks to the dictatorship, discovers Europe,
lifelong friends, and poverty pure and simple

JOSÉ SALGAR: Gabo had a great desire to see Europe, to go and
make movies, and write something, and then came the coincidence of the Big Four Conference [happening in Geneva]. Then
he obtained an invitation to go and take some film courses in Italy.
There were some coincidences and the paper paid for his trip. I
don't know how much because the paper has never been rich, but
some possibility, in any case, got him the ticket . . . Nobody was
happier at going to see Europe. And he didn't realize the danger
of his being stranded there, no. That they'd close the paper, he
had no idea, none. Besides, that enriched him a good deal too.
Because it pushed him toward absolute reality.

FERNANDO RESTREPO: Fernando Gómez Agudelo and Gabo
meet on the flight to Europe. He was going to cover the famous
meeting of Eisenhower and Khrushchev. He was sent by *El Espect-*
ador to cover the famous summit and my buddy, Fernando, goes
to carry out some investigations into European television to try
to select equipment and other things, because Rojas Pinilla had
ordered him to initiate television in Colombia. Fernando, in his
twenties, was the director of National Radio of Colombia at the
time of General Rojas Pinilla. The general ordered him to carry

out an investigation in order to establish television, something that was accomplished in a very short time, less than eight months. And for that reason he's traveling to Europe and on the plane he meets Gabo, who is, at the time, a reporter for *El Espectador.* That was the year 1954. Gabo doesn't return to *El Espectador* because he stays. It's my understanding that he sells his return ticket and stays to live in Europe.

JOSÉ SALGAR: He's totally fascinated by the new world he discovers: he had already been a figure on a newspaper, he already had his title of journalist, he was going to represent an important Colombian newspaper in Europe, he was already the man and had his image as a writer, a successful writer who had published a novel. *Leaf Storm* is the beginning of *One Hundred Years.*

GUILLERMO ANGULO: I went to *El Espectador* and they told me: "No, he went to Europe as our correspondent and is going to study film at the Centro Sperimentale in Rome." And I said: "Ah, that's good, because I'm going to study film at the Centro Sperimentale." And he left me a letter telling me where I could find him. I could find him on Piazza Italia, No. 2, second floor. It said: "You get there, go up to the second floor, and a lady will come out singing opera with a towel around her head, then you ask her for . . ." I forget the name of the guy, the director, he's an Argentine film director who then became director of the film school Gabo started in Havana. What's his name? Well, maybe I'll remember it soon. The fact is that Alzheimer's really is a mess. Anyway, when I got to Rome, I went to the Centro to look for him and I ran into the editing teacher, what the Italians call *montaggio,* and she said with good reason that Gabo was the best student she'd ever had. Why? Because what Gabo does is editing. In his works, no. That is, it's something he learned from American novels but that he handles very well. He's a great editor. So then I arrive at Piazza Italia and the lady comes out, and I laugh. The lady is annoyed at my laughing, but the fact is she comes out singing opera with her head wrapped in a towel. I asked for this friend, whose name I can't remember, who's a director and was studying film and afterward did a lot of things in Argentina, he even acted in *A Very Old Man with Enormous Wings.* Oh yes, Fernando Birri. Eh, and she said: "No, he went back to Argentina." And I say: "And Gabriel García Márquez?" And she says: "*Chi lo conosce?*" Of course, no one knew him then. Then Gabo sent me a letter through a mutual friend and said: "Look, I had to go to Paris."

SANTIAGO MUTIS: Because Gabo says Paris, but what did Paris give him? Gabo is pulled out of the Colombian coast with forceps. Gabo's from there: it's his father, his family, his town, his people. It's his friends. It's everything. No need to go to Paris for inspiration. Gabo goes to Paris for something else . . . What happens is that he gets stuck there, since the paper is closed because of political problems here.

GUILLERMO ANGULO: Our mutual friend Pupa, he sent her to me. "Allora," the story about Pupa, is very nice because Pupa was in love with a Romano named Romano who played the guitar. And Romano took no notice of her, he didn't notice her at all. So she decided to go to bed with every Latin American she could find. She was Costa Rican, and they had sent her there so she wouldn't create a scandal by going to bed with everybody, or at least she'd make a scandal over there in Europe, where that isn't considered bad. She was the daughter or granddaughter of a former president. He was a very important person, so she was first secretary of the Costa Rican embassy in Rome, but she lived in Paris. Naturally, they hadn't sent her over to work.

I still have it around somewhere [the edition of *The Colonel* that Gabo sent me]. On yellow paper. He sends it to me in Rome so I'll read it, and I told him that I liked it; I wrote to him and made some commentary or something. He said: "I'll be in Paris. I'll be at *seize* on the Rue Cujas." That was where Gabo lived with this famous lady. What was her name? Madame. Madame La Croix I think was her name. So then I said: "Well, I have to go to Paris. I'll be in Paris for about six months, so we'll see each there. I'll come to the hotel."

SANTIAGO MUTIS: What Paris gave him was a woman who kept him for a year, the owner of a boardinghouse, an older woman, and a person who wasn't Paris either. I mean, yes, well, she's the profound Paris, let's say, but Paris doesn't give him Leonardo da Vinci. What Paris gives him is brutal confinement, and he uses that to say: "Well, who am I? What am I doing here?" And it obliges him to define himself. And what he decides to be is what he has always been: a man who comes from Barranquilla, from Cartagena, from Aracataca, and who loves [the music of] Escalona, who loves Alejandro Durán, who loves La Guajira, who saw the most beautiful women in the world there. That's the thing.

GUILLERMO ANGULO: The hotel was called Hôtel de Flandre, on the Rue Cujas, and in front of it was this black Cuban poet, Nicolás Guillén. He was exiled in a hotel poorer than the one on the Rue Cujas. He went out every day and came back with bread under his arm, the way all the French carry it, so that you think it's very strange that they use bread like a deodorant. Afterward Guillén was ambassador in Paris, and of course, there's a very nice story. They asked him: "Well, what about . . . Diplomacy, so, is it very hard?" And he said: "Yes, yes, yes. Diplomacy is hard, but working is much, much harder."

So then I come to *seize* on the Rue Cujas and the lady tells me: "No, García Márquez went for a little trip around the Iron Curtain." When he made his reports about the Curtain with Plinio. I had decided that I'd never see him again. Then I said: "Señora, I need a room, the cheapest one you have." And she says: "How long will you stay?" I said at least three months. And she said: "Ah, good," and she gave me a room on the top floor, which was very uncomfortable because the roof was there. You hit your head when you got up.

One day there's a knock at the door and I see a guy in a blue sweater and a scarf wrapped around a few times, and he says: "Maestrico, what are you doing in my room?" It was Gabo. And that's how we met. I have a photograph made there, right at that time.

SANTIAGO MUTIS: He can't pay and he stays there writing, going hungry. The days go by . . . What could he be to La Croix? Nothing. He was the journalist who's there, poor, working.

GUILLERMO ANGULO: Gabo was very, very poor then. While I was there, he would come every day to eat with me. He would come, I kept five metro tickets, he was living in a maid's room in Neuilly, a very elegant area, but in a maid's room. It was a tiny room with an outside bathroom, and he had a small stove where he heated water and fixed coffee and eggs. That was all he could eat. He was very, very poor. So I invited him to supper every night. He would say to me: "What do you have to read? Remember that it's a forty-five minute trip on the metro." I've been a magazine reader my whole life. I had *Cahiers du Cinema*. I had *Paris Match*. He chose whatever there was and said: "I'll bring it back tomorrow," and he'd take a double ticket, round-trip. That was when we became very very good friends.

JOSÉ SALGAR: The other day he says to me: "Tell me about when I went to Europe and they closed *El Espectador* and I was left stranded and without a newspaper. Then I sat down to tell all my troubles, to tell you all the adventures I was having in Paris in some very long letters, and I ended up begging you to get me the check that the paper was going to send me." It was the only income he counted on. "Do you remember anything from those letters I sent to you?" And then my answer is, it's the saddest thing, that like all the things that are sent to a paper and aren't published, they were tossed out. Please! What that was! Of course, he's reconstructed all those changes of fortune throughout his work.

But those letters were firsthand and very, very personal. Stupendous letters, because the man doesn't venture to sit down and write something if he doesn't do it very well. It's another mania. He told me he was writing about that time the two of us lived through, and that's why he asked me for some facts for the first volume of his memoirs. He's reconstructing everything in minute detail, and he's surely going to talk about things I didn't know about.

JUANCHO JINETE: There was a Society of Friends to Assist Gabito, the SOFTAG. But it was a fraud, a fraud because the society never existed as such. SOFTAG collected money to send to him. I didn't give even five cents. But Julio Mario and Álvaro, they did.

GUILLERMO ANGULO: Then I'll go on with the story, I didn't finish telling about Pupa. When I had already met him, I said: "Listen, how did you meet Pupa?" And he says: "Ah, that's a long story. Look, I was very bad off for money and one day I receive a card from Barranquilla, from my friends at La Cueva, signed by Vilá, by the Kid Cepeda, by Alejandro, it was covered with palm trees and sun, and they said: 'You fool, you're there putting up with the cold and we're here terrific in the sun. Come here.' Then I said: 'Assholes, damn it, you could have sent me money!'"

HERIBERTO FIORILLO: They made that postcard here on the bar of La Cueva. The one who knew how to make that sandwich was Jorge Rendón, owner of the Mundo Bookstore. Germán Vargas sent the telegram that alerted Gabito to the existence of the hundred-dollar bill inside the postcard.

GUILLERMO ANGULO: Then after a while he received a special delivery letter from Barranquilla that said: "Since you're very dense, you surely haven't realized that the card is a sandwich with a hundred dollars inside."

QUIQUE SCOPELL: In the old days the image would detach from postcards. The glue was bad, you put it in water, and the image would detach. Álvaro put in the hundred dollars. Back then it was illegal to send money by mail, which is why he didn't send it on the outside.

GUILLERMO ANGULO: Then Gabo went down to look through the hotel's trash—imagine, condoms, everything. Searching. He finds the card and there really is a hundred dollars.

QUIQUE SCOPELL: Álvaro put in ninety and I put in ten. And we fastened them inside.

GUILLERMO ANGULO: But it was Saturday and it was the time when the dollar was like black market, it was very difficult because you didn't change them in a machine like today, and he was desperate because he was hungry. Then he began to ask where he could change money and somebody told him: "Look, there's a friend of ours named Pupa. She arrived yesterday from Rome after changing her salary, so she must have lots of money, so go see her."

He left, wrapped up as always, dying of the cold. We were in winter, and Pupa opened the door. A tidal wave of heat came out of a room that was *ben riscaldata, vero?* And Pupa was completely naked. Pupa wasn't pretty but she had a marvelous body. And at the slightest provocation, or even without one, she would strip. You'd say to her: "Look, what pretty spectacles. Ah, and where did you buy them?" Then she would strip and in all her splendor she'd show off her eyeglasses. And, well, Gabo entered and then Pupa sat down. "What bothered me most," says Gabo, "no, not bothered, surprised, is that she behaved as if she were dressed. Very naturally. She crossed her legs and began to chat, and she talked to me about Colombia, the Colombians she knew, and I said to her: 'Look, this is my problem.' And she said: 'Yes, of course.' Then she stopped with great elegance. She went to the other side of the room, where there was a small chest. She opened it. She took out some money. She said . . . and I saw that what she wanted was to go to bed with me, but I wasn't thinking about that. What I was thinking about was eating. And she said: 'Listen, why don't we have something to drink?' 'If I drink anything now'"—Gabo told me—"'I won't be able to help getting drunk.' I said to her: 'No, no, no, look, we'll see each other later.' Then I went to eat and I ate so much that I was sick with indigestion for a week, I had been hungry for so long."

HÉCTOR ROJAS HERAZO: He's had great friends who loved him a great deal. Most friends betray you at some point. They do you enormous harm. But friends have been extraordinarily faithful to him. Man, that's a beautiful essence of a destiny. Why is it that he's never complained that his friends hadn't valued him or done something . . . No, no. They always wanted to work for him. That's indisputable.

PLINIO APULEYO MENDOZA: Every night Gabriel wrote until dawn, working on a novel that would become *In Evil Hour*. He had just begun when he had to interrupt it: a character, the old colonel waiting in vain for his pension as a veteran of the civil war, demanded his own sphere. A book. He wrote *Nobody Writes to the Colonel* in part to clear the way for *In Evil Hour* and in part to exorcize literarily his ordinary troubles at the time: like his character, he didn't know how he would eat the next day and was always waiting for a letter, a letter with money that never arrived.

QUIQUE SCOPELL: At that time I was living in Havana. He knew I was living in Havana. My father was Cuban. I had my parents as a base in Havana, but I bought pieces of alligator skin here in Barranquilla, took them to Havana, tanned them in Havana, made wallets and shoes in Havana, and went to Miami and sold everything in Miami. In other words, I'd spend two or three months here in Barranquilla, one in Havana, and two or three months in Miami. I left after the revolution, the year that Fidel came in my daughter was born in Havana ... He knew I was involved with roosters, and he sent me a questionnaire. Gabito personally asked me questions. He called me and said: "Quique, I'm going to send you a questionnaire, man, because I'm writing a chapter . . ." about I don't know what damn thing about roosters. Then he asked me: "What are roosters like?" "What color are roosters?" "How do you catch a rooster?" "When do you wring a rooster's neck?" Well, something like two thousand questions.

JUANCHO JINETE: Quique has been a fan of cockfights his whole life.

RAMÓN ILLÁN BACCA: I heard about García Márquez in '58. I didn't know *Leaf Storm* or García Márquez's first stories, I had no idea. When the Barranquilla Group appears here, I was studying for my bachelor's degree at a seminary very far from any of these things. Then in '58 I still remember that *Nobody Writes to the Colonel* was published in *Mito*.

PLINIO APULEYO MENDOZA: *Nobody Writes to the Colonel* was published in a literary magazine without its editors asking for prior authorization or paying for any rights at all: they thought, in good faith, that it was a generous enough gesture to bring out a manuscript turned down by publishers.

SANTIAGO MUTIS: One can't say that *Nobody Writes to the Colonel* is a political book though it is an immense denunciation of the deception the government perpetrated in this country. And yet, the amount of humanity in that book is so strong.

RAMÓN ILLÁN BACCA: I liked *Nobody Writes to the Colonel*, but it didn't produce the kind of upheaval in me that you get when you're reading Thomas Mann; it wasn't *The Magic Mountain*. I was reading *Demian*, *Steppenwolf*. Those were the things I was reading, the things that impressed me.

CARMELO MARTÍNEZ: He hears stories and he takes hold of them and puts them in his books. In Montería there was a woman named Natalia. Lame Natalia. She was lame, they had cut her ankles, she walked on crutches, and when she didn't have anything to eat, she'd put stones in the pot so the neighbors would say: "Natalia's eating." That's what she told my father; Natalia was a friend of my father's. Her house was near the cemetery, a little house . . . She would put the pot outside and put in water and put in stones. "So nobody would think that Natalia was hungry." Do you remember that detail from the book about the colonel? His wife boils stones to save face with the neighbors.

Mercedes Barcha.

13

Sacred Crocodile

In which, thanks to his enormous ability to choose good friends, he obtains work in Venezuela and returns to Barranquilla with the "sacred croco-dile"

PLINIO APULEYO MENDOZA: The only thing he had in his room in Paris was a red Olivetti typewriter I had sold him, and tacked to the wall the photo of Mercedes, the sweetheart he had in Colombia. The first time I visited him, he pointed at the photograph and said: "The sacred crocodile."

GUILLERMO ANGULO: He comes back from Paris and begins to work as a journalist in Venezuela with Plinio. I don't remember the name of the magazine. The "crocodile" was always very steady and they decide to marry when he's in Caracas.

GERALD MARTIN: With Tachia, his Paris sweetheart, there was no way the relationship would survive; it was stormy, but very significant.

MIGUEL FALQUEZ-CERTAIN: Plinio is the one who helped him throughout this period. The period when he was dead broke, in the 1950s in Paris, when he was stranded because Rojas Pinilla closed down *El Espectador* and he was unemployed and didn't have five cents. And as it happened, it was the same period when Vargas Llosa lived there, though they say they lived a block apart but didn't know each other. So he was broke, without money, and Plinio arrived with Delia Zapata Olivella and a dance troupe, the folkloric ballet or however you call it, and they were on tour in Europe. Plinio was always a journalist. His father was a famous politician who was a friend of Gaitán's. Gaitán died in the arms of Plinio's father. He was there at the moment they assassinated him. His father was also named Plinio Mendoza, Plinio Mendoza Neira.

Gabo wanted to go to Russia with the ballet and they couldn't justify the expense of taking him. So that he could go, Plinio talked to Delia and they hired him as a *maraquero*, and he went as if he played the maracas. They traveled by train to the Soviet Union.

He lived in Venezuela with Plinio at the time of Pérez Jiménez's coup,* and that was where he met Alejo Carpentier.** That's the origin of the theory I have that the famous magical realism is not magical realism. It's the marvelous real: that's what they called Carpentier's literature, before García Márquez.

JAIME ABELLO BANFI: One of the great moments in his journalism happened in Venezuela. He makes huge strides in Venezuela. Plinio, who was managing *Momento*, a magazine which was in the Capriles Group, calls him in Paris to offer him a full-time job. And Venezuela is also in an enormously prosperous

---

* General Marcos Pérez Jiménez ruled oil-rich Venezuela with a firm hand from 1952 to 1958. García Márquez landed in Caracas to work at a magazine as the Pérez Jiménez days were coming to an end. This gave him firsthand knowledge of life under the rule of an authoritarian dictator, a subject he returns to in *Autumn of the Patriarch*.

** Alejo Carpentier, a Cuban novelist, essayist, and ethnomusicologist, has been baptized as the father of the term "magical realism" to explain how in Latin America the real and the surreal live side by side. He writes in the prologue to *The Kingdom of This World*, a novel about the revolution in Haiti: "But what is the history of Latin America but a chronicle of magical realism?" Both writers lived in Caracas at the same time but it is unclear if they ever met. Alejo Carpentier was Cuba's ambassador and a worldly man with literary recognition; García Márquez was a lowly staff writer at a gossip magazine.

state. The society was all about oil, and growth. He lives through all of this and the fall of Pérez Jiménez. He writes some memorable articles, like "Caracas with No Water." Now I'm going to point something out: the Gabo of "Caracas with No Water" is very different from the Gabo of *News of a Kidnapping*. In *News* he boasts that he invented absolutely nothing. On the other hand, he's recognized that in "Caracas with No Water" the German in the article is himself; Gabo was the man who supposedly shaved with peach juice, a half-invented anecdote meant to demonstrate the situation. To dramatize the journalistic tale he was recounting. Saying: "It's a news article, everything is true, but I put in a little grain of fiction." But with *News of a Kidnapping*, he insists that everything was super-verified, investigated, researched, confirmed. Total fact-checking. And that's why he insists so much at the Foundation on the ethics of not inventing. That is, now he's a mature Gabo, much more careful because he himself had been the victim of a lot of inventions. That's why he was concerned about the way they conducted interviews, misusing the tape recorder.

PLINIO APULEYO MENDOZA: After the first weekend he came back married. Mercedes didn't say a single word until the third day after we had met.

MARÍA LUISA ELÍO: When did he meet Mercedes? When she was a girl, isn't that so?

RAFAEL ULLOA: They met when they were kids. She's from Sucre. Those Barchas are from Magangué, but they went to live in Sucre and Gabito's father went to Sincé. And after Sincé he went to Sucre and that's where they met.

MARÍA LUISA ELÍO: Once, when Mercedes was about eleven years old, she was in her father's pharmacy. Gabito went into the pharmacy and said to her: "I'm going to marry you when you're older."

MARGARITA DE LA VEGA: She's not only from the coast but is also a mix of Spanish and Turkish. What we call "Turkish," they could be from Syria or Egypt, but they were Turks because they came with a passport from the Ottoman Empire. They were much more established than García Márquez's family. It's in Sucre when the García Márquez family achieves a bourgeois kind of prosperity, and that's why *Chronicle of a Death Foretold* takes place in Sucre, when his father was a pharmacist.

MIGUEL FALQUEZ-CERTAIN: Her father was a pharmacist and had a higher status than García Márquez's father. He would spend his vacations with his parents, and on one of these he met Barcha, who was a little girl, and he said to the girl: "I'll come back for you when you're big so we can get married." And he left. And came back when he was thirty-three years old at least. He had no relationship with her, and it was like one of those love affairs in India where they're engaged when they're children and marry without knowing each other. Not at all. He went, picked her up, got married, and left with her. That's the story.

CARMELO MARTÍNEZ: This isn't for you to repeat. He was in love with a girl named Uricoechea, the daughter of Dr. Uricoechea, from Bogotá. Her name's Camila. Camila . . . no, Camila is her sister. Camila's here, married to Orval's brother. This girl was the younger one. Amparo. He was in love with her but Dr. Uricoechea was a class snob and refused to accept Gabito because Gabito didn't dress well. He was a poor man. Besides, he didn't like dressing well. So the old man was opposed. Then Amparo went to Bogotá. She entered nursing school, and like every nurse, she marries a doctor. She married a Bogotan doctor, they went to California, but they separated and so she married again and so did he. But as far as I know, she never came back to Colombia. Mercedes was a friend of Amparo's, the Uricoechea girl. Of course she didn't take him away from Amparo. Dr. Uricoechea drove Gabito away.

MARGARITA DE LA VEGA: Mercedes was very pretty. She had beautiful eyes. Maybe she wasn't pretty in the traditional sense, but I always noticed her. She had very large eyes, very pretty hair, a lot of expression. She was much better-looking than Gabo.

MARÍA LUISA ELÍO: Then, talking with her, he said: "It's a good idea for you to marry me because I'm going to be somebody very important." I think he really did know everything that was to come.

MARGARITA DE LA VEGA: That story in *One Hundred Years of Solitude* about how he met her, all of that is true. She was very young because she was his neighbor. But there's a lot of machismo in that too, isn't there? You spot them when they're very young and she's going to be the ideal woman because nobody else is going to see her. And he marries her and she's in love. I call that bolero philosophy. It's a part of machismo, all those melodramatic songs. Because "only once," because love like that happens only once, and it doesn't matter what happens, there's something above reality, which is that special union with the person one loves for the first time, that the man behaves badly but it isn't that he wants to, it's that he has certain instincts, but in reality you're the first one. It's like a disease. It's part of the entire culture. It's adoration, devotion, the apparent veneration that flatters you so much and also that romantic thing that also comes from romanticism, that there's one special man for you. Don't tell me the gringos don't have it, of course they do.

14

"That Communist Newspaper"

The true and little-known story of how García Márquez comes to Prensa Latina, *the official organ of the Cuban Revolution*

PLINIO APULEYO MENDOZA: When I decided to leave Venezuela and return to Colombia, I intended to become fully connected to political activity inspired by what was then, for me, the fascinating Cuban experience.

Gabo planned to go to Mexico and continue writing.

We said goodbye one night at the door to his house in the San Bernardino district in Caracas; our Venezuelan experience was coming to an end.

We didn't know that in less than a month we'd be reunited in Bogotá. Thanks to Cuba.

GUILLERMO ANGULO: One day a Mexican came to Bogotá. Gabo has never told this because he says it's more important to say it was a guerrilla who came. He's been cultivating his image. But the truth is this: a Mexican came whom I knew—I had lived in Mexico for five years—and he called me. He was in the Hotel Tequendama, and I said to him: "No, bro, you come stay in my house." I was a bachelor. I brought him home, and the guy, whose name is Slim Rodríguez, always had his valise with him. He went to the bathroom with the valise. He never left the valise. And I thought: "A novel." Of course, who's going to leave a novel lying around? And I said to him: "Listen, why don't you ever put that fucking suitcase down?" "Because I'm carrying dough." (He was carrying dough. Dough!) He was carrying money to set up *Prensa Latina*. And he was carrying a sum that today may even sound ridiculous but which was a lot of money then. Ten thousand dollars. "Wow, what? What's that for?" "To set up *Prensa Latina* here and you'll be the first manager." I told him I'm not a journalist or a manager. "You're the only person I know. The only one I have confidence in, so you'll be the first manager." So then I started *Prensa Latina*. Afterward I met Fidel and I said to him: "You people owe me a statue because I'm the founder." Fidel thought that was funny. Then I called these two guys [Plinio and Gabo] and said to them: "Look, this is for you two. This isn't for me. What should I do?" That was when the two of them began working for *Prensa Latina*.

PLINIO APULEYO MENDOZA: I called Caracas: "Listen, Gabo, there's something important happening here that I can't talk about on the phone. Come to Bogotá. A press office, I'll tell you all about it . . . we'll be the bosses."

I was already talking like the Mexican.

In four or five days, Gabo and Mercedes come down the airplane steps. Mercedes was expecting.

RAFAEL ULLOA: That Castro loves him to death.

PLINIO APULEYO MENDOZA: Of course, that period has a dramatic connotation seen from the perspective of the years, when one looks at the implications of the Cuban Revolution, its illusions, the rhetorical notions that were developed around it (Régis

Debray's unfortunate "foco theory"), the influence they had on many individual destinies that touched ours.

But on the margin of this political excitement we led an organized, easy life, circling around our daily news dispatches, and in the apartment of Gabo and Mercedes, where I, still a bachelor, was a daily guest: at breakfast, lunch, and supper.

With Gabo we had bought identical blue raincoats, and everywhere (editorial rooms, cafés, the houses of mutual friends) they would see us come in at the same time, like two boys dressed by the same mother.

When Gabo (who, with admirable discipline, was writing the final version of *In Evil Hour* at night) stayed home working, I would take Mercedes to the movies.

GUILLERMO ANGULO: Afterward they went to Cuba to work there.

PLINIO APULEYO MENDOZA: Still, each time I returned to Havana (García Márquez would go later), the growing intervention in everything by party members was revealed to me and the demarcation between them and the rest of the agency reporters was accentuated.

Now they were organizing vague indoctrination meetings and letting the idea of collective management of *Prensa Latina* circulate in the corridors.

JUANCHO JINETE: A Communist from *Prensa Latina* kept showing up in Barranquilla from time to time.

PLINIO APULEYO MENDOZA: The appearance in Bogotá of one José Luis Pérez as a special visitor from the agency was the first alarm signal for García Márquez and for me.

GUILLERMO ANGULO: Then Gabo leaves for New York.

PLINIO APULEYO MENDOZA: Gabo returned after a few weeks of training in Havana. Instead of Montreal, he'd be sent to New York. He was boiling over with information . . .

GUILLERMO ANGULO: The *gusanos* begin to call Gabo to accuse him. His first child had just been born and then, too, Gabo is very fearful.

PLINIO APULEYO MENDOZA: In case of any attack, Gabriel worked with an iron bar within reach.

GUILLERMO ANGULO: Plinio retires.

PLINIO APULEYO MENDOZA: Mercedes turns to me with a smile, while the child she is holding onto jumps around beside her:
"So then, *compadre*, the Reds took over the *Prensa*?"
"They did, *comadre*."
When I tell her of my resignation, she, placid and calm as always, remarks:
"Gabito already wrote his. But he was waiting for you to turn it in."

GUILLERMO ANGULO: He travels to Mexico City by land. But it felt like he had already seen that, because *Leaf Storm* is like Faulkner. It's *As I Lay Dying*. He sees the true Faulkner. He sees him in images. But he already knows Faulkner as a twin soul. I think he's his most important influence from a technical point of view because afterward he invents an entire world. I don't know whether he helped or harmed literature, because although Gabo is very good, Gabo's imitators are very bad.

PLINIO APULEYO MENDOZA: Now Gabo intends to finally carry out his long-standing and postponed project of going to live in Mexico City. Without any money, it's an adventure as mad as the one years earlier, when he decided to stay in Paris without the means to do so.

WILLIAM STYRON: Well, I think that's the reason for his great admiration for Faulkner, because Faulkner without the tag of magic realism nonetheless visualized and created an entire world, a universe based on an actual world, which was the Mississippi he made his own and called Yoknapatawpha. Macondo is the equivalent of Yoknapatawpha. And I think that was an important contribution of Faulkner to Gabo's own sense of a literary creation.

EMMANUEL CARBALLO: Well, how did Gabo get to Mexico City? I'm thinking Álvaro Mutis must have said to him: "Come to Mexico City." Mutis came to Mexico City running from a fraud he had committed in Colombia, and here in Mexico he was in Lecumberri.* He has a book about Lecumberri, which is the most famous prison in Mexico. When he got out, he worked in television. He was the voice of a character in a very famous North American series. When Gabo arrived in Mexico City, he went to

---

* In 1958, at age thirty-six, Álvaro Mutis spent fifteen months in prison in Mexico City, facing embezzlement charges that were later dropped. The Mexican magazine *Letras Libres* wrote about Mutis's experience: "He came out of Lecumberri, which had imprisoned such others as the murderer of Trotsky, Ramón Mercader, the painter David Alfaro Siqueiros, the writer José Revueltas, the novelist José Agustín, and William Burroughs, a different man, convinced that 'we may not judge our fellow man,' an essential certainty that guided the voyages and efforts of his literary alter ego, Macqroll, the lone sailor."

see his friend, who had been his friend in Colombia and introduced him to all of us who were writing literature at the time.

DANIEL PASTOR: It was *The Untouchables*. A black-and-white television program about Eliot Ness's team, the ones who put Al Capone in prison. Mutis was the off-camera voice that came on at the start of the program.

EMMANUEL CARBALLO: His voice was very famous and he earned money and prestige. He met the most interesting people in Mexico. When Gabo arrived, Mutis introduced him to everyone.

15

"Tell Me More"

In which Gabriel García Márquez goes to Mexico City
and recounts to an acquaintance the story of the
book he would like to write

MARÍA LUISA ELÍO: Where did we meet? He wasn't living in Mexico yet. He was working with *Prensa Latina* and was going to Paris via Mexico City. Very young, very young. Skinny, skinny. I don't remember. I don't know exactly where. With Álvaro Mutis. At one point Álvaro says to him: "Gabo, tell that story about the ship," and Gabo told the story of the ship that appears in *One Hundred Years of Solitude*. You must remember a ship that they find in the middle of the jungle. Do you remember? That's when I met him the first time.

RODRIGO MOYA: One day I go to my mother's house and she was having a party. I was already studying photography with Guillermo Angulo and see a man who's occupying almost the entire chaise longue, there was a motley crowd, a lot of people in the chairs, on the edges of chairs, and I see a young man I didn't like because of his arrogant attitude. It was Gabriel García Márquez, stretched out on a sofa like an Indian Madonna, as if the sofa belonged to him and he was in his palace. At that moment he was a writer, one of many Colombians, he had won some prize. But he had everyone spellbound listening to him talk.

When he arrived in Mexico City, he went to my mother's house very often. Years later he said to me, as he was chatting about my mother, that he loved her very much, he said to me: "The truth is your mother often killed my hunger." He would go to eat at my mother's house, food from Antioquia. My mother cooked Colombian. She'd fix flank steak in a hurry and there was always cold brown-sugar water. In the icebox, before she bought her first electric refrigerator. Then I see Gabo there and we're introduced this time and somehow we like each other, and on other occasions I ran into him again. I remember a long walk that he recounts in a piece at some point: "I would go out walking with Rodrigo Moya, who had a cat that knew how to walk outside." I remember that he asked me a lot of questions and we talked a great deal.

GUILLERMO ANGULO: I'm responsible for the first prize given to Gabo. The Esso Prize.

Yes. That was the first prize in the Esso competition that was held for ten years or more. A very important prize in Colombia. I worked with Esso. I wasn't an Esso employee, but I took photographs for them, and made films. I made some documentaries about the unknown coasts, about the city, Bogotá, two others. At that time I was very involved with the people in public relations. Botero was there. Botero did the magazine. He was the designer of the magazine, Fernando Botero. And one day I saw there was a competition, a very important competition. Do you know how much the first prize was? Fifteen thousand pesos. It was very, very important. With that you could buy yourself a car, with fifteen thousand pesos. The first Volkswagen they imported here sold for thirty-eight hundred pesos. So I said: "Man, I have a friend who's very important." Gabo already had a name here as a journalist, he hadn't done many literary things, but people knew, with *Leaf Storm*, that we had a writer here.

Gabo already had respect, but it was more about an expectation because he'd already done something solid. Then they said: "Then ask him to send in something." And he sent me his novel tied up with a necktie and a title that I removed. Because I said: "With this title you don't win the prize." It was called *This Shit Town*. So I told them: "Look, the novel doesn't have a title. It's missing a title." I told them: "There's a very important novel out there, it's Gabo's. No chance they give the prize to anybody else." So then the prize went to Gabo. The novel's *In Evil Hour*.

MIGUEL FALQUEZ-CERTAIN: Germán Vargas was a juror for the competitions, and in the 1960s, he was very important because García Márquez wasn't appreciated in Colombia. All they had published of his, thanks to his friends on the magazine *Mito*, were two or three sections of *Nobody Writes to the Colonel*. His first novel, which he paid for out of his own pocket, *Leaf Storm*, was published in the 1950s. It was a small edition, and it didn't amount to much, as they say nowadays in Colombia. He wrote stories that won prizes in Bogotá, in *El Espectador*, when he was a journalist. Afterward he went to Europe and to Mexico. Then he didn't come back to Colombia anymore and wrote that novel that's called *In Evil Hour*, though it wasn't called *In Evil Hour* but *This Shit Town*. He sent it in like that, with that title. The Esso Prize was given by Esso, the oil company, which had a Jesuit priest, Father Whatever, who was very important. And he was the president of the Colombian Academy of Language. And since he was a priest, that man was very prudish. Germán had a lot to do with their giving the prize to his friend García Márquez. And they gave him the prize.

García Márquez was the first to win that prize. Germán Vargas was always a juror and he always helped his friends.

JOSÉ SALGAR: He won the Esso Prize and it was his first published work. He says: "With this I twist the swan's neck because I finally published my book." A few copies that he gave as gifts were in circulation, but nobody bought it. He gave me this one. He gave it to his friends as a gift.

EDUARDO MÁRCELES DACONTE: He wins the prize and that does a lot for him. That's when I really find out that he's from Aracataca. His stature grows. My family would say: "Listen, Gabito . . ." "Listen, things are going really well for Gabito, how nice!" and so forth. They held Gabito up as an example. They all call him Gabito. Gabito, Gabito . . . Since they remember him as a boy, he's Gabito. Nobody can call him Gabo or Gabriel, nothing but Gabito. Especially those who knew him when he was a kid.

SANTIAGO MUTIS: He's had the best luck in the world with friends and boardinghouses. In Barranquilla it was Alfonso Fuenmayor. The landlady at the boardinghouse in Paris, and then in Mexico City the story is more or less the same.

GUILLERMO ANGULO: Álvaro Mutis was an advertising man, or he was an advertising man for a long time. One day I was with Mutis and we went to an agency in Mexico City and all the women threw themselves at him; they embraced him and kissed him. I said to him: "Maestro, you make me jealous. How do you do it?" And he said: "Look, maestro, I'm going to tell you a secret. You have to make all the women think you are always an available man." And I have a book of his where he writes: "For the only friend I know is always available." I was in Mexico City when Gabo arrived and I had the impression that he had already retired from literature because he was very involved with film people.

EMMANUEL CARBALLO: Mutis put him in touch with writers, with publishers, with newspapers. And with film. He worked with the Barbachanos. They put out a weekly newsletter and made movies. Lots of people worked there. He met Carlos Fuentes, who unfortunately can't tell you anything now.

MARÍA LUISA ELÍO: My husband Jomí and I made an experimental film called *On the Empty Balcony.* We filmed it in Mexico City. And each time they showed this film—it couldn't be shown in movie theaters but only in art houses—Gabo's face would appear, hiding so we wouldn't see him again. But Gabo was there watching it. I think he's seen that film twenty thousand times. He was always watching it. In that film a huge number of people appear. There's Jomí, who's the one who made the film. There's Emilio García Riera. José Luis González de León. Jaime Muñoz de Baena. Diego de Mesa. There's Salvador Elizondo. Juan García Ponce. Tomás Segovia. Who else appears? They're stories I wrote that were unified afterward. My husband directed it. Gabo didn't act in it. Salvador Elizondo plays a seminarian and John Page is a priest. Gabo isn't in it because he didn't have the face of someone born in Spain. Gabo has that exotic face. Marvelous cheekbones. A beautiful face . . . enormously beautiful, but it isn't a Spanish face. A solemn face.

GUILLERMO ANGULO: He's had some incestuous love affairs with the movies and it's gone very badly for him. There's not a single great film by Gabo. There's not a single great screenplay by Gabo. And they're marvelous ideas. Stupendous. But Gabo's so literary that his literature can't be transferred to the screen, or it would have to be done by someone very special, someone like Bergman, who I thought at a certain moment, I don't remember which one, was going to let us see God opening a door. No? Then you need a very special genius that corresponds to Gabo's genius. On the other hand, I think it's a little . . . how shall I say it? . . . exaggerated to try to demand of Gabo that in addition to being a great writer he should also be a great filmmaker.

CARMEN BALCELLS: He never wanted a film made of *One Hundred Years*. And even today it's a desire respected by his family, which I think will be upheld forever. And I don't really know why, except because of the impossibility of transferring the brilliance of that text and that work of art and turning it into a different product. It's absolutely unthinkable that it would be as brilliant as the book. This would be true of any book by García Márquez. But I've often insisted that he accept offers or cinematic proposals for reasons that were sometimes financial, other times because of the reliability of the people involved in the project, but in fact it's very difficult to transform an inspired sentence into an image.

EMMANUEL CARBALLO: Well, I met him because I was very connected to ERA Publishers. ERA was Gabo's publisher in Mexico. ERA published *In Evil Hour*, with a note saying that he withdrew authorization from the first edition that had won the prize offered by an oil company in Colombia. They had translated it from Colombian into Castilian and he was very annoyed with the book. So then ERA published it and it said: "This is the first edition in Spanish." The other one was in a language that resembled Colombian but wasn't Colombian or even real Castilian. At that time I was married to the director and owner of ERA Editions. A Catalan. Neus Espresate. Vicente Rojo is another person who was very good friends with Gabo. Vicente Rojo brought Gabo to ERA. I met him there, introduced by Vicente. Neus Espresate met him, I met him, and we became friends. We saw one another frequently. We talked once or twice almost every week. With Mercedes, his wife. With him. We had a very good friendship.

QUIQUE SCOPELL: Ah, this is with Gabito, who was already in Mexico City. Kid Cepeda calls me one day. Get ready for Carnivals. We're going to have a really wild time. Since I knew that he always had plenty of cash because at the brewery they didn't pay shit but there was money, he says: "I am flush for the Carnivals. I need you to film them. The two of us are going to make a documentary about the fucking Carnivals because the two of us know Barranquilla and what the parties are like. So get ready." I said, okay, the first thing you need is film to be able . . . Immediately he says, "There's no problem at all." Calls Panamá: "Send two hundred rolls of 16 millimeter." There was nothing like what we have today, digital, but 8, 16, and 35 millimeter. "Send me two hundred rolls." Álvaro said to me: "You're not going to pay for this. Don't worry." We had two hundred rolls of that stuff. A brewery truck. "I already have a brewery truck ready. It's all set for us. I'll pick you up at three in the morning" (because parties begin at three, four in the morning). We did it: I was filming, Álvaro beside me drinking rum, and Gabito behind us. Álvaro sent it to Mexico City to be developed, and Gabito edited it there. A little while ago they showed me the film. The film is narrated by that radio personality who died. What's his name? Marcos Pérez. It comes out. Credits: photographs by Gabriel García Márquez, edited by Álvaro Cepeda. Enrique Scopell doesn't appear anywhere. Same thing happened with *The Blue Lobster*.

GUILLERMO ANGULO: The fact is he liked making films as he says to me: "Look, this is the only thing I studied, right?" Remember that he studied film at the Centro Sperimentale di Cinematografia de Roma.

EMMANUEL CARBALLO: He was a writer known by the intelligent people of Mexico, Latin America, and Spain, but he wasn't famous. We overgrown boys knew him, boys who were going to be interesting in time but who were ordinary and commonplace, not worth very much. We were his friends. Well, Vicente Rojo brings him to ERA, the publishing house where I was an editor. And ERA published all his Colombian books and the new books he wrote in Paris and in Mexico City. We eat lunch, we eat dinner, we talk, we get drunk for months.

CARMEN BALCELLS: That year of 1965 when I sold that first group of short texts was the year I met him for the first time in person during the trip I took to Mexico City after Washington, where I went for the first time with my husband Luis, and we were there in Mexico and met Gabo and Mercedes. The meeting was a marvelous meeting, and from then on our relationship grew stronger and stronger. That first trip to America was an extraordinary discovery and the start of everything my professional life has been, and even today I have a phrase that sums it up: "My destiny is America."

MARÍA LUISA ELÍO: It was the third time we saw each other. We went to have supper again at Álvaro Mutis's house; he hadn't married his wife, Carmen, yet. Carmen was preparing Catalan-style rice, and when we left a lecture we went in a group to eat the Catalan-style rice. Then Gabriel was sitting close to me and began to talk and talk and talk talk talk. To everybody.

EMMANUEL CARBALLO: He was defensively simple. He seemed like anything but a writer. He wasn't presumptuous. He didn't speak a language filled with literary figures and exquisite words, he spoke the way everybody else does. In fact, he played at being so simple that he disarmed the pedants.

MARÍA LUISA ELÍO: And then, when we reached Álvaro's house, a tiny apartment, people had already heard him but he kept walking up and down and talking. I was so moved by what he was telling me that I stayed right beside him. I said: "Tell me more, what's next? And then what happened?" Then everybody left and I was alone with him and he told it all to me, all of *One Hundred Years of Solitude*. All very different from what's written, but all of it already there . . . And I remember, for example, when he told me that the priest levitated, that I believed him, I totally believed him. What he was saying was so convincing that I said: "Why wouldn't a priest levitate?" and I said to him: "If you write this, you've written the Bible, you can write a Bible." And he said to me: "Do you like it?" And I answered: "It's marvelous." He said: "Well, it's for you." And I said: "Don't do that to me, please, don't do that to me!" I think he saw me as so innocent that he said: "I'll dedicate it to this fool."

GUILLERMO ANGULO: I remember a famous ad that Gabo did. There was a brand called Calmex. Calmex is California-Mexico. Calmex is a brand of canned fish and things like that. So what Gabo did was something like this: "If you're not expecting a visitor, and your mother-in-law or someone else stops by without letting you know beforehand: Calmex, señora, Calmex." He did very clever things.

MARÍA LUISA ELÍO: And then Jomí, Mercedes, Gabriel, and I went to the house by car, with Jomí driving . . . And Gabriel said to Mercedes: "Do you think it's a good idea for me to dedicate my next novel to María Luisa?" And Mercedes says: "Of course." "And do you think it's a good idea, Jomí?" "Yes, of course." And that's how it happened . . .

EMMANUEL CARBALLO: Well, I think they became great friends. Besides, it's a very nice dedication. Jomí García Ascot and María Luisa Elío. A very beautiful, very intelligent, very receptive woman, she made films with her husband. Jomí was charming, handsome,

María Luisa and Jomí.

and he rode around on a motorcycle. I managed the magazine of the University of Mexico and he would go to my house to drop off an article on his motorcycle. María Luisa is very interesting, very intelligent, with very bold opinions, and she always hit the target, in other words, it's a very good dedication. A woman with a lot of talent. Very pretty, good-looking. She dressed very well. The friend of the best people at that time in Mexico City, and everywhere. She attracted attention wherever she went because of her beauty and her talent. She was very nice to García Márquez, and García Márquez repaid her by dedicating the book to her.

CARMEN BALCELLS: I was triumphant with my contract in the United States for five books. I don't remember but I believe it was an advance of a thousand dollars, and when I showed it to Gabriel García Márquez in triumph, he made a memorable comment and said: "It's a shit contract." A few days ago, as a consequence of his death, I gave an interview on Peruvian television, and the commentator on the program asked me if that story and that answer were true. And he said to me: "What did you think of that answer?" And I said: "At the time I thought it was arrogant, but after many years, and having dealt with great, highly esteemed writers, I've discovered that the highly esteemed writer is the first to know that he is, and that the esteem is legitimate." So now I don't think it an arrogant answer but an answer appropriate to the magnitude of the literary project he was working on at that time.

16

Solitude and Company

In which the desperate writer endures eighteen months of solitude and some company

MARÍA LUISA ELÍO: Gabo said: "I have to retire for a year and I'm not going to work. You see how you can arrange things," he said to Mercedes. "We'll see how you do, but I'm not working for a year." And Mercedes arranged things the best she could.

GUILLERMO ANGULO: She got credit.

MARÍA LUISA ELÍO: Borrowing the meat from the butcher.

GUILLERMO ANGULO: She got money from one place and another. And he began to write. To write with that discipline that only he has. Like the architect Rogelio Salmona, who lives in the apartment next to mine. Like him. Salmona doesn't have a cent (he's done the greatest buildings in Colombia) because he says: "I don't like it" and he does the building all over again, paying for it out of his own pocket. They're very good friends, besides. He designed Gabo's house in Cartagena, and the presidential guesthouse there too.

EMMANUEL CARBALLO: He left everything. He worked. He saved. He borrowed money and began to write *One Hundred Years of Solitude* like a desperate man. Like a madman. He didn't do anything else. He stopped seeing friends. Doing things. Working on things that paid him some money. He borrowed money so he could sit down and write *One Hundred Years*.

MARÍA LUISA ELÍO: He had written notes but nothing else because that room Mercedes made so he could go in and write the whole blessed day wasn't made yet. They lived in a little house on Calle de la Loma. In the living room Mercedes had a wall built with a wooden door that went all the way up so there'd be no noise, and a pine table like a kitchen table with an old typewriter. Gabo went in there and spent the whole day, all day, writing. The room was a very tiny thing, tinier than this, which is very small, like from here over to that point. There was room for his table, a chair, a small armchair, everything that fit was very small. Above the armchair was a painting and something like a calendar. But a very tacky calendar.

EMMANUEL CARBALLO: He dressed like a peasant. He dressed very badly. Very ugly. Shabby, a peasant trying to be elegant who ends up being just the opposite. That's what dressing like a peasant means.

MARÍA LUISA ELÍO: Then we would go there every night. Since Gabo wasn't going out, we would go to see them every night. We'd arrive around eight o'clock. One day with a bottle of whiskey. The next day with a piece of ham. And there we'd stay, drinking a little and eating things Mercedes made. We'd see one another every day. We would also see the Mutises there. The kids upstairs, in their rooms, doing wild things.

EMMANUEL CARBALLO: And now here comes something that only I can tell you about. When Gabo began to work on this novel, he asked me if I could read the pages he wrote every week. So every Saturday he'd come see me with what he had written during the week.

MARÍA LUISA ELÍO: I stayed home a good deal, reading all afternoon, not doing anything, and he would call me. Gabriel would say: "I'm going to read you a little bit, let's see what you think." And he would read me a passage. He would call me and say: "I'm going to tell you how the aunts are dressed. What else would you put on them? What color do you think the dress is?" And we would talk. Or he'd say to me: "Look, I've put this word here but I don't know what it means. Did your aunts say it? Because mine did." Like that. It was marvelous. We spent time talking on the phone. How the women are dressed, I don't know which one, just a minute, when she goes to catch the train . . . I think it's from a magazine I had in the house about things from the 1920s.

MARGARITA DE LA VEGA: You know the story when he's writing *One Hundred Years of Solitude* and I heard him telling it. He needed the *Encyclopaedia Britannica* to verify the things he wanted to use that were part of the world. Because that's the really nice thing about *One Hundred Years* for me, that it's a vernacular, universal, and encyclopedic book all at the same time. That's why *One Hundred Years of Solitude* sells so much and is read so much: because you can be a Colombian janitor (not a gringo janitor who goes to Columbia and graduates, like the one who was in the paper yesterday or the day before, but a Colombian), read *One Hundred Years of Solitude*, and understand it on a level different from the level of the scholar who looks up all the references and all that nonsense. He lives the story, the tragedies, the family, the evolution, the historical context, because he's somebody who has lived it and suffered it and heard it talked about in his family. It isn't something they read in books. It's part of their culture.

EMMANUEL CARBALLO: From the beginning I admired García Márquez a great deal. I liked his stories and novels very much. I thought he was a great writer. I mean, he brought me the first installment of what he was writing; he brought it punctually every Saturday. Every Saturday he brought me the novel until he finished it and said to me: 'What defects do you find in it? Tell me the things you don't like, why you don't like them.' And I said: "Yes, well, yes I like it. The novel's stupendous. Keep doing what you're doing. I have nothing to tell you and nothing to criticize you for. On the contrary, I praise you." And that's how it went until he finished the novel. At the most, I deleted two or three things and added something. That's what my work on *One Hundred Years of Solitude* was reduced to. It was perfect. I didn't have anything to do except tell him: "It's wonderful, this character is growing, this one you're moving to the side, I don't know why, but in the next few weeks you'll tell me what that's due to." We talked about the characters. They were our friends. We talked for two or three hours, but not as teacher to pupil but as friend to friend, and I was a fan. I use that word that perhaps belongs more to soccer than to literature. It's a novel made almost with a superhuman gust of wind. I've been a literary critic for sixty years, and I've never seen a novel written with so much skill, so much talent, so much dedication as I saw in Gabo writing *One Hundred Years of Solitude*.

He chose me, then, because I'm very talented. If not, he wouldn't have chosen me. I don't believe in modesty. I had written about all the novels he had previously published. He knew I was implacable, that if I didn't like something I would say so, I would tell him why it was bad or why it was good. And that's why he chose me. And he found in me a person excited by a talent I hadn't seen before in literature in Spanish, that boy's talent was larger than him. I say "boy" because he's a little younger than I am, but only a little. We're almost the same age, old men by now.

MARGARITA DE LA VEGA: Gabo needed the encyclopedia and so they bought the encyclopedia. At that time one bought the encyclopedia and collections of classic books. They were sold throughout Latin America, in my day Aguilar sold them. There were people who came and offered you the books for a monthly payment, so you bought the entire collection. That was in '65 or '66. Gabo said that he was using them, and Mercedes said to him: "You don't need this volume anymore," because the man was coming to pick it up for lack of payment. Then Mercedes would give him the ones he had already used. Because Mercedes was always the more practical one. That's why in his first interviews, especially the one in *Playboy*, which is very good, he said that men are the dreamers, the poets, and that women are the practical ones; without them the universe would not exist. What he said infuriated me and I even asked him about it once. Of course, he didn't answer me. He answered only what he felt like answering. But I think that Mercedes is the model for Úrsula, the wife of the first founder of Macondo, Úrsula, the wife of the founder, she invents the business of the little sugar animals; she's the one who makes the family survive.

EMMANUEL CARBALLO: I'm a pretty old man now, my dear girl. I don't remember a lot of things, but I'm going to tell you what I do remember. So, we had lunch, we had supper, we talked, we got drunk for months. When he began to write *One Hundred Years of Solitude* he told ERA: "I've given you all my books because, well, you're my friends. This is the most interesting publisher in Mexico, but too young; the book I'm writing now, and I have a lot of hopes for it, I plan to give it to an important Spanish-language publisher." And then it was between Spain and Buenos Aires. He forgot about Ediciones ERA, telling us it was very small for the hopes he had for the novel.

GUILLERMO ANGULO: Then Ms. Gabo, when they finally got the money to mail the manuscript (money they didn't have, since their car was in hock and they owed money to the butcher and to everybody), what she says is: "Now all we need is for that novel to be a piece of shit."

EMMANUEL CARBALLO: He was totally certain he had written a very important work.

RAFAEL ULLOA: Then he sent it to be published by Editorial Sudamericana, in Argentina. And he spent everything he had to mail the fucking book. Then he said to his wife: "Now all we need is for that fucking book not to be worth a damn." And just think what the situation was like . . .

EMMANUEL CARBALLO: There were three of us in my house who were close to him. At Comercio and Administración, No. 4, next to University City, and we'd see one another there on Saturdays at about five and work until seven. Then we'd talk, drink, gossip, do what young friends do. He spoke about his mother, his friends, his brothers and sisters, his life as a journalist in Bogotá, in Barranquilla . . . He talked about all that very enthusiastically. Our friendship was a literary one. He respected me. I respected him. I was enthusiastic about his novel and he was enthusiastic about my having spent time reading it. I would read the chapter two or three times (it took me a week) in order to talk about it to him the following week. The work ended and our friendship ended. The year we were working was a very beautiful year. We'd wait for Saturday to come in order to talk to this man.

MARÍA LUISA ELÍO: I recall that Aureliano Buendía's first death hurts him so much that he revives him. He gives the story another direction so that he doesn't die.

RODRIGO MOYA: He lived in the Colonia Florida. He was married and had the two boys. Sometimes I'd go to his house with Angulo. I remember one or two visits we made to Gabo's house because Angulo visited him a great deal and Gabo was writing *One Hundred Years of Solitude*. We'd arrive early, at about seven, and everything was dark, and Mercedes tells us: "Gabo's working but he'll be down soon." We waited an hour and Gabo didn't come down, so then we started to smoke marijuana and in a while Gabo comes down and joins us. And we were talking and I never can remember what we said. Imagine, it's fifty years ago. But we were very happy next to the fireplace, where there was a fire burning, and he talked to us about *One Hundred Years of Solitude*, and what I do remember is that he was swollen. Then Mercedes told us that when he was writing a very intense part or moment, he would swell up. His face swelled up. The process of a work like that is a little superhuman, and so those things happen.

17

"There Was a Blinding Light"

In which One Hundred Years of Solitude *is launched,*
causing an earthquake throughout the world and elevating
its author to other spheres

CARMEN BALCELLS: I already represented Gabo when *One Hundred Years of Solitude* came out, and I read it in manuscript. I was enthusiastic. But it was sent directly to Paco Porrúa by the author. The author sold it to Editorial Sudamericana and only many years later did García Márquez tell me to also take care of that sector that was out of my hands because of the direct contract he had made with Sudamericana.

MARÍA LUISA ELÍO: I remember that day. He comes in, very friendly, bringing me the first copy. I read: "A Jomí García Ascot y María Luisa." With a pen he adds a comma and signs: "Gabo." He doesn't write Gabriel. He writes Gabo. It's clear. It can't be more dedicatory. Then we go from bookstore to bookstore. I'm buying books for my friends and having him dedicate them. Like crazy people. Gabo said to me: "You'll go bankrupt!" because I was going to bookstores in his car. I bought one so he would dedicate it to Diego, my son. In it he writes something like: "For Diego, an uncle of yours wrote this book when you were just learning to talk." That is, very small. We pick up Jomí, we go to their house and get Mercedes, and we all have supper. The next day, I . . . You

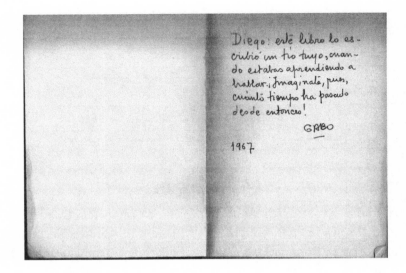

remember that there's a moment in *One Hundred Years of Solitude* when it rains yellow flowers. Then I buy a very large basket, it's immense, the biggest one I could find, and I fill it with yellow daisies. Back then I wore a gold bracelet. I take it off and put it in the basket, and look for one of those little gold fishes and a bottle of whiskey. I put everything in the basket and Jomí and I go to the Gabos' house. That's where we go. Jomí took his book and I took mine, and back home we didn't go anywhere until we had finished reading it.

MIGUEL FALQUEZ-CERTAIN: And when he comes to Bogotá in '67 to introduce his novel, nobody pays any attention. In Colombia they ignore him completely. In Bogotá, because he's with Vargas Llosa, who comes to introduce *The Green House*, and everybody wanted to be with the young, good-looking man. Everybody crowding round him, the reporters and so forth, and

Gabo was in a corner. Nobody even noticed him or gave him the time of day. Look at the photograph. García Márquez is there in a corner dressed in a tie and jacket like a wannabe Bogotá dude with his little mustache and his curly hair. Vargas Llosa is out front.

Then he goes back to Barranquilla. That's when he meets in person, after many years, with his buddies from Barranquilla. This is what happens: García Márquez stayed in touch with his group of friends from Barranquilla, principally the literary group, which was Germán, Kid Cepeda, and Alfonso Fuenmayor. He corresponded with them wherever he was, Europe, Mexico. All those years, in the fifties and sixties, he was always in touch with them.

RODRIGO MOYA: Before the publication of *One Hundred Years of Solitude* he went to my house with Mercedes so that one of my photographs would illustrate the first edition, but unfortunately for me, the designer was Vicente Rojo, whom I considered for a long time a terrible designer; I would say that he was public enemy number one of photography, and here they adored him, said that he was an innovator in graphic design. And it was a fairy tale. He was never a graphic designer. He would copy things a little, mostly North American, newsprint, Warhol, but in my opinion he was a bad designer. He mistreated photography. You'd give him a photo, he'd make it tiny, he'd make it grainy, he'd make it a negative, he'd put a color over it. The photographer would say: "What's this?" In that style of doing things, he thought the photo wasn't appropriate, wasn't necessary. And so the first edition of *One Hundred Years* appears without my photograph. I was happy that my photograph was going to appear. It's in the first North American edition, in Penguin Books, and it made me happy, but I would have been happier if it had appeared in the edition in

Spanish. I didn't even show up when it came out. I was very elu-
sive back then, I didn't go to see him when it came out. I bought
One Hundred Years of Solitude in a bookstore, and it's not dedicated. My sister Colombia said to me: "Let's go see Gabo so he
can sign the book." I never asked him to dedicate a book to me
and yet I have several with dedications. My mother died recently,
and in her house I found one dedicated to her by Gabo. It said:
"To Alicia Moya, for the love I have for her because I didn't marry
her."

MIGUEL FALQUEZ-CERTAIN: In Colombia that first edition was
never available, with that ship abandoned in the middle of the
jungle, the Sudamericana edition. I was studying medicine in
Cartagena, and I saw a woman in Cartagena who had it, and my
friend Braulio and I hated her because the novel wasn't available.
Later the first edition arrived, early in '68, and I bought it. The
edition I have was printed "April 25, 1968, in the Graphic Workshops of the Compañía Impresora Argentina, S.A., Calle Alsina
2049, Buenos Aires, for Sudamericana Publishers (Calle Hum-
berto I 545, Buenos Aires)." I bought it on June 15, 1968, in the
Nacional Bookstore. The cover is by Vicente Rojo.

In those days I had money because I put on magic shows. I
bought the book in the Nacional and it was the edition with
playing cards. I rescued it and brought it with me from Colombia.
It's not the first edition but something like the third reprint. But
that was the Colombian edition.

MARGARITA DE LA VEGA: I had already read some other things,
but what's curious is the letter my mother wrote when she sent me
One Hundred Years from Bogotá. And she sent me a clipping of

the interview of Gabo's father. She didn't send me social notes or anything like that, but she was fascinated by *One Hundred Years of Solitude* because she said that at last she understood this damned country. My mother was French. I was already expecting my son Mario Henrique, who was born in January of '68, and I was feeling very sick. They kept me in bed for something like eight months, and that's where I read it.

MIGUEL FALQUEZ-CERTAIN: Before I could read the book I ran into him in Barranquilla, when he came there to see his friends, his closest friends at that time. I'm walking along 72nd and I recognize him from his photograph. Nene Cepeda I knew, and I had seen Alfonso Fuenmayor in photographs; I knew who he was. I saw them at their table and went up to them. That was at a hotel on the corner, across from the Mediterráneo. It was called the Hotel Alhambra and they were sitting on the terrace. There were something like five people at the table and the table was covered with empty bottles of Águila beer. He was in Barranquilla meeting his friends whom he hadn't seen for ten years because he certainly didn't have the money to travel back then. That's why he wrote that book, *Cuando era feliz e indocumentado* ("When I Was Happy and Undocumented").

I was drunk, staggering. I interrupted the conversation he was having with the others. I said: "Are you García Márquez?" He said: "Yes. What can I do for you?" "I'd like you to give me an autograph because I have two of your books." Then he was weak with laughter because I was drunk. Then he said to me: "Come to the Nacional Bookstore on Monday and it will be my pleasure if you buy a book and I'll sign it for you." Then I said: "The thing is I'm leaving Sunday night because I'm a student in Cartagena."

Then I stretched out my arm and took the napkin that was under a beer. I gave him the napkin and said to him: "Sign this for me." And he said to me: "What, do you think I'm María Félix?"*

RAFAEL ULLOA: I bought *One Hundred Years* at the Nacional Bookstore, which was in the center of town back then. Right across from the Club Barranquilla.

MIGUEL FALQUEZ-CERTAIN: The Nacional had delicious fruit juice that they made right there. Tamarind juice. And with air-conditioning. And then there was a part where one looked at books. They were very expensive and they permitted lots of people to take them to read there at the table. It was a meeting place. It replaced the Mundo Bookstore.

RAFAEL ULLOA: I bought it there . . . I must have the date when I bought it and the title page with that boat. You don't have that? I'll give it to you and get myself another one. If you love Gabo, and I love Gabo, then, as they say: "Two things equal to a third thing are equal," so yes: I've begun to love you too.

MARÍA LUISA ELÍO: *One Hundred Years* changed the world's view of Latin American literature.

SANTIAGO MUTIS: And I think that's when many things begin to weaken. But because real contact with things is lost. It's awful. That title's like a premonition.

---

* María Félix, one of Mexico's iconic movie stars from the forties and fifties, the golden age of Mexican cinema, is like a Mexican Elizabeth Taylor.

MARÍA LUISA ELÍO: He was shy but I think he almost, almost still is, right? A very strange, marvelous human being. He dedicated himself to running away all his life. Running, running, running away.

RAMÓN ILLÁN BACCA: Everybody was dazzled, weren't they? There were people who learned by heart entire paragraphs, entire pages of *One Hundred Years of Solitude*. I liked it. I thought it was a great novel, but I wasn't dazzled because I felt it was very close to the things I knew. When he talked of life in the banana plantation and the mister so-and-so . . . Yes, terrific, but since I had seen it growing up with my aunts, at all the parties . . . it continued to be the same life I already knew. I had that feeling to some extent.

MARÍA LUISA ELÍO: More than Latin American, Spanish-speaking . . .

SANTIAGO MUTIS: You can't say that *One Hundred Years of Solitude* is a work with a structure, that it follows a path. There's no path to anything, to anything literary, what's there is a distinct vision of Colombia, not the one seen in the capital.

JOSÉ SALGAR: Twenty, thirty years later, what Gabo did was never to abandon journalism but to apply his love of literature to his journalistic work. All his works have a journalistic base of exactitude.

EDUARDO MÁRCELES DACONTE: In fact, everything—in *One Hundred Years of Solitude* I saw nothing but familiar people, people I knew. Besides, I had a geographical space very clearly in my head. I imagined their movements when they spoke, about the river and the irrigation ditches, and where they lived, and I don't know what. I imagined the town because I was walking physically with the town in my head. And I knew the town well. He mentions lots of places. El Prado, for example, where the gringos lived. The train. The river. Now, of course, it's a microcosm.

SANTIAGO MUTIS: I read *One Hundred Years of Solitude* in secondary school, and for me it really was a revelation. A revelation not because of literature but because he was recounting the country you were in. Then I read it, I don't know how old I was, fifteen or sixteen, and it turns out that you read it and thought: "Colombia isn't Bogotá." Colombia exists, and that's a marvelous life. He opened up a different life that you didn't respect in Bogotá where I'm from.

GREGORY RABASSA: When I was translating it, I was also teaching a class on Cervantes. I saw in the narration—of course, not the same words—the same modes as in Cervantes. You can take a sentence out of the paragraph and it turns into a parable. Gabo and Cervantes did that. Besides, Macondo is an imaginary place and that's what Cervantes did too. Perhaps he did it more furtively, like when the duke and duchess promise Sancho Panza the island and play with that. That's where the novel comes from. If somebody wants to write a novel the best thing to do is read the *Quijote*.

QUIQUE SCOPELL: And now they dare to compare that *Hundred Years* to the *Quijote*.

18

Geography Lesson

In which the region that gave rise to Macondo is discussed

EDUARDO MÁRCELES DACONTE: Aracataca has about five thousand people. I don't know how many, but a lot of people there have read the novel. Well, reading is more emotional when a person can recognize things. Perhaps in another person it would be more intellectual. But I'm referring to the case of someone who recognizes the town, the place, and the people, isn't that right? There's a more emotional relationship, even a sentimental one, if you prefer . . . For the people from there many of the things are no surprise; in fact, for the people from the Coast. You know, we exaggerate a lot of things, and we say things, many things that, well . . . So I think things are taken more naturally.

Let me draw it for you here on this napkin. This is the coast: here's the Magdalena River, here's Barranquilla. Santa Marta is here. All this is the Sierra Nevada. Then Aracataca is here. Fifty miles to the south is Aracataca. It's on the spurs of the Sierra Nevada. The Magdalena River. Here's Fundación and here's the road to Bucaramanga and the interior of the country. Do you see? According to this, Mompox is more or less here, on the banks of the Magdalena River that comes through here. The departments of Atlántico and Bolívar are here. Riohacha is over here.

One Hundred Years of Solitude is from the river to here, from the Magdalena River to the east, the northeast of the coast. That

177

is, everything that would become the region of Santa Marta, Ciénaga, the banana zone, and then from the Sierra Nevada to Riohacha, which is where the founders of Macondo come from. You know that Aureliano Buendía killed Prudencio Aguilar in La Guajira; then there's a kind of exodus, and the ones who leave are the ones who found Macondo. He takes this from his grandfather's story.

PATRICIA CASTAÑO: On the trip we made to retrace the journey of *One Hundred Years of Solitude*, his English biographer Gerald Martin and I went from Maicao to Barrancas, Guajira, which is an important town today because of the coal mines in El Cerrejón. It must have had something then as well because Colonel Márquez left Riohacha for Barrancas. I think it was an area of colonization, like an opening of the frontier. And it must have been a town rich in cattle, maybe. Then we go there looking for the history of the family, the arrival of Colonel Márquez in Bar-

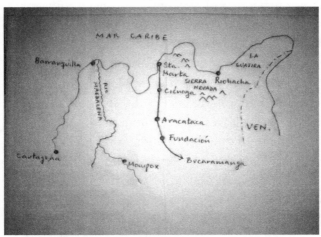

Map of the region that was originally Macondo.

rancas. And Doña Tranquilina doesn't arrive right away. That is, he goes first. Then when Doña Tranquilina comes and they move into the house, he'd already had a series of lovers (it seems he was dreadful). And one of those lovers seems to be Medardo's mother, who was a lady of rather easy virtue.

We interviewed a lot of people there who were either relatives or who knew the story. In other words, that history and its relationship to the town is very vivid. Here's something very interesting. We met a little old man, very very old, who says he witnessed the death of Medardo. He says he was very little, a boy of seven or eight, and at that moment he was delivering something. He reached the corner just as Colonel Márquez fired his revolver and killed Medardo. But the marvelous thing about the oral tradition is that on the night we were there in Barrancas, on the street, on those benches that rock back and forth, and the granddaughter of one of the ladies, who must have been about twelve years old, showed up and said: "My grandfather told me the story of that death." And then, standing in the middle of the street, she began to recount the story, and you can't imagine how delicious it was.

I don't know why I didn't have a camera with me. Well, at that time cameras were very heavy: "And then Colonel Márquez was waiting for Medardo. He knew that because it was the day of the town's patron virgin . . ." Medardo lived on a farm. "He would come with feed for the animals because he was going to stay there for a few days, for the fiestas. The colonel said to him: 'I have to kill you, Medardo.'" And then Medardo said something about the bullet of honor, I don't remember. But the girl told it as if it had happened yesterday. I think it's in Gerry's book, but what impressed me was the oral tradition. This little girl. It was as if she were narrating Euripides, as if she had learned it by heart in a book. That really impressed me because it happened in 1907 I think, and in this town, in 1993, the story was still alive.

EDUARDO MÁRCELES DACONTE: Even though Aracataca is hot, it's a town that's on the spurs of the Sierra Nevada. That's why it has "a river of clear water that ran along a bed of polished stones, which were white and enormous, like prehistoric eggs," as he says in *One Hundred Years of Solitude*. Why? Because it's a river that comes from the Cristóbal Colón and Simón Bolívar snow peaks. It's the Frio river, the Fundación river. It's hot, but at the same time, at night the weather's cool because of the mountain and the rivers and streams that come down from the Sierra. The vegetation's very dense. In other words, it's really beautiful around there.

There's a dry season and a rainy season, the typical climate along the coast. So if you go there in the dry season, you'll see that it's dusty. But it had to be rainy because bananas need a lot of moisture. When there are rainstorms, they're tremendous downpours, like the ones in "Isabel Watching It Rain in Macondo," which are interminable.

All of Aracataca is in the novel. There's the river of crystalline water, the Aracataca River, a really beautiful river. Because it's like this: it has little beaches. And almond trees. Almond trees all around the main square in Aracataca. There's the heat. The afternoon siesta. There are all the people who travel through Aracataca, which is a travel center. It's the place the Indians from the Sierra Nevada come to. Many people passing through. There's the train. And, well, ideas. For instance, during the banana bonanza in Colombia, people danced the *cumbia* using bundles of bills as candles. That's in the novel.

You realize that in Gabo's narrative the environment has a great deal of influence. Superstition plays a great part. Things of those towns. Natural phenomena. The rain. The heat. They had to have that influence. And you know that the rainstorms there can last two or three days, when it seems that pellets were falling from the sky because they're downpours, rivers, and that must have had a big influence on him. He begins to absorb all these things that happen around him while there are natural phenomena with tropical intensity. Aracataca didn't have electricity until a short while ago. It had a small generator.

All of this area that goes from Ciénaga to Aracataca to Fundación, all of this is the banana zone. It's very fertile land because it's the alluvial deposit from the mountains that comes down to this little valley, a broad valley. Aracataca was an agricultural town. It was beginning to see the inroads of bananas. All the banana plantations were here in this region. At first the owners lived there, there were plantations.

My grandfather, Antonio Daconte, comes there from Italy, and he's an impressive figure in the town. He opens a store that was called Antonio Daconte's Store. He isn't just anybody. My grandfather emigrated from Italy toward the end of the nineteenth century and came to Santa Marta. He was one of the first colonizers in Aracataca; he comes there and practically helps to found the town. When he arrived, and when the Turks arrived, and the Italians, Aracataca was barely a tiny hamlet.

IMPERIA DACONTE: Three young siblings arrived: Pedro Daconte Fama, María Daconte Fama, and Antonio Daconte Fama, who remained in Aracataca. Very young people when they arrived. Things went very well for him in Aracataca. Oh yes. He had three farms there. And most of the houses in Aracataca belonged to my father. He traveled to Europe, my father. The rest didn't travel.

EDUARDO MÁRCELES DACONTE: He arrives, and I don't know, either he brought money with him or made some deals that went very well, because from the time when he arrives he sets up a tremendous store and organizes the movie theater. He had one of the biggest houses on what they call Four Corners, which is, in a manner of speaking, the Times Square of Aracataca. It's called Four Corners. It was an immense corner house. It took up a quarter of a block, I'd say, because in the courtyard is where he set up the theater. The movie theater. In the courtyard of his house. There were chairs, and he brought the machines, and then by train they sent him films from Santa Marta. He had his people who fetched and carried, and there was a projectionist and everything. He brought the movies and the jukebox. All the new things that were appearing, he brought them to Aracataca because he would travel to Santa Marta.

IMPERIA DACONTE: My father would take us to the farm very early so that we'd have the morning air. There were a lot of bananas and they would fall, then they would cover them up and I would pick from this bunch and then from another.

EDUARDO MÁRCELES DACONTE: Later on the United Fruit Company arrives, and it acquires many of the farms. Although all the original owners were kept on, United Fruit is practically turned into a banana monopoly there. They're the ones who buy the bananas, process them, export them. They have their own ships.

RAMÓN ILLÁN BACCA: But of course moving up wasn't so difficult at a given time because all the people came and set up a store
and then bought land. The value of land increases again in '47,
after the Second World War. And people found themselves rich.
That's what they call the banana bonanza. My aunts, the Nogueras
of Santa Marta, had been rich from before.

ELIGIO GARCÍA MÁRQUEZ: In order to protect top management,
the United Fruit Company had built its encampments, far from
town, in the middle of the plantations. The one in Aracataca was a
kind of neighborhood called El Prado, wooden houses with burlap
windows with wire gauze as a protection against the mosquitoes,
and pools and tennis courts in the middle of an unbelievable lawn.
And so, on one side, separated by the train tracks, in the middle
of the coolness of the plantations, the citadel of the gringos, the
"electrified chicken house" as García Márquez calls it, immune to
heat and ugliness and poverty and foul smells. On the other side,
the town. With wooden houses and tin roofs or simple cane and
mud huts with straw roofs. The town where, attracted in a certain
sense by the bonanza, the Márquez Iguarán family had come to
live in August 1910.

19

BOOM!

In which the Latin American novel explodes and some people think it's because of Gabo and others don't agree

RAMÓN ILLÁN BACCA: Then came the business of the Boom and I read Carlos Fuentes's *The Good Conscience*. I tried to retrieve Carpentier a little, but Gabito wasn't in that thing. The explosion happens in '67 with *One Hundred Years of Solitude*. I'm talking about this whole period when you didn't assimilate García Márquez with magical-fantastic literature. When you talked about magical-fantastic you thought a little about Carpentier, in *Écue-yamba-ó!*, in *The Kingdom of This World*. You didn't associate it with García Márquez. That came later. Much later. For people like me, who tended to read in spurts, but in a steady way.

WILLIAM STYRON: It was a *very* important contribution, but I don't think it was alone. I think that all of the writers of the so-called Boom including Carlos [Fuentes] and Vargas Llosa, and one or two others contributed something. Cortázar, of course, was very important. I think all together their collective impact could be what it was because these writers each added something. There was the force of their works that brought Latin American literature to the fore in the consciousness of non-Latin American readers. I would say that. I think the important fact is that Spanish-language literature was almost nonexistent, as Carlos has pointed out himself in various writings. There was practically nothing after *Don Quijote*. The novel was not a compelling art form. I'm not including Spanish-language literature in the drama form by García Lorca and others. I'm talking about the novel, purely and simply. It just did not exist in the world's consciousness until this boom almost miraculously gained the attention of readers in Europe and the United States.

SANTIAGO MUTIS: Yes, he's the one who breaks the barrier.

WILLIAM STYRON: Many were living in exile. Often this was due to the fact that their works were not only criticized but attacked by the establishment in each of the countries they came from. I think that Gabo's work was preeminent, but I don't think he could have existed by himself. I believe his work needed the work of the others I mentioned.

JOSÉ SALGAR: I remember when he came to do publicity for *One Hundred Years*. They come to do publicity and try to make a lot of sales. They were public relations guys . . . The Boom begins!

WILLIAM STYRON: Yes, I think that is absolutely true: he was the crown's jewel. But he wouldn't have existed without the others.

GREGORY RABASSA: I don't know whether he was the paladin or whether things were already changing. Vargas Llosa came later but Julio Cortázar and Borges were already there. Benito Pérez Galdós* was also there, for example, a solid but forgotten writer.

---

* Benito Pérez Galdós is a leading literary figure in nineteenth-century Spain, second only to Miguel Cervantes Saavedra.

Doña Pefecta. Nazarín. None of them was a follower. They were all writing their own things. Nobody writes like Julio. He's the most international. Paris has a great deal to do with this. He writes better than any Frenchman. He parodies all the French intellectuals.

WILLIAM STYRON: It's a fact that he was representative of this multinational literature, so to speak. So I don't believe it would be quite accurate to say that Gabo alone brought Latin American literature to the world's consciousness. Although probably the most famous single work of the Boom is *One Hundred Years of Solitude.*

SANTIAGO MUTIS: It's a Bible. It recounts life from the beginning to the end. A version of human beings told with the truth of people who are very Colombian, which is what is lived here . . . What Gabo has, and what the whole world has thanked him for, is humanity. That's it precisely.

GREGORY RABASSA: My word is going to be a word that's no longer used. In my day, in the swing era, the jazz era, we would say *I dig that shit.* The Brazilians have the word *jeito.* It can also be *duende,* but I like the concept of the *ángel. One Hundred Years* has *duende,* and *duende* brings the reader to the *ángel.* Of course I think that Gabo is Cervantean. What exactly does he have? Why doesn't the moon leave its orbit? He has the *jeito* of a writer.

HÉCTOR ROJAS HERAZO: I've been asked many times which of those who participated with him in the boom, which of the Latin American writers and novelists share the Boom with him. And I say none of them. After him, the rest are mediocre. He's the real creator there; the rest are individuals, men who have had good publicity, among other things. Because the creation of the Boom is an invention of the publishers. Publishers created that because the writer can't. So, who deserves the title of best? He is . . . the best writer . . . that's undeniable.

SANTIAGO MUTIS: But, for example, Juan Rulfo isn't part of the Boom and neither is José María Arguedas. I think because in Arguedas and Rulfo they saw something very hard. And most of the media, compelled to demonstrate that poverty has to do with salvation, that we can all be rich, that happiness lies in certain objectives in which you play the lottery of life. But Rulfo is the opposite of all that. He's a being trapped among his own dead. But that wasn't so easy to digest either because Rulfo is the greatest of them all. It was Rulfo, Argueda, Guimarães, Gabo . . . Now, I think Europe was dazzled too. For very valid reasons. Because Spain too, that knew how to tell a story, forgot how. And all these people were magicians in telling stories . . . Spain was shattered. It was in its own terrible spiritual story. And you have to recognize that sometimes literature changes countries, and the people who were telling stories and saying things were here. And that brought him attention too.

GREGORY RABASSA: It seemed Latin American because it was Latin American. But it didn't seem like any other book. It seemed original. Denser, but also easier. It was going out of bounds, playing off the court. Melquíades! I loved it. I gave it to my friends from India to read, that part when he says that Sanskrit looks like clothing put out to dry in the sun. That moment when he realizes that the Gypsies originally come from India. I don't believe Melquíades came from India because the Gypsies didn't maintain roots in India. But obviously the strongest Gypsy roots were in Spain. You see it in García Lorca. In Alberti too. And in the great bullfighter Belmonte, in Mexico.

ROSE STYRON: I had read it three or four years before I met him, when it came out in English. It was published in Spanish in the late sixties, but it didn't come out in English until 1970. I read it when it came out.

GREGORY RABASSA: I translated it by chance. It was also by chance that I became a translator. I was finishing my doctorate at Columbia, and with a couple of friends from Columbia and another from Brooklyn College we put out a literary magazine called *Odyssey.* I was responsible for finding new work from Spain and Latin America. In each issue two countries were chosen: two from Europe and two from Latin America. I would go to the public library at 42nd Street to look through all the magazines for things that might interest us. We chose four or five stories and then we had to translate them. Among them I remember Onetti, the Uruguayan. They all had Italian names. Onetti. Alberti. I translated them, and since I translated all of them, I used different pseudonyms.

Sara Blackburn was Julio Cortázar's publisher in New York. Her husband, the poet Paul Blackburn, was his agent. Julio was unknown here, though he was well known in Argentina. *Hopscotch* had come out with great éclat in the early sixties. Sara called me, since she knew *Odyssey* and knew I was the translator. She asked if I'd like to take a look at this Argentine novel and translate it. I told her yes, and she sent it to me. She wanted me to translate a chapter as a sample. I did the first chapter and another one. I sent them out. She liked them. Then Julio liked them. And said he'd like for me to do the book. I said I would, but I hadn't even read it. Then I made the case that this was the best way to translate. Without having read the novel.

MARÍA LUISA ELÍO: From here he writes to the famous writers of the day. One was Vargas Llosa and the other was the Argentine, what was his name? . . . Cortázar. He writes and sends them the novel to see what they think. It was finished but hadn't been published yet. And they both answered, amazed, astonished, as if they were saying: "What can we say? We're going to have to ask him ourselves."

GREGORY RABASSA: Then Julio and Gabo got together in Paris. They were friends, and Gabo needed a translator for *One Hundred Years*. They met because of politics. They were Latin American exiles in Paris, working for certain leftist causes. And they also read each other's work. He wanted me as a translator, but I was busy with another translation. I told them: "Let me finish with Asturias." I think it was Asturias, though it might have been Clarice Lispector. I had just come back from Río, from having been divorced, I remarried, and it was when I returned that they gave me the news that *Hopscotch* had won the National Book Award. In those years they gave prizes to translations. Not now. And I won it. I don't recall their giving me any money.

In short, José Guillermo Castillo, a Venezuelan sculptor who was also involved with literature, was the literary adviser at what is today the Americas Society. He waged a great campaign with the publishers here, and obtained the money to translate Latin American books. He was the one who obtained the money for

Gabo's book with Cass Canfield Jr., who was the publisher and son of Cass Canfield, one of the founders of Harper & Brothers, later Harper & Row. They had bought *One Hundred Years* and put up the money for the translation. They gave it to the Center and the Center paid me. Without royalties. Translators didn't receive royalties. It didn't even occur to me. I didn't have an agent. I suppose I should have had an agent, but that complicated everything. When it came out, that was the end of it.

PLINIO APULEYO MENDOZA: In March of 1968, Gabo tells me about his impression of witnessing, almost with surprise, the enormous success of *One Hundred Years of Solitude* in Italy.

GREGORY RABASSA: I don't think it was more than ten thousand dollars. Of course, back then, that was worth more than it is now, but they certainly could have given me more. But that's how it was done. Cass did get me royalties for the edition of the Book-of-the-Month Club, which no longer exists, which amounted to small payments of three or four hundred dollars a year, not much. But then I woke up. For the last translation I did, I skillfully got a dead author: Machado de Assis. So I'm Machado de Assis. All the royalties come to me.

MARGARITA DE LA VEGA: When I came to the United States in '74, I would go to the bookstores to see where García Márquez was and have them place him where he belonged. Because he was always under the letter M, and nobody understood that he had to be under the letter G. I think that even in a library I saw him in the M's. In the United States they think García is his second name and that Márquez is his first surname.

GREGORY RABASSA: I think the translation took me less than a year. I was living in Brooklyn Heights and we had a beach house in Hampton Bays. We had a very pleasant porch there, and I would sit there with the book. It was the edition with the purple, white, and red designs. I worked on my Olympia, which I still use, though it takes me a little longer now than it used to. I worked with the book and a dictionary. I made one copy. I sent finished pages to Cass so he could begin to edit them. No, it wasn't as if I thought I had written it. But I did think the translation read well. That was all I thought. Afterward you begin to think, but while you're doing it you concentrate only on the words. It was fairly easy. I can be a little mystical now and tell you that he was telling me what to write through the word he had chosen. For the word he had chosen in Spanish, there was only one perfect equivalent in English. It's not that I'm praising him, I don't give praise. But he did it well. It came out right away and he became famous. Very quickly. I think the continent was pleased that someone had finally begun to represent it. He was the first writer to receive worldwide attention, and he brought a whole group of people with him.

SANTIAGO MUTIS: How old was Gabo during all that? It was in '67. Gabo was born in '27, '28. In other words, he was forty. After *One Hundred Years* another person begins to appear.

GREGORY RABASSA: I met him once when he was in New York. His children were very young. The book had just come out, he had to attend some meeting, and we saw each other for a little while in the hotel. I don't recall which one. One of those traditional midtown hotels. Clem, my wife, came a little late because she was teaching that day. We didn't have much to say to each other. It was very hot, and the moments of friendship came and went, but I didn't know him the way I knew Julio. He isn't like Julio, who's an open person. Gabo is more reserved. And there was another difference. Julio was a few feet taller.

SANTIAGO MUTIS: One can't think that fame doesn't have an influence, but if you're isolated, you're alone with your problem. So I believe that Gabo submitted to that. No! Not submitted, no. He was gored by it. It attacked him like an animal, like a bull. And then gradually, slowly, another person begins to appear. He's no longer there.

20

Gabo Is Adjective, Substantive, Verb

In which García Márquez is transformed into the famous author of One Hundred Years of Solitude

RAMÓN ILLÁN BACCA: There's *gabolatría* on the part of critics, commentators, journalists, and they create a crushing, definitely overwhelming presence. Especially for those of us who came later and were trying to write. Everybody aspired to writing the other novel that would define an epoch. I even recall that in the novel of Aguilera Garramuño—*A Brief History of Everything,* it was called—there was a strip of paper, a sticker, that said: "*The Successor to* One Hundred Years of Solitude." Everything was sold like that. Ay! The ravages of *garcíamarquismo.*

JOSÉ SALGAR: I believe he influences everything. He had a bad influence on the generation immediately following his. Something similar to what happened with Watergate. After Watergate all the professional journalists felt obliged to bring down their presidents. When Gabo had the great success of the Latin American literary boom, all the journalists believed they were obliged to write better than he did in order to succeed. And many of them thought Gabo was a poor writer and that they wrote better and they began to imitate him.

RAMÓN ILLÁN BACCA: I remember Juan Gossaín, a journalist

who acquired a good deal of prestige writing like García Márquez. It was very clear that he garcíamárquezed all the time.

QUIQUE SCOPELL: I remember one day in Kid Cepeda's house when Gabito told Gossaín to stop imitating him.

JOSÉ SALGAR: It's a normal development. I lose the thread with Gabo and he begins to make his own character different, but he quickly returns to Colombia. He never lost the connection to journalism except for those five years. Until we all suddenly convinced him, especially Guillermo Cano, to write his columns. He began with one about a brilliant minister; he wrote from wherever he was, and he sent it in on time, but now he was a different Gabo.

RAMÓN ILLÁN BACCA: Then came the overflow about him. That's when he becomes Gabriel García Márquez. And it's when everyone is trying to know things about the man, right? There were even gabolaters. Gabolatry began, which still exists, of course. Universally. Here there were people like Carlos Jota who was involved in gabolatry, he began to write down facts about García Márquez, to collate things; if he was here, if he was there. It was a little later, when Jacques Gilard, the Frenchman, arrived . . .

MIGUEL FALQUEZ-CERTAIN: Jacques Gilard arrived in Colombia maybe in 1977. When he arrived, he communicated immediately with Álvaro Medina, since he already knew about him from references, and he helped him find all the necessary research materials to write his doctoral thesis on García Márquez and his friends from La Cueva, whom Gilard would later baptize the Barranquilla Group.

RAMÓN ILLÁN BACCA: That's when I become involved in the complicated story. I come back from the interior, I return to the coast, and then I hear things about him, I meet Jaime García Márquez, his brother, yes, but I wasn't one of the gabolaters. I didn't have much interest in looking for information.

FERNANDO RESTREPO: When I return to Colombia, the figure of Gabo always appears among us, and the first thing we did when I came back was to produce *In Evil Hour* for television. And that's when Gabo's real interest in visual media is born. We began to talk a lot, a great, great deal, about the possibilities of his plots being transferred to television. *In Evil Hour* was the first work by Gabo brought to television, to the screen.

RAMÓN ILLÁN BACCA: Well, every great author really arouses a great deal of interest, not only in his work but in his person. What hasn't been written about Thomas Mann? The other day I read a very long biography.

Even in minor authors, a great deal of interest is suddenly awakened.

For example, there's a character who attracts my attention, that is, Somerset Maugham, and I, for example, read almost all the pieces I see about Somerset Maugham. If you do that for a minor author, how will it be for the authors whose presence is so imposing?

NEREO LÓPEZ: He wasn't made in Colombia. He lived in Paris and in Mexico City but Colombia . . .

FERNANDO RESTREPO: I come back to Bogotá in '68 from Europe. So I encounter the presence of Gabo everywhere.

QUIQUE SCOPELL: I assure you that if you ask one of those types from the capital, they won't understand half the novel. They don't understand it because it's a regional novel about Barranquilla, about the coast. Because Colombia has three regions: the Paisa region; the Cachaco region around the capital; and ours, the region of the ignoramuses to them. That book, half of the Cachacos don't understand it because they can't imagine that a man would do the things the novel says. It's a completely regional novel. Nothing's imagined.

SANTIAGO MUTIS: That's a world lived by him, which I don't have. I'm from the city. I have a family life that's totally different. My education was different.

EDUARDO MÁRCELES DACONTE: It's difficult. Not only for a person from Aracataca but for any writer. What Gabo marked out in literature is a very high point, so one often feels . . . What shall I say? He's a figure that somehow has weight within the literary trajectory, not only of the coast but of Colombia. Of course, of the world too, but let's leave it there. So it's a very high fee we writers from that region paid, but filled with admiration in any event.

SANTIAGO MUTIS: Gabo has traversed almost all of my life. The first books I read were by Gabo, and Gabo still continues to be an important influence; so the relationship with him has been real. For any person of my generation who has written it is permanent, because ever since I began to read until I became a man, until I became a writer, Gabo is there. One cannot deny that. He is a tremendous presence. But it's also very different, let's say, to reread him now than when one read him as a boy. As a boy, *Leaf Storm* or *The Colonel* is the truth. What an intense way of approaching life and literature! From then on you began to make your own way. The only thing that's an influence is that one attempts to have the same intensity with things, but with one's own things. That's the lesson. His intensity. How much one can demand of oneself. But with things that are one's own. And each person has his own.

ROSE STYRON: Bill had met Gabo with Carlos Fuentes in Mexico City. At a very, very large party where they both were, but I didn't have the chance to meet him and talk to him until '74. I really didn't know that he was going to be there. I had been in Chile at the time of the coup and returned early in '74. I think this was later in the year, in '74. It may have been in '75. It was during one of Bertrand Russell's tribunals and a conference of some prominent Chileans who had been imprisoned by Pinochet had finally gotten out: singers and diplomats, all kinds of people. The tribunal brought them to Mexico. So I flew to Mexico City to meet Orlando Letelier, who had just arrived, not knowing that Carlos and García Márquez would be there too. We were all activists at the time, and we were all anti-Pinochet. We had all been involved the previous year in the Chilean fiasco. So that's how we happened to meet, and then the three of us became very good friends, and since then we've spent a good deal of time together.

QUIQUE SCOPELL: Besides, a person who had his beginnings, so humble . . . As I've said, for me that's no sin or offense. On the contrary. He's a tenacious guy. Honest. Because he's been honest his whole life. A working man. Persistent in his work. What else can you ask of a man? One can be furious with him as a person.

Not as a literary man, but as a person. He deserves it. That place he has in life, he's worked it.

EMMANUEL CARBALLO: There are two García Márquezes: before *One Hundred Years* he was a common, ordinary person, and after *One Hundred Years* he began to be another person . . .

A.C.
AFTER *CIEN AÑOS DE SOLEDAD*

This has all gone to hell. An average of three lizards fall in on me every day, from all over Latin America, and so after the summer we'll move to a secret apartment. They all come to tell me about their connection to the anguish of the world, and then they leave me 800-page originals. If this is glory, I prefer to enjoy it when I'm a statue.

Gabriel García Márquez, in a letter to Alfonso Fuenmayor from Barcelona

Gabo and Fuentemayor in Barcelona.

21

Rich and Famous

In which García Márquez pays his debts and distributes money

MARÍA LUISA ELÍO: They go to Spain and spend a few years there. When he comes back and I see him, you can't go outside with him. I, who hadn't gone back to Spain, go back and see them. And yes, he was already famous. In Spain he was already a celebrity.

CARMEN BALCELLS: Starting in '67 he settled in Barcelona, and there I saw him practically every day and participated in his ideas and all his projects. He would put on like a private rehearsal to see how I responded and how I reacted.

GUILLERMO ANGULO: When he's about to write *Autumn of the Patriarch* he decides to go to a place where an important patriarch still ruled; that is, he went in pursuit of Franco. To Barcelona. Being in Franco's environment, seeing how he was, how Franco was. After that, he also studied other dictators a great deal. That is, *Autumn* is probably more centered on Venezuela's Juan Vicente Gómez. But he studied all the dictators in America, Rafael Léonidas Trujillo from the Dominican Republic in particular. And he told me something about Trujillo that he never used, because, of course, he has so much more information than what he ends up using. It turns out that Trujillo was once walking with his bodyguards and he saw an old man, a classmate, but older than him, and he remarked: "So-and-so is still alive." Later his bodyguards told him: "Not anymore."

MIGUEL FALQUEZ-CERTAIN: He misses the Caribbean and returns to Barranquilla supposedly to find the smell of rotting guava.

JUANCHO JINETE: Quique rented him his house. He went there with Mercedes and the kids. He wrote . . . But as I'm telling you, he was withdrawing.

QUIQUE SCOPELL: No, we weren't so angry that we'd never talk to each other again no matter what, but we grew distant for the reasons everybody grows distant: either because of money or women. That's the only reason why you grow distant from a person, because of money or because of women. There's no other reason.

JUANCHO JINETE: He was already García Márquez. He wasn't a Nobel winner yet.

QUIQUE SCOPELL: He wasn't García Márquez yet. He was halfway to García Márquez. Not yet. I was living in that house and Álvaro says to me: "Don't fuck around, Quique, Gabito is stranded. Move out of your studio, you can go to your mother's. He'll pay you. He's going to earn big bucks with that book he's publishing. He's going to earn big bucks and he'll pay you." That's why I left my house and rented it to Gabito. Then, when I made the mistake of charging him, he became angry with me because I was charging him. "Don't fuck around, but pay me, you sonuvabitch, if you owe me the money. You've lived in the house for two years and you haven't paid me." In the end he paid me. We were both angry, but we didn't stay angry.

MARÍA LUISA ELÍO: When he became rich, he finally paid the butcher for all the meat he had given him on account.

CARMEN BALCELLS: The relationship with money is fundamental, not only for Gabo but for the whole world. So that when you don't have anything you do everything to have money. When you have some you hardly suffer at all because of money, and when you have enough, maybe more than enough, you can indulge your whims and not do anything anymore just for money.

In fact he liked the best restaurants and the finest-quality champagne. We had many memorable dinners. I don't recall who paid the bill. I certainly paid for just one reason, because Gabo didn't like to pay bills and he would say to me: "Kame, pay the bill and add it to what I owe you."

ARMANDO ZABALETA: I learned in *El Espectador* that García Márquez had won the Rómulo Gallegos Prize, worth a hundred thousand *bolívares*, and had given the prize money to some political prisoners. Then he won another prize worth ten thousand dollars and gave that money to another prisoner. And I . . . I'm very fond of the town where García Márquez was born and I knew the house where he was born very well: the courtyard was full of weeds and brambles. The only difference was the front, there was a half a façade there. I saw the condition of the house where he was born—abandoned—and the town too needing an aqueduct, needing a hospital, a secondary school . . . And him giving the money to others. Because of that I wrote a song. The song says:

> *The writer García Márquez*
> *The writer García Márquez*
> *We have to make him understand*
> *That the land where one is born*
> *Is the greatest love of all*
> *And not to do as he did*
> *When he abandoned his town*
> *And let the house tumble down*
> *The house where he was born.*

JUANCHO JINETE: He came to Colombia and said that he had given the money from the Venezuela prize to the guerrillas, to the revolution. When that thing with the guerrillas started here, there was a disagreement with a boy there in Bogotá, at a demonstration. A photograph that went around the world of them setting a fire in the university; he ran out and they threw things at him. And Gabo wrote that he was taking part in the revolution. Then Pacho Posada, who was a Conservative and the editor of *Diario del Caribe*, came and discovered this and wrote an editorial that said it was easy to come and make the revolution this way. From a distance. Now he had money. Now he was famous. He had a flat, as they call it in Barcelona, and I don't know what else. Pacho crammed an editorial down his throat. Pacho said to him: "And why don't you come and make the revolution here? Come on, come here." He even said to me: "You're going to Mexico City, you're going with a camera and you're going to photograph that house he has there. Damn! What is that? Have you seen it?" Finally

Alfonso Fuenmayor went to see Pacho and said: "No, Pacho, leave that alone now." But Pacho hit him hard. He wrote, "He writes to all the dictators . . . Like that, yes, delicious . . . They host him at the presidents' house."

EMMANUEL CARBALLO: His friendship with Fidel Castro bothered me very, very much.

WILLIAM STYRON: I think Fidel admires Gabo because he's a great writer. And this isn't a strange phenomenon. It's a mutual attraction and respect. Not only because of his great literary work, but because he has a fascinating mind and because he understands the respect and admiration that Gabo has for Fidel's revolutionary principles. In a sense, Fidel represents *The Autumn of the Patriarch*. They have a mutually inspired relationship based on shared principles, and that has shaped a kind of friendship that doesn't require an explanation.

EDUARDO MÁRCELES DACONTE: Aracataca did change, of course. García Márquez put it on the map. Life changed there because tourists began to go there. So then they had to build a new hotel. They had to open more restaurants. The town's economy improved. One way or another people who go there spend money, they eat lunch, they stay in a hotel. All of this resulted in the house where he was born being declared a museum. They rebuilt the back of the house. The front is like one of those reconstructed houses because the first house (it seems it was made of cane and mud) collapsed. Then they built one of solid materials, in the front. In the back they left the kitchen and many other things like that just as they had been when he was born. I always go and visit Aracataca. My aunts and cousins are there. I have so many cousins by now that on the street they call me "Cousin!" and I answer "Cousin!" without knowing who they are because they're the cousins of cousins. As many as the Buendías.

JUANCHO JINETE: All kinds of gringos fell all over us, foreigners too, so we'd take them around in a jeep and show them the region. Some would ask us to get them marijuana; it was around the time of the bonanza.

ARMANDO ZABALETA: After I composed the song, I ran into him in Valledupar and he greeted me and said: "I liked it. Your song was very good, congratulations. I was very annoyed for about three months, with how restless people were, but after three months the furor over the thing began to pass and I began to calm down. I wanted to reply to your song with my own *vallenato* but I didn't find a composer in Colombia who could write a song that was any better. And so then it all passed." Then he congratulated me and invited me to lunch one day when they were celebrating. And he was very happy with me, yes he was. We sang in Darío Pavajeau's house, in Valledupar. They had a party there because of our reunion. He likes *vallenato* music very much. I met him in Aracataca when he wasn't as famous as he is now. And after *One Hundred Years of Solitude* I saw him again. He's always the same. A smile and everything. He always tells me: "Maestro, this is good, this is elegant."

There in Valledupar he said: "I'm inviting you to spend some time with me, to accompany me these two days here in Valle." Then I accompanied him and one of the Zuleta brothers was also with us. That was a two-day party. A great party. Wherever they invited him to have lunch or dinner, he invited Emiliano Zuleta, the old man, and he invited me. It was his program and we came along. They would prepare a meal, a typical meal. Goat. Stew. Fish. Chicken. They always did it as if it were a party, singing along with a box, a guacharaca, and an accordion. And singing in the real *vallenato* party way. *Vallenato* is not for dancing but for listening. The elegant thing is that they improvise. When the party's at its best, you improvise and listen to the verses. Nobody dances. Because that music, its brilliance, is for listening, listening to the words, who the words are directed to. Because the music there is *costumbrista*.* It tells the story of a character from the department of Cesar. In the region at least, the song is composed to an individual.

EMMANUEL CARBALLO: The García Márquez I knew was a modest boy not interested in having people speak marvels about him, and when he published the novel and experienced the amazingly great success of *One Hundred Years*, I didn't see him again. I haven't seen him for years. He became famous and pedantic, and pedantry and feeling important bother me a great deal. I didn't seek him out again, and he didn't seek me out. Once when he came from overseas, when he was already very elegant, he came to see me in my office, at a publishing house I had, and he wasn't the same. We had met at a certain moment in life and had been very good friends. Not afterward. He was looking for other things, and so was I. Fame, recognition, his going in and people saying: "There's García Márquez." But what I'm telling you is nice because, without having a friendship, I still have good memories of that moment in life.

---

* *Costumbrista* refers to the depiction of everyday life in Spanish and Latin American art.

ALBINA DU BOISROUVRAY: I met Gabo García Márquez when we founded the journal *Libre* in Paris in the year '71. I knew Juan Goytisolo, the Spanish writer who was very avant-garde, and that year he came to me because he had this idea of gathering together all the writers of the Latin American boom, whether they were leftists or rightists, in a literary magazine. Many of them lived in Paris, others didn't, but they visited the city frequently because Paris was the intellectual and literary center at the time. Goytisolo wanted its purpose to be not so much different national politics but ending North American imperialism in Latin America at every level: economic, intellectual, cultural. He came to me because I was already involved in many movements that were very 1968 and I gave them some money, and he asked me to finance the magazine that didn't cost very much. I thought the idea was fantastic, not only to promote Latin American culture and literature but to bring together well-known writers—like Gabo—with those who were not well known, like a Paraguayan whose name I can't remember. Juan chose Plinio Mendoza, whom I didn't know, as editor. Plinio worked at the Colombian embassy in Paris, in other words, he was already there, and besides, Plinio is a very meticulous person, very precise in everything, in that Colombian, Bogotan way of his; that English-dandy way. Juan thought he was the perfect person. The idea was to put out four issues that year. Plinio made a list of writers and the committee would decide whether to include them in the edition. I was on the committee. I remember there was one who was not approved because he was on the extreme right. If I remember correctly, it was Guillermo Cabrera Infante. Yes, Cabrera Infante. But there were two whom Plinio said we absolutely had to include. Gabo and Octavio Paz. If we got those two, fabulous, because we'd get the rest. They were the two. And it was true. After them came Vargas Llosa and Cortázar, who lived in Paris. There weren't many women. I remember Claribel Alegría.

It all began perfectly. Plinio informally asked the writers for essays, and it was at that time that I met Gabo. For me, Gabo was the great author of *One Hundred Years of Solitude* that du Seuil had published, I think it was Severo Sarduy who had brought him to the publisher so that they'd translate *One Hundred Years*, that is, I was clearly very moved to meet him.

Plinio brought the writers for me to meet. Besides, in the beginning the offices of the magazine were in the living room of my apartment on the rue du Bac. Then we moved them to the rue du Bièvre. Since in those days we didn't have so much access to images of people, I had no idea what García Márquez looked like, and I remember that when I saw him I thought he was a combination of a hedgehog and a teddy bear. Vargas Llosa and Cortázar always looked impeccable. Not him. Nothing to do with the writers I knew like Bill Styron. He was not the image I had of what one expects of a great writer. Besides, I felt he was extremely shy. I remember that when I spoke to him the first time he was not at all open, I'd say, in fact, that he was fairly cautious. As if he were asking Plinio: "Who is this woman? Where have you brought me?" I don't know, but he wasn't very communicative. Gabo was never very extroverted and I always felt that there was a good amount of timidity in him. I felt that he was a contradiction, there was a certain insecurity regarding his place and at the same time he had a huge ego, he knew very well the person he had become as a writer. So he was a great contradiction. He wasn't someone with whom you could feel totally comfortable. You had to zigzag around his sensitive areas, you had to be careful not to wound hidden feelings, which were there but which he didn't show. He was precisely solitude and company. A solitary person with a feeling about who he was, but at the same time he needed his friends, and sought out affection and admiration.

MAURICIO MONTIEL: When García Márquez decided to found the magazine *Cambio* in Mexico City in the mid-eighties, I was the editor of the section on culture. Several times we went to lunch, and he never, ever let me pay. One day I told him that if he didn't let me pay, I wouldn't eat with him anymore. And he said fine. And he chose where he wanted to go. At the end of the meal, when the bill came, he pulled it out of my hand and said: "Look, since we sat down at this table I've sold thousands of copies of *One Hundred Years of Solitude*. How many books have you sold?"

JUANCHO JINETE: I remember that I moved away from Gabito because he said that Kid and I were the lackeys of Santo Domingo and things like that. But you know something: Gabo is a good person because my niece ran into him on a flight not long ago and went up to him and said she was my niece, and Gabo invited her to travel with him in first class.

22

The Death of Five Kings

*In which various theories are discussed regarding the relationship of
García Márquez to the dead*

FERNANDO RESTREPO: He had endless situations that worried
him very much. Very, very much. Very nervous. Those phobias
and fears that he displayed. Like not wanting to stay in a house
where anyone had died. There wasn't the slightest chance it would
happen.

GUILLERMO ANGULO: I don't know if you know what *pava*
is. *Pava* is very complicated . . . The intellectuals in Venezuela
invented the expression: "That's really *pavoso*, my friend," when
Venezuelans were oil-rich—naturally, that wealth of the new rich
meant they had things in very bad taste. The intellectuals would
say that to protect themselves so they wouldn't have things or do
things in bad taste.

Do you know what the height of *pava* is? Serving tripe in a
goblet. So *pava* has two connotations. It's what we call *lobo* here.
Colombian *lobo*, Bogotan *lobo* is a little classist. To use the word
lobo here is very well educated; very, very educated in its origins
because there has always been a well-educated bourgeoisie here. It
comes from *lupanar*, the low-rent brothels in Rome. So *lobería* has
to do with the cheap girls offered by the madam. When the upper
class talks about these things they refer to them as lovers and there's

nothing bad about it. But saying that a girl is a *loba* is putting her down, minimizing her. So obviously that *loba*'s taste is at the level of her education, at the level of her class, that's what became *lobo*. In Cuba it's *picúo*. In Mexico it's . . . what is it? I ought to know because my children call me that name. It's something that sounds as if it's Indian. *Naco*. Well, as I was saying, Gabo wrote about *pava*. So the Venezuelan connotation is that things in bad taste bring bad luck, and that's *pava*. Some of his characters have *pava*. In his daily life, he believes in *pava*. He fears death more and more and believes in a series of things that one doesn't believe in. In salt and in every kind of omen. He believes in all that.

FERNANDO RESTREPO: He stayed several times at our farm in Zipaquirá. Our farm is above the salt mines in Zipaquirá. It is relatively large, more than three hundred acres and the house is relatively old, more than eighty or ninety years old; my father-in-law built it. So Gabo was there because he wanted to retrace the steps of his stay there when he was a student.

The first thing he demanded was that we tell him its entire history because he was supremely superstitious. But he considers all those things terrifying, as he told us, and it was incredible how superstitious he was about that kind of thing. "Had people died in that house?" he asked. Because he said that if there had been dead people, he wouldn't stay. Then I guaranteed that nobody had died in that house. I was absolutely new to that kind of situation. But he took it seriously. I thought it was a joke but he was *very* serious. If I had told him that someone had died there, he wouldn't have stayed in the house. That really surprised me, because I thought, at first, that he was making a kind of ironic comment. Not at all. His superstition about that kind of thing was very deep.

MIGUEL FALQUEZ-CERTAIN: *Pava* leads to pathological extremes. When Alfonso Fuenmayor was dying, he didn't go to see him, the friend who took bread out of his own mouth to give to him.

QUIQUE SCOPELL: In my opinion, whoever dies is already fucked. That's a phrase of Álvaro Cepeda's: "The one who died was fucked." Why remember anything else? My mother died, and you go to the cemetery . . . What flowers or what shit! If she died, she died. What else are you going to bring?

JUANCHO JINETE: Let's say, when Álvaro Cepeda died in '72, Julio Mario Santo Domingo wasn't in Colombia but he came right away. He arrived one day before the funeral. Everybody came, the president of the republic and all of that. And Gabito said he couldn't come back because he was in Bolivia (*extending his arm, trying to get the waiter*): Maestro . . .

QUIQUE SCOPELL: The one who died, what does he care about flowers? Or cemeteries, or funerals, or the Day of the Dead . . . You have to give people whatever it is you want to give them while they're alive, whatever you want, and not get all upset when they die.

JUANCHO JINETE: Afterward, with what happened with Fuenmayor, who was talking to him a couple of days before he died, he also had an excuse for not coming to the funeral.

GERALD MARTIN: Well, about Alfonso Fuenmayor, what I can tell you is that Gabo made no exceptions. You know what he says:

"I don't bury my friends." He's terrified of death and sickness. He didn't go to any funeral. Not his mother's or his brother Yiyo's, the number-two writer in the family. The only important exception, curiously, was his father's funeral. Strange, don't you think?

GUILLERMO ANGULO: I have a story for you. There's a very good film director in Venezuela. Her name is Margot Benacerraf. Do you know who Margot Benacerraf is? Margot Benacerraf was a famous woman. She made only two films. The two films were very successful, and afterward, when you talk to Margot Benacerraf, she tells you: "I was in Antibes with Pablo." Pablo is Pablo Picasso. "And then Henri took me dancing." Henri is Cartier-Bresson. "And Pablo painted my thigh."

Then she decided one day that she wanted to make a movie about Gabo, and Gabo told her: "Look, there's a short paragraph this small in *One Hundred Years*, which is the story of Innocent Eréndira. It can be made in La Guajira. It's very nice." "Ah yes, let's do it!" So he wrote the script for her. Then she began to get the money. She went to Europe. She took me to Europe. At a certain moment Gabo and I arrived at one of the most elegant hotels. The hotel where Nixon stayed, which was the Grand Hotel in Rome. And so the reservation for Guillermo Angulo was fine. For Gabriel García Márquez, who wasn't famous yet, not so famous (*One Hundred Years* had just come out) they hadn't made a reservation, even though in Rome, in Italy, they really like him. So they said to him: "No, forgive us, but we'll give you the Royal Suite. You can sleep there tonight and tomorrow we'll find a room for you." They take us to something full of brocade. A marvelous palace, and suddenly Gabo said: "Shit, maestro, Alfonso XIII died here." "What shall we do?" "Let's take a walk." We walked the whole night through Rome. We saw everything. I was dead tired. "No, look, let's go to the Fontana dell'Esedra." We went to the Fountain dell'Esedra. "Let's go to the Fontana di Trevi." We went to the Fontana di Trevi. Damn!

The next day . . . It was a very elegant hotel where you didn't have to sign the bill. Gabo, when it was time to pay the bill, since you don't sign, but they just ask you for your room number, Gabo says he was there, in that room where a king died. The desk clerk says: "Excuse me, señor, but five kings have died in this hotel!"

23

"Excuse Me, What's Your Name?"

In which the hick is transformed into a slick sex symbol

FERNANDO RESTREPO: Gabo bought an apartment near the Boulevard Montparnasse and he invites us to go there because he wants to see the possibility of our forming a company to make films with a friend of his, a French producer, and a Portuguese-speaking film director from Madagascar, an extremely nice man, in whom he had a great deal of confidence. I don't know whether he had already done some things, I don't think so, but he had made some attempts to produce a film with him. So he decides that we'll form a company with Fernando Gómez and with me, with this friend, the Frenchman . . . I don't remember his name . . .

By the way, something very nice occurred. By now Gabo was Gabo, and we went to have lunch, to talk about business, to talk about the movie project, at the Closerie des Lilas on the Boulevard Montparnasse, up there, that place famous for its artists and so forth. The four of us were eating lunch and a very pretty girl, in a corner, was looking at him and looking and looking. He realized that she was looking at him. At a certain moment an employee of the restaurant or café comes over and says: "Are you Señor García Márquez?" "Yes, that's right." "Well, the girl who's looking at you wants to know if it's you, and if it is, she wants an autograph." Then he takes out a piece of paper and Gabo says: "No, look. I

221

don't sign autographs on blank papers." He took out a fifty-franc bill, I remember, and said: "Tell the girl to go and find a bookstore near here, the closest one she can find, and buy a book by García Márquez. When she buys it, I'll be very happy to dedicate it to her." And we continued chatting. In ten minutes the girl left the restaurant, went and bought a book by Gabo, and brought it over to him. The man signed it. "To . . . your name? What's your name?" Just like that. Very bold, because knowing that in any bookstore near the Boulevard Montparnasse there would be books by Gabo was something pretty . . . Well, I don't know how sure he was, but it made an impact. This is, for example, an incident about impressive confidence because, *caramba*, I don't know how many authors can say: "Go to such-and-such bookstore, in Paris, and buy one of my books." That happened. I saw it with my own eyes when the guy came over to talk to us. He dedicated the book to the girl and she, of course, was delighted.

HÉCTOR ROJAS HERAZO: Once he went to Barranquilla and they took him to dance where there were some girls. And he changed his name. The thing had already begun: not the Nobel but before that, when he was beginning to have a name. So he was dancing with her and suddenly she says to him, when they finish dancing: "Listen, tell me something. What's your name?" Gabo says: "Okay, I'm going to come clean with you. My name is Gabriel García Márquez. Why?" And she says: "Oh, because you're a damn fine dancer!"

ROSE STYRON: I love all the things he says about love, about being possessed by love. I asked him about *Of Love and Other Demons* and he said love *is* the demon that possesses you, that love is a personal disaster you can't live without, that it starts out very purely, as I'm sure he sees his parents' love or the first love of his life. But as one gets older society sort of confuses that, but love is still the moving force.

I've always been fascinated by the young girls in his books, like Fermina, who was about fifteen years old, and then there's that girl who is about twelve in *Of Love and Other Demons*. And how he associates with them, and sees that sort of purity of love. Then, as you know, in *Love in the Time of Cholera* he's more interested in Florentino's view of love, because he is always falling in love, again and again and again, searching for the pure love he had with Fermina. I'm very curious to see how he sees his mother and father's love from a child's point of view.

JUAN CARLOS CREMATA: I took a film workshop with him in San Antonio de los Baños, the film school he started in Cuba, and he said that he feels more comfortable with women than with men. In the workshop he paid much more attention to the female students.

ROSE STYRON: And, of course, he is so wonderful with women, not only the women in his books but the women in his real life. He is a man who loves women . . . It's just a totally sensual and spiritual feeling. I don't know how you sense it. It's just the way he behaves with women, as if he loves and appreciates them, and understands them. And has a good time with them. He is so fun to be with . . . I'm expressing this as a woman. In his books, you know, women are pretty sensual and a lot of what he writes is seen through the eyes of female characters. It's a man writing, but a man who you know understands and cares about women enough to put himself inside their heads. And I think that just as he gets inside the head of his male characters, he does the same with his female characters. And as I said: he treats dictators the same as lovers or killers or, you know, whoever it is . . . But the fact is that I'm a woman, and as such, it's wonderful to be in his company.

GUILLERMO ANGULO: La Gaba, that's what we called Mercedes, a woman of incredible intelligence and serenity. That's a woman. She's much more intelligent. Gabo has more talent, no doubt about it. I mean, Gabo has the talent, but as for intelligence and strength, she's the one who dominates. Not in the sense that Gabo wouldn't have been a writer without Gaba, nothing like that, but she is a very, very strong support. So strong. More than maternal. She's a fortress. She's in command. She commands. No doubt about it.

MARÍA LUISA ELÍO: The two of them have a very nice relationship. Besides, I never saw her looking upset because there was no money. Never. Or in a bad mood because he spent the whole day in that room. Never. Not once. Yes, I believe that one doesn't do things by oneself. You have to be with someone.

EMMANUEL CARBALLO: A woman in her house. I never spoke about literature with her. With Gabo, yes. I never spoke with his wife. Gabo would go alone to the meetings we had on Saturdays. No one accompanied him. Just the two of us.

FERNANDO RESTREPO: Marvelous. An enchanting woman and she was really the one who organized everything. I have the feeling that she organized his daily life because he gave the impression that he wasn't very ordered in his daily habits. She coordinated and straightened him out, let's say, and so they have a very nice relationship, very nice, because I imagine it can't be at all easy to live together in that way and to mix with all the people he was friendly with. But she managed very well and was very well liked by all of us. A very nice friendship between Elvira Carmen, my wife, and Mercedes. She was often here, and when she came here we saw each other, even if Gabo was absent.

MARÍA LUISA ELÍO: I can't say he's one of those people who gives himself entirely to another person. No. He can even be a little distant at times. You talk to him and you know you're talking to someone very intelligent. And that's very pleasant: talking to someone who's very intelligent, isn't it? You're talking to someone exceptional and you know it. I knew he was someone very distinctive. The proof is that I left all the rest (it was a very select group) and stayed exclusively with him, listening to him. I think that's why he said: "The book is yours," because there was no motive. We barely knew each other. I always tell him: "Gabo makes me, I haven't existed. I'm going to be an invention of yours. That's what I'll be. I'll appear in encyclopedias tomorrow. María Luisa Elío, a character invented by García Márquez."

GUILLERMO ANGULO: Then I said to him: "Well, you've told me how you met la Pupa but not why you broke it off." Because he sent her to me almost as a gift. He said: "No, some women are strange." "But why?" I asked. And he: "No, well, you tell them things and they have their own way of understanding it . . ." "But you, what did you say to her?" And he says: "Pupa, you fuck so much, why haven't you learned how?" La Pupa was famous among us for being the worst lay in the world. But no, it wasn't her. We were the bad lays! One day she got a Tuscan and that man made her climb the walls, she shouted too, and that was some incredible fucking. So good and bad don't exist. Two people who at a certain moment understand each other. There's nothing else.

KAREN PONIACHIK: This is the letter I wrote to Gabo:
My dear Señor García Márquez:
I feel embarrassed just asking to request an interview with you. I'm afraid I won't impress you enough for you to be willing to receive me. Even worse, I'm even afraid that you'll be willing to receive me because I wouldn't know what questions to ask you. You intimidate me, señor. The only time I saw you, a couple of years ago when you came to New York to open a cycle of Latin American films, I didn't even dare to greet you. It was you who approached me. I don't believe you remember: I was dressed in green. It was the first time I wore something that color. Since I was a little girl, for some reason I still can't explain, I had avoided green. The day before the launch, I found a very pretty dress on sale, and in spite of its being the forbidden color, I bought it. I'm in the habit of wearing a new outfit the day after I buy it, and so I put on the dress to go to the cocktail party at the Mexican Consulate. I felt tremendously uncomfortable, and for that reason I tried desperately to go unnoticed. I stood in a corner, far from the celebrities. You must have noticed my anguish because you approached, and citing someone I don't know, you said something like: "The lady must be very certain of her beauty for green to flatter her." That was all. You turned and left. Since then I no longer avoid green. Since then I've also reread your *One Hundred Years of Solitude* several times; I devoured your *Strange Pilgrims* and was in anguish over the one about the girl who

only wanted to use the phone. I ought to confess that I broke off with a gringo I was dating because he told me he hadn't liked your book. No, señor, I'm not going to write to request an interview. Furthermore, I don't even want to interview you. Your books are enough. And the green dress, of course. I wear it each time I'm going to do an interview.

GUILLERMO ANGULO: The saying is: "Whoever wears yellow is certain of her beauty." There's a story I'm going to tell you. It's a story that happened to him and he had to give it away. Who did he give it to? Carlos Fuentes. Fuentes published it in a book called *Blind Men's Song* because Gabo thought he'd be found out. He sees a very beautiful woman at a cocktail party and loses sight of her. He sees her again and loses sight of her again. Suddenly he realizes that the woman was noticing him. Then—Mexican women are outstanding; Mexicans and Brazilians—she goes up to him and says: "Would you like to have coffee with me?" He said he would. When they get into his car the woman says: "Shall we have the coffee before or afterward?" They go to a hotel and with such bad luck Gabo falls asleep. When he wakes it is already morning, the sun is already shining through the window. "And now what do I do?" he wonders. They leave the hotel, he drops her off and he's left thinking what is he going to do and decides one thing that's very important: one shouldn't go home so late—or early, in this case—and not smell of drink. So he takes a beer, or half a beer, and spills it on himself so that the smell is very strong. He buys a peasant hat, takes the car, and drives it into a pole. He smashes up the car. When he arrives home, La Gaba is waiting for him. "I almost killed myself . . . I'll tell you about it later." He goes to sleep. And it was never discussed again.

ODERAY GAME: We met at a film festival in Cartagena. I was dressed in white. So was he. He wore a white watch, white shoes. He didn't detach himself from me for the entire festival. But always with Mercedes. I'm a girlfriend who has Mercedes's blessing. In my case it was an adoption. I felt like a daughter. When I returned to Madrid they often called and told me: "We're coming to your house to have some of the fish soup that Juanita makes." They were fascinated by Juanita, my cook, worked wonders in the kitchen. And they would arrive and spend the evening with me. Or they'd call from Paris and tell me to go see them there: "Come see this film with us." When I had to go back to Ecuador to live he gave me a hand. I would have wanted to stay in Europe but it was impossible. He called to ask how I was. And then Mercedes would get on the phone: "How are you, my dear? Go out, don't be depressed." He gave me an affectionate hand. I remember the first time he called Quito. My mother almost fainted. She answered the phone and since her voice is identical to mine, he began talking to her, thinking it was me, and my mother said: "Who is this?" "Gabriel García Márquez." And so each time the phone rang and it was him, she would almost die. She would drop the cup, the tray, or whatever she had in her hand. "Honey, it's García Márquez for you." And so I was accompanied by him on my return. I haven't known anyone who isn't a relative, who isn't in the family, who's been more generous to me than Gabo.

MARGARITA DE LA VEGA: He didn't get along with his father because he was a bad husband, but the fact is that Gabo hasn't been like an innocent boy at first communion. Mercedes has put up with a lot in terms of fidelity. That is, he has the traditional fidelity of the coast.

GUILLERMO ANGULO: There's a friend of ours who is Goytisolo, one of the Goytisolos, I don't remember which one, who had a girlfriend in New York: he would write to his girlfriend and she would answer him. One day they decided that they would see each other, something very romantic, see each other in Manhattan, go to Staten Island and come back, all of that. So he goes on the trip and leaves all the letters in his locked desk. He tells his wife: "I have a meeting with an editor about publishing some things of mine in the United States, let's see if the thing works out." As soon as he catches the plane, his wife (all women with a pin, with a hairpin, can open any lock) opens that desk and sees all the letters. They're telling the story to Gabo and Gabo says: "What an idiot to have left the letters there." And Gaba says: "No, she's the idiot for having opened the drawer." So that demonstrates a little of Gaba's philosophy: don't open the drawer.

24

Persona Non Grata

In which García Márquez becomes an enemy of the United States

FERNANDO RESTREPO: He was very critical of the United States and the crisis with Cuba and all of that. He took a very radical position and for a long time they didn't give him a visa to enter the United States. Now I think he has one, permanent and everything.

ROSE STYRON: He was on that list for so many years . . . I organized the Committee for Free Expression at PEN, and we were trying to bring to the United States, for our own edification, various prominent writers whom the American government, especially the Nixon–Kissinger administration, considered dangerous leftists. And García Márquez, like Graham Greene—and Carlos Fuentes for a time—couldn't enter the country. There were a lot of writers who couldn't. And then suddenly, and very quietly, they let him come to New York. He wanted to go to Mississippi and pay homage to Faulkner, go to his house, and the first time he entered the country they didn't allow him to. He had to wait. The whole business of their not letting him enter the country angered him and amused him at the same time. Fuentes came in every year because he taught at Pennsylvania and at Brown, and he spent several months at a time in various universities in the United States.

But each time Fuentes had to request permission and each time he did they authorized him.

If García Márquez made the request, he was turned down.

JUANCHO JINETE: Everything we did here in Barranquilla, all the petitions we signed asking that they give him that visa. We were friends of those gringos from the consulate who went around with us here. Later we learned that some of them were even in the CIA.

WILLIAM STYRON: The McCarran-Walter Act was a delicate subject with Gabo for a long time. This awful embargo on intellectuals like Gabo. A time in 1985 comes to mind, I recall. It's a particularly memorable moment for me because it's connected to the depression I suffered from and that I wrote about, and I remember I was flying from New York to Martha's Vineyard. He called and said he would be at the house of a mutual friend, Tom Wicker, who at the time was still writing his column for the *New York Times*. He told me he was going to have a get-together at his house and I remember it was the beginning of that colossal depression. I remember flying to New York, going to the party, and being profoundly sick. Gabo's extremely amusing comments on how he had managed to enter this time with the McCarran-Walter Act, which still prohibited his coming in, scarcely registered in my mind. I remember that he took it with a mixture of anger, good humor, and cynical acceptance.

FERNANDO RESTREPO: At a certain moment he was invited to teach a class, a seminar, at Columbia University, and he was issued a special visa so that he could go. At that moment Fernando

Gómez Agudelo and I were in Paris on some television business. We called Gabo and decided: "Let's go to New York."

WILLIAM STYRON: We shared recollections of his love for New York, and what I want to say is that he came and went very quickly because of the immigration problem. The time they allowed him to spend in this country was limited. But I think that one of the many things that acted as a catalyst for our friendship, though it would have existed all the same without it, was the war in Nicaragua at the beginning of the eighties. The war was a delicate subject, almost a painful one, for him and for me. Later I went with Carlos Fuentes to Managua, at the most heated point in the war, because it was a cause of great sorrow for many people in this country, myself included. And then there was the fact of his friendship with Castro, which has always been an uncomfortable subject. Many Latin American intellectuals have been concerned, of course, about his relationship with Castro.

PLINIO APULEYO MENDOZA: Fidel is a myth from the confines of his recovered childhood, a new representation of Aureliano Buendía. If anyone's looking for a key to his Castroite fever, here it is in eighteen carats.

FERNANDO RESTREPO: Gómez Agudelo and I decided to take the Concorde, since they had recently initiated the supersonic flights of the Concorde. We told Gabo we were traveling on the Concorde, and Gabo says: "I'll meet you at the airport." When we landed, there he was, and Gabo asks: "Well, and how's the Concorde?" Fernando says: "A fast-as-shit DC-3." Gabo wrote that description in one of his columns.

CARMELO MARTÍNEZ: His father, a Conservative, and him, a communist. With the money he has he can't be a communist. He has a lot of money.

BRAM TOWBIN: The scene is the 1982 Cannes Film Festival. I was ensconsed aboard the *Sumurun*, the most beautiful sailboat in the harbor that year, which belonged to my father. I was spending my spring vacation from Dartmouth in Europe. I was on deck alone while the crew and a good number of cosmopolitan European and American guests were down below. A South American gentleman in his forties appeared on the dock and came up the gangplank. He behaved with determination and authority, but with a low profile. I didn't think he was an intruder, but rather one of those minor actors. When he came on board he asked for one of the guests, saying only her first name, Albina. I told him in English that she was busy but would soon be up and invited him to the table, in the middle of the ship, which was set to receive guests. We sat there.

In my defense for what I'm going to relate, I should make it clear that at this time Gabriel García Márquez wasn't the recognized name that it is today for most people in the United States. Our dialogue begins here. He claimed not to know English. I don't know Spanish. We decided on French, which I speak very badly. Taciturn and obviously unimpressed by my qualities as a host, he put me in a bad humor and I imagined him acting, reciting the usual phrases, but he was our guest and I rushed to show him the marvelous benevolence and good manners of the ultra-privileged gringo college student. It may be that we don't have the panache of the French or that old-world overconfidence of the English, but we do have our strong points:

I: Where were you born?

He: In Colombia.

I: Is it nice in Colombia?

He: Yes.

(*Uncomfortable silence*)

I: Do you want something to drink?

He: No.

(*Uncomfortable silence*)

I: The chef is preparing cheeses and bread. They're terrific. Do you want cheese and bread? It's delicious.

He: No, thank you.

(*Uncomfortable silence*)

I: Do you have a film in the festival?

He: No.

I: I heard that *Annie Hall* and *E.T.* are super fine . . . but to each his own.

(*Uncomfortable silence*)

I: It's a nice day . . . a very nice climate . . . a little hot but much better than in New York. I live in New York.

He: Yes.

I: Have you liked any of the films they've shown this year here in Cannes?

He: *Missing.*

I: I haven't seen that one yet.

(*Uncomfortable silence*)

I: I didn't like *Annie Hall* at all. It's pretty stupid. Really.

At this point people began to come up. I realized immediately that he was no second-rate actor. For all these people adulation is as sinful as wearing velour, but there they all were, fairly servile and tittering like embarrassed children. Who the devil was this guy? Well, then, for the next few days I didn't do anything but hear them all preach to me about *One Hundred Years of Solitude* . . . And I said to myself what the hell, another writer. I return to the United States and it seemed as if the whole country was reading that novel, and I begin to realize its significance. In a few months, he's awarded the Nobel Prize in Literature. Wherever I go I hear everybody talking about García Márquez. And I'm silent. I return to my university and decide to take a course on William Faulkner. The first day of class, the professor, very well versed in the subject matter, who had spent years teaching Faulkner, begins: "This year the Nobel Prize in Literature was awarded to the great Gabriel García Márquez. Of all our contemporary authors, he is one of those who share with William Faulkner the sense of place. I want all of you to know that at this moment this formidable talent is not allowed to visit the United States thanks to our antiquated immigration laws. This is an embarrassment. What I wouldn't do to spend a few minutes with this man." I didn't raise my hand.

25

Something New

In which we come to understand why he writes
The Autumn of the Patriarch

SANTIAGO MUTIS: The other Gabo appears. Lots of luminaries.
Lots of things.

RAFAEL ULLOA: They praised him to the skies when he wrote
One Hundred Years of Solitude... All the world's press. So the
venom of pride grew in him and made him get involved in that
Autumn of the Patriarch. He wrote it as if he wanted to write
something better than *One Hundred Years of Solitude,* but since
the man wasn't sober but emotionally in the clouds ...

MIGUEL FALQUEZ-CERTAIN: He said that after he became
famous with *One Hundred Years of Solitude*, in '67, he fought with
that novel and didn't write anything; he couldn't write anything.
He talked about dismantling his style. You can quote me because I
remember it as if it were yesterday: "I have to dismantle my style."
That means that he had to destroy it. Return to the beginning
and find a new style for writing a new novel. Not keep doing
the same thing; I'm saying that, he didn't say it. Like in painting:
for me, I don't like a painter who repeats his painting because he
doesn't look for other alternatives, like Picasso did. Picasso tried
everything and not everything he did was good. Gabo wanted to

dismantle his style, and he spent seven years in the process. And then he decides to write this novel that is *The Autumn of the Patriarch*. Really I admire him because he wants to do something new. Probably he's reading Joyce and Woolf, the great stylists and modernists in the twentieth century, to write a new novel. And what happens is that the critics destroy it. But in my opinion it's one of García Márquez's most valid efforts.

GUILLERMO ANGULO: That's one of the most beautiful things there is . . . And there's a very curious thing: even critics have said that it has no punctuation, but it has all the punctuation in the world. The only thing it doesn't have is separation of chapters, so some people feel as if they're drowning.

HÉCTOR ROJAS HERAZO: The thing is that *The Autumn of the Patriarch* was against the dictator of Venezuela, who was Juan Vicente Gómez. The dictator Gómez. He spoke in general about the dictator. But, of course, he had triumphed with *One Hundred Years* until he had become a myth. That's why he had enemies in Spain. Then he thinks that he has to write a novel against *One Hundred Years* and so he writes *Autumn*. His detractors say: "Let's read it first to see what happens." Then they were impressed because García Márquez's best novel is *The Autumn of the Patriarch*. Something very typical of him. There were even people who said: "It isn't the autumn of the patriarch, it's the autumn of García Márquez."

WILLIAM STYRON: I think that every writer who has created a work that in the eyes of the world is his most distinctive wishes that the world would focus on his other work too. I think it distracts from the other works and it isn't fair to the rest of his work to have all this attention lavished upon one book. So that is probably the reason—or one of the reasons—that he has these reservations regarding *One Hundred Years*.

JOSÉ SALGAR: He has the journalistic sixth sense to know where the public's interest lies, their literary interest. He knows what the public that reads him expects. That's why he attempted to write something strange, just as James Joyce wrote, without periods or things like that. That's how he wrote *The Autumn*.

HÉCTOR ROJAS HERAZO: A great novel from the technical point of view. I love it. He handles the narration, he especially has a great ability to capture an entrance. He grabs the reader. I used an example the other day. For example: "The world woke up sad on Tuesday." Then you become interested. What happened? It's a way of entering. Well. I don't remember in which novel. The great novel for me is *The Autumn*. As a novel, as a technique, because it's handled extraordinarily well. How would the technical handling of the novel be that treats this man with a tenderness that makes one, at the end, let's say, sad because of the passing of the leader. Of course, every authentic narrator has great tenderness. Just look at the tenderness of the girl falling asleep and talking to her grandmother. *Innocent Eréndira* is extraordinary. The character who rides the bicycle. Everything, everything.

RAFAEL ULLOA: *The Autumn* is a brick because it's a runaway horse without periods or commas. *Papapapapapapapa*. Then you get bored. The fact is that the manner of writing that, I don't know, it's like a terrible pain, it's like a . . . It's a strange way of narrating, but, of course, here he's recounting the excesses of dictators. But in any case one doesn't know, one hasn't lived that . . . As I told you, I read that book in parts, but not . . . The style is different. He wanted to write an extraordinary work. You know that fame makes people crazy.

GUILLERMO ANGULO: At a certain moment Gabo threw himself to the floor in desperation, in Barcelona, because he couldn't find the ending for *The Autumn of the Patriarch*.

GREGORY RABASSA: I knew a doctor on Long Island who was from Barranquilla and a friend of Gabo's. I'd call him occasionally to ask him about the meaning of a word. I forget his name. A nice guy. Translating *The Autumn of the Patriarch* was more difficult because it's more savage and there's something untamed in the language. But what an entertaining book.

When *The New Yorker* was going to publish an excerpt from the book they told me they didn't print the word "shit." I told them that if they took out that word, it would be better not to publish anything. Because that word is the whole story. Now it's used more in English, but not so much earlier. I remember I lived in the Village, and in the world of jazz they liked the word because it had so many connotations. Some of them positive. You would hear them playing and you would hear them say: *Man, that riff is shit*. That word was the spirit of the spirit. The word was in the spirit, in the Village of Fourth Street. I had a friend who made jewelry and worked in silver. We would sit and talk and one day a black man came in the door and we heard him say *shiiit*. And my friend Bob says: "There goes the zeitgeist." At the end, *The New Yorker* came around and it was the first time they published the word shit.

FERNANDO RESTREPO: When he wrote *The Autumn of the Patriarch* . . . As I said, one of the connections with him was music. He enjoyed music a great deal, from *vallenatos* and *ranchera* music to classical music. And I took part in that because I'm also a melomaniac. So there were always conversations around the subject of music. For example, he thought Bruckner was boring. He didn't listen to Bruckner because it bored him . . . Then one day we sat down to talk about his two fundamental works, which are *One Hundred Years* and *The Autumn of the Patriarch*, and he himself created a very nice simile that says: "Look, *One Hundred Years of Solitude* is the Ninth Symphony and *The Autumn of the Patriarch* is the Fourteenth Quartet," which was a quartet we all loved and that, according to the melomaniacs, is the most profound quartet Beethoven wrote.

26

"Shit, He Died"

In which Gabriel García Márquez wins the
Nobel Prize in Literature, 1982

GUILLERMO ANGULO: Gabo invited Fernando Gómez Agudelo and me to a party, and we went from Bogotá to Mexico City via New York. We were in a cab in New York when they announced that the Nobel Prize in Literature had gone to Gabriel García Márquez. We didn't hear it clearly, did we? We didn't believe . . . That wasn't in the range of the possible. Then we changed the station and they confirmed it.

FERNANDO RESTREPO: Do you know the story about Alejandro Obregón, when he went to restore a painting of his in Gabo's house in Mexico City? Well, in Gabo's house we saw the famous painting, which is by Blas de Lezo, the Stubborn Man*. The story is that one day he goes to Alejandro's house in Cartagena, and

---

* Blas de Lezo, the "Cool Dude," is a folk figure in the Caribbean Coast. A Spanish admiral during colonial days, he is known for his victory in the Battle of Cartagena de Indias in 1741 when Colombia was part of the Spanish Viceroy and for all his missing body parts. He arrived in Cartagena having already lost his left eye, his left leg, and use of his right arm and is known as Half-Man. Alejandro Obregón loved Blas de Lezo's heroism and loved to exaggerate when recounting his version of the one-eyed admiral's resistance to the siege commanded by British admiral Edward Vernon. "Because of him," a Colombian saying goes, "we don't speak English." When Obregón painted his portrait, he wrote in the left-hand bottom corner: "Blas, the cool dude of Lezo, half a gaze and half a hug, seven balls and seven seas bringing victories and gangrene. A bullet hole for history and a silence made of copper for Blas de Lezo."

after a few rums, I don't know why, at a certain moment (I heard this personally from Gabo when he showed us the painting in his house in Mexico City) he takes out the rolled-up canvas and it's of Blas de Lezo, "Cool Dude," with a hole from a bullet that he [Alejandro] shot in his eye. And he says that it was because his children began to fight over the painting, disputing who owned the canvas, and in a fury he shot out the good eye in the painting. I believe Alejandro had a certain obsession with blindness; I think his father had a vision problem. At a certain moment he says to him: "I don't want that damn painting. It's for you." And he raises his hand, like this, "For Gabo," and he gives it to him. Gabo leaves very happily with his painting. And he has it the whole time. Obregón promised to restore it for him, but he never did. And one fine day Alejandro goes to Mexico City.

JUANCHO JINETE: There's a good story. I don't know whether you've heard it. When Maestro Obregón was at the filming of the picture *Quemada* in Cartagena, this man who was Marlon Brando wasn't going around with anybody. You know those guys are strange, and he saw Maestro Obregón in some scenes. He came out on a horse. He was a nobleman with his sideburns. Then he met the maestro and they became friends. Afterward Marlon Brando would go every day to the maestro's house to drink white rum. What was the name of that rum? Tres Esquinas.

The filming continued in Morocco, and when he was on his way back, Gabito told him to stop in Mexico City. He was coming by way of London, and he made all the connections and arrived in Mexico City. So the address he had for the house where he lived, where the rich people lived, the movie stars in Mexico City . . . Well, long story short, a house he had. So the maestro took a taxi, arrived there, and saw the terrace of the house filled with flowers and things. He arrived and said: "Damn, he died." Those flowers were the ones used for tributes. That's a good story. And when he arrived here in Barranquilla, that was the first thing he told me: "Juancho, listen to what happened to me. When I'm ready to get out I see all these flowers and think he died. 'Shit, he died.'" It was the day they had given him the Nobel Prize.

GUILLERMO ANGULO: When we arrived, well, the party was in full swing, and we wondered (Gabo always denied it) whether he had known earlier. Yes, he invited us to a party, but his insistence was far bigger than an invitation to a regular party. It did seem as if he had known.

MARÍA LUISA ELÍO: I find out because friends call me from Spain saying they had heard the news. They call me from Spain at about four in the morning here. Then I put on pants and a sweater and I rush out to his house. When I get there Mercedes has all the phones off the hook; she's talking. "Here comes the woman *One Hundred Years of Solitude* is dedicated to. Talk to her." She's holding the telephone so that we can hear what they're saying. On a big sign on the door of their house, here in Pedregal, they had written in yellow: CONGRATULATIONS, GABO. His eyes were shining.

García Márquez greeting a *cumbia* dancer in Stockholm.

27

"I Don't Want to Be in Stockholm by Myself"

In which the entire nation travels to the Nobel celebration

GUILLERMO ANGULO: [The then president] Belisario Betancur told him: "Make a list of your eleven closest friends so that they go with you to Sweden," and he said: "No, then numbers twelve and up are going to hate me. So I won't do that." Then I said: "Mr. President, it is up to you to do it," and he said: "I won't do it either. You take care of it." And I did. I chose the ones I thought were Gabo's best friends and we took them, at the government's expense.

GLORIA TRIANA: I was the one who coordinated the delegation of musicians who traveled to the celebration of the prize. The idea came from Gabo, though he surely said it not thinking they would do it but just as a way of expressing himself. "I don't want to be in Stockholm by myself. I'd like to have *cumbias* and *vallenatos* with me," was what he said. I went immediately to the director of Culture, what's called the Ministry of Culture today, and I said to her: "If he says he wants this, then let's organize it." The boss, Consuelo Araujo Noguera, chooses the *vallenatos* and the rejection begins; our ambassador in Sweden thought it was terrible that we were going to do that. That was playing the fool, acting like an imbecile. There's an article by a Colombian reporter, D'Artagnan, who's dead now, called "An Act of Silly Tackiness." He used the

247

Bogotan popular slang, *"hacer el oso,"* which means to do something embarrassingly tacky, uncouth. So that was the attitude of people except for Daniel Samper, who defended the idea.

NEREO LÓPEZ: The director of Colcultura, Aura Lucía Mera (we called her la Mera) tells me to go as the photographer for the delegation. And so we went. And so we got there. Certainly very late. We left Colombia at about five. One hundred and fifty people in the delegation. Folkloric groups. La Negra Grande. Totó la Momposina. A group from Barranquilla. A group from Valledupar. Special guests went by another route. It was in December '82 that we went.

RAFAEL ULLOA: The old man, Gabriel Eligio, Gabito's father, loves to talk. In Cartagena he always went to the park to talk to people and there they congratulated him. But more than anything he was a simple man. He's not like Gabito. Gabito threw a dim-witted party with that Nobel Prize thing, taking even *vallenatos* groups there with him. Well, they were extravagant with strange things.

QUIQUE SCOPELL: It was a few people. They suggested I go but I said: "No sir, I'm not spending all that money, what did you think!" Alfonso went. And Germán went.

JUANCHO JINETE: Álvaro had already died.

NEREO LÓPEZ: In any case we reached Stockholm at dawn. It was so cold!

QUIQUE SCOPELL: They brought along some *vallenatos*. The ones who wrote those songs about yellow butterflies, lying *vallenatos*, lies to sing there.

NEREO LÓPEZ: They told the *vallenatos* that Swedish women were very loose and so the men were ready to devour all the Swedish women they ran into, and on the third day one of the men says: "They haven't called us yet." So that night we went out. Seeing that the mountain didn't come to us, we went to the mountain. To some damn striptease! Striptease for nuns. There was more covered up, a little bit of nipple uncovered, and that was it. Then the *vallenatos* said: "No more of this!" We were there for something like two weeks.

After two or three days the folkloric groups rebelled because they took us to eat in a typical Swedish restaurant. That is, food full of fat for the cold. Codfish. And these people used to yucca, plantains . . . they didn't like it. So they rebelled. A real rebellion. So much so that they had to give in to them. "What do you want?" [they asked them]. They said: "No, we want the money for food." So they gave them the money. Then they ate hamburgers . . . I was with them and we were living on a boat. It was nicely fixed up and cheaper, because the special guests were staying in a first-class hotel.

PLINIO APULEYO MENDOZA: I see the Grand Hotel, its huge façade with flags waving up high. I see corridors carpeted in purple: a suite as big as a royal chamber, its high windows looking out on the Nordic night. I see thin slices of smoked salmon and disks of lemon on a tray, bottles of champagne chilling in a metal bucket, and beautiful, large, fresh roses; yellow roses exploding on every table above porcelain vases. In the middle of the salon I see Gabo and Mercedes, calm, unconcerned, talking, completely removed from the coronation ceremony that's approaching, as if they were still in Sucre or Magangué on a Saturday afternoon thirty years earlier, in the house of Aunt Petra or Aunt Juana.

GLORIA TRIANA: As an official I had an allowance for staying in the Grand Hotel, where everybody was, but I was responsible for sixty-two people. I had to pay attention to all those Colombians who had been against it and report on our foolishness.

NEREO LÓPEZ: They asked me where I wanted to stay and I was interested in being with the folkloric delegation. My roommate was the doctor. So the doctor told me that one night a girl from Barran-quilla came up to him and says: "Listen, Doctor, now when we get to Barranquilla you'll give me a laxative so I can get rid of all this junk I've eaten here." And a man from the plains comes and says to me:

"Don Nereo, you up there . . . I don't know. I want to go back."

"Go back? Do you know where you are?"

"No, I'm going no matter what."

"The plane took twenty-four hours to get here. Look. Remember that the plane left Bogotá at five in the afternoon and we arrived here at two in the morning. Look at how far we've traveled. And we got here at two in the morning. That means eight in the morning in Colombia. Why do you want to go?"

"No, it's just that I have a problem. And I want you to resolve it for me and talk to Doña Aura Lucía."

"And what's the problem?"

"No, it's a men's problem. Well, I go out to urinate and I don't find my willie."

"Well, and where do you go to urinate?"

"No, I go to the deck."

Of course, the deck with one or two inches of snow.

"Find the bathroom, that's why it's hiding from you," I tell him. "And what's the problem? That happens in the cold."

"No, it's that . . . How will I go back to my country if I have . . . three wives there. How do I respond to them?"

"No, man, for God's sake, the very idea. No. Look, there's a bathroom down here."

"No, but I've taken off all those layers of clothing and I don't know where they are."

Then I had to take him to the bathroom. He wanted to go back! Another case I remember was in that restaurant. Just imagine, winter, heavy food. Suddenly the woman at the counter screams. A scream. Nobody understood. The only thing we understood was the scream. Well Rafael Escalona was going to take a glass of what apparently was fruit juice and it was what they put on salad. The dressing. In a glass. Escalona thought it was juice. First, the harm it could have done him, and then . . . he'd ruin the salad we were all going to eat! Then Escalona said: "What happened?" Somebody said to him: "Don't you see that you're drinking the salad dressing?" Aracataca came to the world! They were expecting the Nobel Prize winner but they weren't expecting a show. The entire nation arrived. They didn't know where to put the show.

GUILLERMO ANGULO: One of the two Nobel speeches wasn't written by him but by Álvaro Mutis. He wrote the official speech, but the other one, which might be something about poetry—I can't really remember—Mutis wrote because the moment arrived and there was no time. Gabo told him "You write it." Yes. The man sat down and wrote it. Afterward he told the story. I knew that as a secret and I didn't tell anybody until I saw that Gabo told it one day.

PLINIO APULEYO MENDOZA: In Suite 208 of the Grand Hotel there's an atmosphere of great preparations . . . It's three in the afternoon, but the cold night of the Swedish winter, peppered with the lights of the city, colors the windows black . . . A photographer has come exclusively to take the picture of Gabo with his friends. And it's at that moment that Mercedes remembers the yellow flowers. When she begins to put them in our lapels. "Let's see, compadre."

I know the secret reason for that ritual. Gabo and Mercedes believe, as I do, in what is called *pava*, what I explained earlier . . . There are adornments, behaviors, individuals, articles of clothing that are not worn for this reason, kind of superstitious reasons. Tails, for example. That's why Gabo decided to wear a *liquiliqui* at the ceremony, a traditional suit in Venezuela, and in another time, throughout the Caribbean . . .

And now Gabo's friends, who came to Stockholm to have a photograph taken with him minutes before he receives the prize, have arranged ourselves, our backs to the high windows. Mercedes officiates at this rite too. "Alfonso and Germán beside Gabo," she has said, referring to Alfonso Fuenmayor and Germán Vargas, her husband's oldest friends.

GLORIA TRIANA: He was wearing a *liquiliqui* and not tails. He was the one who gave the most poetic and beautiful speech heard at the Nobel prizes: "The Solitude of Latin America." He was the one who had a banquet party in the Royal Palace accompanied by all the musicians.

NEREO LÓPEZ: The banquet was where that presentation took place. The nice thing about the dance at the banquet is that with so many people, the chief of protocol was worried. Naturally permissions were required, but the guy who organized all of it dedicated himself to having a good time. He picked up a sailor somewhere. He enjoyed his sailor and forgot about the rest of the world. He didn't look at my credentials. Then I had to disguise myself as a dancer to go up onstage. And the detectives saw. What kind of dancer is this who goes around with a camera hanging around his neck! The day of the banquet. The presentation of the prize was in the morning and the banquet was at night. The show we had prepared was two hours long. And then the guy said: "Come here, this isn't on the program. You can't do this." Another one said: "You can't place that cable. Because the King (they're like gods), the King can't see the cable." The King can't see . . . And on and on: the King and the Queen this, the King and the Queen that, like gods. And the spectacle can't last more than fifteen minutes.

When they come down those steps with the drums thundering . . . What an emotional thing! But really emotional! The spectacle they had given fifteen minutes to lasted forty-five. Because these guys applauded like madmen, like madmen. Very emotional. Very emotional. So much so that the guy who had put pressure on us said: "This isn't programmed either but the King has ordered us to invite you to lunch and have the palace cook hurry up and prepare lunch for one hundred and fifty people. So please excuse us." They gave us a meal and these guys are begging our pardon. They gave us a lunch much better than anything we could dream, of course, but for them no, they were apologizing for its simplicity. But the King, the King had them attend to us. That was very emotional. Very emotional.

MARÍA LUISA ELÍO: When they give him the Nobel I'm in my house. My son Diego is in their house with their son Rodrigo. They're watching television, they're seeing the Nobel. I'm in my house talking to them on the phone, my son Diego and his son Rodrigo and I are watching at home in Mexico City. I was crying like a hysteric.

GLORIA TRIANA: The next day the most important paper in Sweden had a four-column headline: GARCÍA MÁRQUEZ'S FRIENDS SHOW US HOW TO CELEBRATE A NOBEL.

NEREO LÓPEZ: Rafa [Escalona] was with us. Gabito couldn't get out of the celebration. He was a prisoner of the moment. He went to all the dance presentations the delegation was doing but they were part of his organized agenda. When we were having a short party, he joined in for a while. We couldn't really party with him. I bumped into him, for example, in the *cumbia*. "What happened? What's up?" and he took me by the chin. "This goatee? How long have you had a goatee?" I haven't seen him since.

GLORIA TRIANA: The next day all of the international press went to the ship except the Colombians. D'Artagnan, who had been so critical, did a very noble thing. He wrote an editorial saying it was a success, that it had to be acknowledged that it had been a success and we had moved the icy inhabitants of Sweden.

RAFAEL ULLOA: They were really proud. You can say whatever you want, but even when Gabito isn't part of your family like in my case, he has roots in your family, everybody knows that Gabito is a cool dude. That imagination of his . . . not just anybody has that. Suddenly I believe what the old man there says: that he has two brains . . . So when they gave him the Nobel Prize I wrote an article with the information I had. I sent it to *El Espectador*. They published it on October 10, 1982, and the next day *El Heraldo* published it. Someone faxed it to Gabito. And he said to me: "Send me something else." I like to tell stories about towns. There's a lady who was a secretary where I work. She knows I'm related to García Márquez and told me: "You inherited that thing from Gabito because those stories are Gabito's."

GLORIA TRIANA: That year the Nobel was thirty-one years old, and nothing like our ceremony has happened since, and I'm still tracking it down. There have been African writers, writers from the Caribbean, a Chinese writer, and nothing like the way we did it has happened again.

HÉCTOR ROJAS HERAZO: When he won the Nobel, we were in Spain. The ambassador, who was a novelist too, invited us. The Colombian ambassador invited us in order to greet him. Gabo, who's smiling a lot, laughed at everything. Then I arrive, very happy, and we gave each other a big hug.

Carlos Fuentes, William Styron, and García Márquez in the US.

28

Ex Cathedra

In which García Márquez confronts fame

MARÍA LUISA ELÍO: I don't know how it is in Colombia, but here in Mexico it's amazing. Women throw themselves at him on the street to kiss him. As if he were Robert Redford.

QUIQUE SCOPELL: What do you call that thing when the Pope doesn't make a mistake? Extreme unction. What is it? Ex cathedra. When the Pope speaks ex cathedra. He can be wrong when he speaks but not when it's ex cathedra. That's how it is here: Gabito said so, and that's it. First with that book, which, if you ask me, is bad, and then with the Nobel. Shall I tell you the truth? I don't understand it, because it's a bad novel. A bad, folkloric novel. Because you say, for example: Romeo and Juliet is a love story, but *One Hundred Years of Solitude* is . . . I don't understand how the hell they can translate that thing into Russian to tell the Russians that yellow butterflies jerk off. How do you translate that into Russian? Now everything's whatever Gabito says and that's it. So after the Nobel, everything began to change. Life is divided into Gabo before the Nobel and Gabo after the Nobel.

CARMEN BALCELLS: The Nobel didn't change him at all.

WILLIAM STYRON: I'd put it this way, in a rather perverse negative way. I'd say this: the extraordinary influence and affection and power that he enjoys because of his talent, that gives him such an appeal to Latin Americans, is something that could not exist here in the United States. The admiration that exists in Latin America for a great writer like Gabo has no parallel here. Because we live in a country that has very little regard for its writers. Most writers are marginalized in this country. Even the best ones. To a degree that's inconceivable. I think that Gabo could not have existed in an Anglo-Saxon world. We have no real tradition. It's not that writers aren't respected in some way in this country. They are. But not to the degree of not only being respected, but venerated.

EDUARDO MÁRCELES DACONTE: Now you'll see: I met García Márquez in Cuba. I met him in Havana. I was invited by Casa de las Américas to take part in a conference, and Gabo was one of its organizers. For Latin American sovereignty and policy. That was in '81. So the day after I arrive in Havana, I come down in the elevator in the Hotel La Habana Riviera and see Gabo talking to the receptionist. Gabo in a gas-station attendant's coverall, and sandals, the newspaper under his arm, talking to the receptionist. I see him and say: "What's up, Gabo?" First time I saw him in person, but as soon as I saw him, imagine. "My name is Eduardo Márceles" and I emphasized the Daconte. Then he says to me "Damn! Then whose son are you?" I tell him Imperia's. "Damn! Another Aracataquero here in Havana. Now the thing is really fucked up . . . Somebody else from Aracataca here in Havana. No, no, no. This is really fucked up. Let's sit down over there, we have a lot to talk about, damn!" Listen, he begins to tell me things. One of the first anecdotes I remember is that he says to me: "Imagine, *caramba*, Antonio Daconte, how well I remember your grandfather. Imagine: when I was writing *One Hundred Years of Solitude*, the Italian who appears there is your grandfather. His name was Antonio Daconte, that's what the Italian's name was. I wrote him thinking of your grandfather, but as I wrote the character was becoming effeminate." Then he says that the character was turning into a fag because of circumstances of the plot and so forth. And then he says: "I had to go through the whole manuscript and erase Antonio Daconte and write in Pietro Crespi, who was a piano tuner my mother had known in Barranquilla. She had told me there was a piano tuner who passed through there, and he was a very beautiful man, and I don't know what else." So the two ideas stayed with him. On the one hand my grandfather, and on the other the Italian piano tuner who had passed through Barranquilla. He says: "I started to think and said to myself that your uncle Galileo Daconte, when he read the novel, would have a heart attack, you know, because, well, your uncle (all the Dacontes) seeing a character like that, an effeminate man . . ." And we talked about Aracataca and I don't know what else and people he knew. And we talked as two people do who are recalling the same town. "Listen, and the so-and-so family, what happened to them? And what happened to such-and-such, to your uncle? What happened about the other thing?" We talked about town things, about what he remembered. Then I say to him: "And so, it seems you've used my family's name in some of your stories." He says: "Damn! You're going to ask me for millions of dollars." I tell him: "No, no, take it easy . . ."

HÉCTOR ROJAS HERAZO: So the thing had already begun when the Nobel business came along. Colombia eats it up. You can't say anything that doesn't have to do with Gabito. So the thing is here and the thing is there. I mean, the country became distorted. What that famous man [the poet Porfirio Barba-Jacob] from Cali said, that it's "a garage with an archbishop." That's what Colombia is.

MARGARITA DE LA VEGA: When he won the Nobel, Mercedes got her revenge on Cartagena. Everybody wanted Gabo to invite them to the house and she didn't invite them or go to the parties of people who had treated them badly before. They had rejected Mercedes much more because she was from a town that was much closer and because women are women, right? In certain circles they were snubbed, and in other circles, not. Never by the men, but by the women. And Mercedes was pretty, but she was different, too. She had lived in Mexico and in Europe. More sophisticated in a certain sense, and in a certain sense not. Do you understand what I'm saying? She belonged to that class that has no class, you see, that isn't marked by its social class. I believe it's one of the advantages one can have in life.

SANTIAGO MUTIS: I believe that the people who left Colombia don't return because they can't. Because there's a dimension so large that it's as if they don't fit. Because it isn't possible. But I think that the nostalgia of someone who has been isolated from his childhood, well, it's like that, it's like not having access. As if the crowd doesn't allow him to return to his former life. So then they became big. And then they no longer fit in anywhere.

JOSÉ SALGAR: With Gabo what happens is that it's wonderful to sit down and chat. Ask. Tell. He listens. So I say to him: "Listen, why do you say it that way?" At a get-together a curious thing happened. My son was little and very excited because Gabo was coming to the house. And he said: "I'm going to put a tape recorder under a chair and record everything Gabo says." That was clever. He recorded him. Then, when it was over, I said to Gabo: "I'll be frank with you. The little devil recorded this. Let's see if we can do something with it. Let's see if there are some things worth saving and we'll publish them."

HÉCTOR ROJAS HERAZO: They don't let him live. He even had to go around with a bodyguard. He feared for his life.

JOSÉ SALGAR: "In fact we have to get rid of many things in Castilian," Gabo said. "Like what?" "The *H*. We have to get rid of the *H*." We talked about that during one of those long meetings in my house. Osuna was there, Argos, Mercedes. Then we started to talk about how the Gabo phenomenon might even change the Spanish language itself.

MARGARITA DE LA VEGA: After the Nobel he keeps living in Cartagena, in an apartment, for a long time. I remember having gone in '83, '84, when they celebrated Cartagena's four hundred and fiftieth anniversary. He lives there and they celebrated him so much . . . I remember pulling his leg and telling him he had turned into an oracle in Colombia, they would call to ask him if it was going to rain, and who was going to be elected beauty queen. And I tell him: "What are you going to do?" And he said: "No, I still write every morning, four or five hours, and I'm writing the novel about Cartagena," which is *Love in the Time of Cholera*. And it's very inspired, of course, by Balzac, and I believe, up to a certain point, that this is a personal contribution of mine, that my father's love of Balzac played a part.

JOSÉ SALGAR: It seems to me that this business of fame is very strange. Gabo loves it, of course, when people recognize him and tell him so.

ROSE STYRON: Yes, he's spoken to me about how fame brought great responsibility, and how each time he sits down in front of paper and writes, he has to be very careful because he's writing for the people out there. And, of course, when he speaks the same thing happens. Because when we were in Cartagena, I think it was at the end of the nineties, he was more famous and was pursued more than the stars who were there for the film festival. And there were always reporters hanging on to his every word . . . I think it's a terrible burden. In '74, '75, it wasn't like that. I mean, he has always been light-hearted and he is very funny, but he had more freedom to speak out and be an activist. And, you know, to curse Pinochet. He said he would never write another word of fiction until Pinochet was defeated and left Chile. He could make wilder statements back then probably than he would now. Now he's still very political and very effective and very much an activist, but he does it in a quieter way. Certainly, if not more cautious, he is more thoughtful and circumspect.

ODERAY GAME: I was living in Madrid. He'd call me and say: "I'm coming to Madrid but don't tell anybody. I don't want to see anybody." Then, after three days he'd call and say: "Come with me to a bookstore, I need to be recognized."

RAFAEL ULLOA: When he was already famous, I saw him again in Cartagena. You know, when he came, the people went out to greet him. Gabito at a distance. Because famous people . . .

JAIME GARCÍA MÁRQUEZ: One Sunday morning Gabo and I were in our pajamas on the balcony, playing Crazy Corner, which was the name we gave to the very long talks we would have when we saw each other, and all of a sudden the president arrives, because he wants to see Gabo.

MARGARITA DE LA VEGA: My father and Gabo talked about anything. I think they saw each other in any social situation, in any get-together, in a restaurant, in my parents' house. But, for example, I remember going to have breakfast in an apartment his family had on Avenida San Martín, when he didn't live in Cartagena and didn't have the Nobel or any of that, and I was fascinated because hearing Gabo talk was a delight. About anything. About food. "Why does the corn bread pair so well with sour cream?" And from there they'd start to talk about X's book or Y's poetry. Or: "Why did Guy de Maupassant die in an institution?" "Why did he have syphilis?" And my father would give him all the details about it, which was what he was writing about: the diseases of writers. My father publishes his first book, called *This Was How They Suffered*, and in a sense he publishes it internationally because Gabo sends it to Carmen Balcells and she gets it published.

CARMEN BALCELLS: All my life I've tried to do what he wanted me to do, which in reality was my job and how I spent my days.

FERNANDO RESTREPO: By the time he was a famous man, you didn't notice it so much, but he was a withdrawn, timid man. I do have that perception of him. Privately he was very pleasant and had that marvelous sense of humor.

HÉCTOR ROJAS HERAZO: Naturally, all that changed him. It had to change him. That's terrible. He has a great sense of humor, so he laughs at anything, but the time comes when he has to be faithful to the success pouring over him, and then come the comic transformations.

MARÍA LUISA ELÍO: It must be very annoying. People don't let you live. It's a phenomenon that doesn't happen . . . because I've gone out with Octavio Paz a thousand times, not once, but a thousand, and I've never seen them falling all over Octavio Paz so easily, kissing him and asking: "Are you Octavio Paz? Sign this for me." No! The phenomenon of García Márquez is very special. He is totally attractive to people . . . It's as if he were, I'm telling you, Robert Redford.

ELISEO "LICHI" ALBERTO: Gabo and I were walking along the walls of Cartagena one afternoon and we saw a couple of young lovers. The boy sees Gabo and begins to signal him to come over. When we get there, he says to Gabo: "Gabo, please, tell her I love her, because she doesn't believe me."

JOSÉ SALGAR: Somebody asks me and I say there's no difference, because as soon as you meet up with Gabo it's as if no time had passed. You go back to a thread broken by distance and time, and it's the same. The same energy, the same connection. There's no difference at all. That's the great advantage among Gabo's friends, the ones he calls friends, and there aren't many, as opposed to the quantity of people who've met him. He's very different with other people. But not with you. Now, he's out of the country a lot, he comes back, here nothing's happened. To the rest of the world he's a different Gabo. It's natural.

GUILLERMO ANGULO: You want me to speak badly about him? There's something that seems bound to happen. People change with fame and with money. Besides, they almost always come together. I mean, you can't compare the earlier Gabo to present-day Gabo. He's much more distant now. He doesn't give himself to you the way he did before.

MIGUEL FALQUEZ-CERTAIN: At the time of that important journal that Plinio edited with Goytisolo, *Libre*, García Márquez arrives in Paris, and he's already famous. Plinio and Marvel organized a private party at the Colombian embassy, which was next door to the Russian. They hired a *vallenato* group and a cook to prepare egg arepas, pork sausage sandwiches, stuffed yucca . . . Food from the coast that he liked. They had white rum. And he arrived and said: "Ay, no, what a drag. What I like is caviar with champagne."

GUILLERMO ANGULO: There's a writer, a friend of ours, who says that Gabo at this moment is the best-known writer in the world. And of course, there's never been a Colombian in the history of the world who's been as well known as him. I mean, in China they probably haven't heard of Bolívar, but they have heard of Gabo.

29

Damaged Goods

In which the history of Chronicle of a Death Foretold* *is discussed and
a Colombian magistrate gives us his version of events*

MARGARITA DE LA VEGA: It's something that had occurred in
Sucre when his father was a pharmacist. That killing happened
and those boys, the twins, were studying in Cartagena at the
School of Medicine.

PATRICIA CASTAÑO: We went to Sucre with Gerald Martin. We
looked over the whole story. We went to the place where the Italian
they killed is buried. The one from the *Crónica*. We saw the grave-
stone, one of those gravestones that has a photo of the deceased.
And everybody tells you a version. "They came in through this
door and went out through this one," and yadayadayada.

CARMELO MARTÍNEZ: Gabito wasn't in Sucre when they killed
Cayetano [Gentile]. He was studying in Barranquilla. His father
and mother were there. So I told Gabito what I knew. What I
had witnessed. He came here to my house and I told him about

---

* García Márquez wrote *Chronicle of a Death Foretold* in 1981 based on real events that
occurred in 1951 in Sucre when his parents lived there. A groom returns his bride hours after
the wedding claiming she was not a virgin. Her brothers go out and murder the man they
thought to be her first lover. It is said he waited so long to write it because his mother had
asked him not to write about it and he only did after she died. His mother, Luisa Santiaga,
has a cameo in the novella.

it right here on this terrace. Look, that happened on Monday, February 21 or 22 of 1951, in Sucre, a town on the water. Cayetano and I had been together the previous Saturday, when the wedding of Miguel Reyes Palencia, a Sucreño who lived in San Marcos, and Margarita Chica, took place. That's Ángela Vicario in the novel. We went to the port with Cayetano to watch the departure of the newlyweds. I haven't forgotten that I almost became a criminal because I took my father's gun to pursue the Chicas. The Chicas took refuge in a house across from the Palencia family's house as you pass the church. When I saw Víctor, who was brandishing a knife, claiming grief as his reason for stabbing Cayetano, I ran out with a gun in my hand. When he saw where I was going, he went inside and locked the door.

JAIME GARCÍA MÁRQUEZ: I was ten years old when they killed Cayetano Gentile. When I heard about it, I ran out to see, and there in the living room I saw him, lying on a cot, very pale, of course, because he had already lost a great deal of blood; there was mud on his shirt along with blood, and at that moment the doctor was removing the stethoscope and declaring him dead. Sometime later, when Gabito was working on his *Chronicle of a Death Foretold*, he confronted a doubt: whether or not it had rained in January, when they killed Cayetano. He's always had the idea that tragic events have to do with the weather. Somebody said that in Sucre it never rains in January. Then I said to him: "Well, it did rain, because I remember Cayetano's shirt splattered with mud." Doubts remained. After the novel came out, talking about this with my sister Margot, she remembered another interesting fact, which was that shortly before the death of Gentile, my brother Luis Enrique and she were talking to him in the port, and it was raining, and a boy tripped and fell in front of them, and Cayetano picked him up and his shirt was covered with mud. In other words, it was definitely raining that day, which is why I remembered the shirt covered with mud.

CARMELO MARTÍNEZ: When Miguel Reyes brought Margarita back, it caused a scandal in the neighborhood farther down. Everybody there knew what had happened. But where we lived, near the plaza, we didn't.

She gets married on Saturday night, and they kill Cayetano on Monday. At eight in the morning. Eight. Eight-thirty. Sunday night he slept in his house and went out to run an errand. He never knew they were looking for him. And I was with him that morning. We went to the port that morning. He was in love with a girl whose last name was Nasser. Her father was from Egypt. Her mother's family was Italian. Her name was Nidia. Nidia Nasser. They had an appointment to meet at the port, and since the sweethearts were talking, what was I going to do there. So I left them alone. The plan was to meet back at the port to take our dugout out to the farm.

We were outside waiting for Cayetano to come back. He had to go look for a maid he had to take back to the farm. He was coming to meet us in our dugout when the Chicas arrived and attacked Cayetano. So then the first thing I did was run to the second floor in my house for a gun, a .38 by the way, my father's white star, and ran out of there. Like a madman. I don't know why, but I went out holding the revolver. I didn't know yet what had happened. Then, when I got to Cayetano's house, I found out that the Chicas had knifed him, that they were already in the house across the street where Víctor Palencia lived. Then I went out heading there.

When I came out, they barred the door. They surrendered. The others came in and handed them over to the police.

RAFAEL ULLOA: Gabito's mother didn't want him to tell that story. She felt sorry for Cayetano's mother. He wrote it after she died.

CARMELO MARTÍNEZ: The wedding was on Saturday, the supposed honeymoon that night, and on Monday the sweethearts would go to San Marcos. But it didn't happen that way, because that night, after the incident that kept them from consummating the marriage, Miguel Reyes returned Margarita to her mother, as if she were damaged goods. Well, he realized she wasn't a virgin. So he returned her to her mother ceremoniously, because he was of Santanderean origin. Then the trouble started because Margarita's family put her in the confessional so she'd say who the man was who . . . Well, who had been the one . . . Well, who was the husband. So she said it was Cayetano. Cayetano Gentile had been engaged to her. But Cayetano broke the engagement because, while he was studying at the Javeriana University, she found a sweetheart from Guaranda. Another town. Possibly for that reason, Cayetano didn't marry her. When I reached the door, he was already clutching his guts so they wouldn't spill out. They had knifed him. Víctor Chica, especially. Víctor is the killer. He was the killer. Not Joaquín. Joaquín went to help his brother. He didn't take part in the killing. He intervened, calming down his brother. Víctor was a butcher, he slaughtered cattle. He's the one who takes them to market, and he had a knife. A knife for killing cattle was used to kill Cayetano.

MARGARITA DE LA VEGA: When Gabo brought out the book, the twins wanted to sue him.

CARMELO MARTÍNEZ: Then, what is it that happens to me? Margarita denounces him, taking her revenge because Cayetano's social and economic position in town was higher than hers. Then, when Cayetano abandoned her, what she did was a typical act of vengeance by a woman who'd been wounded. What I think is that she took her revenge on Cayetano because Cayetano didn't marry her. Now, it's very possible, I think it's almost one hundred percent true, that she was Cayetano's woman. That she did have sexual relations with him. Now, Cayetano left her, and her pointing him out as the one who had taken her virginity, is her revenge on Cayetano.

MARGARITA DE LA VEGA: One of the things that Gabo wanted was information about the trial. The murder trial took place in Cartagena, and another of my uncles, whose name is Antonio de la Vega, was the judge. He had access to the papers and my uncle went to get them. They were in the basement of the Palace of Justice in Cartagena and were covered with damp, like the scene in the movie; I don't know if you've seen the movie, which is pretty bad. It evokes the place but the actors are pretty bad, even if they're great actors. Rupert Everett should be hanged. The same thing that happened with *Love in the Time of Cholera*. I never thought I'd say that the *Chronicle* film was better than something else. So my uncle is the judge. Do you remember that they're going to look for the papers and everything's flooded? Gabo takes that from reality and uses it for the novel.

CARMELO MARTÍNEZ: At that time there was an idea in the penal code, which was the defense of honor. There's no defense of honor there. Since we always lived in an up-to-date way, that was true under Benito Mussolini's Italian penal code, from which the Colombian was copied. Copied. Copied. So there it is. Under the penal code of the year 1936, one could claim defense of honor, but a murder took place there because there was observation. Observation is when I begin to watch the victim to find out his movements, what he does and doesn't do to facilitate the attack.

Miguel Reyes Palencia was from a Conservative family on his mother's side. Liberal on his father's side. But a refined man. A correct man. Miguel Reyes lives in Barranquilla now. Margarita lives in Sincelejo. She wasn't as pretty as the girl in the movie.

MARIELA DE MARTÍNEZ: She's a dressmaker.

CARMELO MARTÍNEZ: There's gossip. I'm telling it to you as gossip. Miguel Reyes came back afterward to Margarita and they had something. They were husband and wife again. But sporadically. That's like living for a while on the ashes of a dead man because those two killed him. Those two are the intellectual authors of Cayetano's death. Why? For one of two reasons: either she'd had previous sexual experience, which is most likely, with some men from Guaranda, boyfriends she had in Guaranda, which is why Cayetano broke it off with her; or else, Cayetano really was her first husband.

MARGARITA DE LA VEGA: He's very interested in the theme of honor. And the theme of honor placed on the woman, because he does that in his early stories and he's done it in other screenplays that he's written. It's part of the film *Time to Die.*

CARMELO MARTÍNEZ: In the villages, everybody has his own version. The story is the death of a man stabbed by some other men for reasons of honor. In my opinion, what happens is that this girl was already an older woman. If she had been a minor, a child, a girl younger than fifteen or twelve years old, there might have been a charge of corruption of minors or carnal violence. But if she's a woman in her twenties, what carnal violence can there be? She went to bed with the man because she liked him. She was in love with Cayetano. Now, I believe that the business with Miguel was a lifesaver, because a woman in her twenties is almost a spinster. Because in a village, a girl that age is already over the hill.

So Cayetano died saying he was innocent. I believe Cayetano because a man who's going to die tells the truth. Cayetano, when I came in, said: "I'm innocent, I'm innocent. I die an innocent man. These people have killed me." So I went out to kill Víctor . . .

PATRICIA CASTAÑO: Sucre . . . Sucre is an incredible city. A tale he wrote also comes from there; it's called "Isabel Watching It Rain in Macondo." That story he gave to a lady named Tachia Quintana, his girlfriend in Paris, and he gave her the rights to that story.

GERALD MARTIN: How could I not include Tachia in the biography? Tachia is woman number two in his life. Tachia's the one who appears in his books. She's in *The Colonel* (they were living together in Paris, suffering from hunger, when he wrote it), in *One Hundred Years of Solitude*, in *The Trail of Your Blood in the Snow*.

PATRICIA CASTAÑO: The year before last, Tachia put on a piece for theater about that story in Cartagena, for the first time, and in Bogotá, for something like three days. And it's very impressive because that story is about a flood in Sucre, Sucre. And the day after Tachia completed her presentation in Bogotá, which was Saturday night, and we were having the worst winter in Colombia, a super photograph appeared that said that Venice is in Sucre. It shows that day's flooding in Sucre. I mean, what's incredible is to think that fifty years after Gabo's description, the people in Sucre, Sucre, continue to live the same drama.

CARMELO MARTÍNEZ: The fundamental fact is true. Afterward, on top of that, comes the magic of Gabito, the style of Gabito. Now, the facts are true, they're certain. What happens is that Gabito has a great imagination, and besides that, a great pen. The work is his and the literary work is his, but the facts are exact. There's no exaggeration or any invention. Those were the facts. Now, when I tried right here to tell Gabito, to give him my explanation, he said: "If you give me your explanation you'll ruin the idea I have. What I want to do is write a novel."

GREGORY RABASSA: Many things that I translated have become clichés. Now they call everything "Chronicle of a so-and-so foretold."

30

Dreams of Power

In which García Márquez dines with dictators and presidents

GUILLERMO ANGULO: Do you know what happened? Gabo has a very curious tendency, which is that he adores power. Whether it's economic power or political power. Yes, he loves all that. That was a change in him for the worse. General Omar Torrijos* from Panama told him: "Listen, you like dictators." Gabo sticks out his chest when they tell him things like that. And he asks Torrijos: "Why?" And Torrijos says: "Fidel's friend and mine." Gabo boasts that there are nine heads of state who take his calls, and he calls himself a friend of Clinton's.

ARISTIDES ROYO: Their first encounter, which was only supposed to last a few hours, became a delightful dialogue in his beachside retreat in Farallón, from which a tight friendship was born. It was the early seventies and the general sent a plane to pick him up at the Cartagena airport. The writer was interested in meeting Omar, because both Fidel and López Michelsen had told him about the fights that the Panamanian leader was spearheading for the recuperation of the canal and the complete sovereignty of our

---

* General Omar Torrijos ruled Panama from 1968 to 1981. He is best known for negotiating the 1977 Torrijos–Carter Treaties, which ended the US hold on the Panama Canal in 1999. García Márquez, an activist for Latin American sovereignty, showed an interest in meeting the general, who also counted Graham Greene among his friends.

territory. They were supposed to talk for a few hours but that first conversation lasted days and turned into a lifelong friendship.

On September 5, 1977, Gabriel García Márquez was aboard the Air Panama plane as a member of the Panamanian delegation attending the signature of the Torrijos-Carter Treaty. He and Graham Greene were traveling without visas to enter the USA but neither had any difficulty because as the trip was presided over by Omar Torrijos, the chief of state, the US authorities let go of the usual immigration process.

The next day, in a meeting with Jimmy Carter, a day before elections and after all of the agenda of the official mission was completed, Torrijos asked the US president to explain the reasons why two important writers, a British one, Graham Greene, and a Colombian one, Gabriel García Márquez, were denied entry. Carter passed the question to his national security advisor, Professor Zbigniew Brzezinski, who left the room for about fifteen minutes while the two chiefs of state kept chatting.

He returned to the meeting saying that Gabriel García Márquez frequently visited Cuba and would meet for many long hours with Fidel analyzing political matters in the American hemisphere. Later, when they realized that the Colombian author was neither a spy nor a conspirator, they gave him a visa that he used when he was given a PEN award. With regards to Greene, they explained that he was denied the visa because he traveled annually to Moscow and stayed with his friend Kim Philby, a British spy at the service of the Soviet Union. Soon after, Greene also got a visa. It must have been made clear that Greene and Philby spent their time together under Communism simply drinking very good vodka.

WILLIAM STYRON: Our connection to presidents, Gabo's and mine, extended very singularly with François Mitterrand, who we both became friendly with because Mitterrand had an enormous love for literature in general. We became friends of his, and in fact, we were present, he and I, at Mitterrand's inauguration. In fact, he and I shared the first luncheon ever served in the Palais de l'Élysée under Mitterrand's administration on the day of his inaugural. Mitterrand invited us separately but together, in the end, because he had read our work. And this is another president who fascinated Gabo and whom he has written about. We both received the Légion d'honneur. We weren't at the same ceremony but he gave it to us roughly at the same time, back in the mid-eighties.

HÉCTOR ROJAS HERAZO: So this is what I want to tell you. He ran away every time they were going to pin an award or something on him, give him a medal here in Colombia. He would run to catch that plane out. But a moment comes when, because of how seriously the world takes this, he became transcendental, transcendental, and of course, he surrendered to the glory.

WILLIAM STYRON: We had a very interesting talk about heads of state. We agreed that we both were almost fatally attracted to presidents. We admitted to each other that we frequently dreamed about them. But we said: "And what's bad about that?" You see . . . I've had a kind of long-term mental love affair with presidents. I've dreamed about Truman. I've dreamed about John F. Kennedy. I'm talking about the good presidents. I'd even include Eisenhower, who in my opinion was one of the least harmful Republican presidents. I confessed, then, my fatal attraction for powerful political leaders and, as you know, I've stated that one of the objects of my attraction was Bill Clinton. And we told each other that there was almost a metaphysical element in this attraction toward powerful men because, in his case, these men, who almost always had mercilessly climbed to power, have an enormous effect on the lives of others. This is a central aspect of national life. A man, let's say, like Castro, like so many Latin American leaders, the presidents of Mexico, the presidents of Central American countries, for example, they exercise control over the entire nation. Which is why they are people who legitimately fascinate writers.

JAIME ABELLO BANFI: In '94, for example, he was very enthusiastic, ready to return to Colombia. It was the César Gaviria government. He had agreed to be part of what they called the Commission of Scholars, a group of thinkers, scientists, commissioned to work on topics of education, science, and development. But he was also thinking about the creation of the foundation [for journalism], and meeting with us. He was publishing his novel *Of Love and Other Demons*. That year he was meeting with Clinton on Martha's Vineyard along with Fuentes and the Styrons. He was considering building his house in Cartagena, but he also decided to buy in Barranquilla in order to have an apartment there. He bought it in a building designed by his goddaughter Katya González Ripoll. Let's say it's a period when he's prepared to return. '94 is a key year.

ROSE STYRON: It came up more than once. I don't remember whether it was in New York or on the phone or just through Carlos [Fuentes], but we'd talked for a long time about him coming to the Vineyard and because Clinton came every summer, you know. It was one or the other, or maybe it was Carlos who said: "Why don't you plan your visit for when Clinton's there and then we can all meet?"

WILLIAM STYRON: What's certain is that by the time he came to supper in 1994, by that date he could come into the country freely. The act had already been repealed.

ROSE STYRON: Carlos visits every year and stays with us. We told Gabo to come, and that year—it must have been '94—was the first time he came to stay with us. In reality he slept in a hotel very close to our house, but he spent the day with us.

WILLIAM STYRON: Well, Carlos, who is one of my oldest and closest friends, we saw each other in New York in 1994, in the spring, and I told him that Clinton had made it a point to schedule a trip to the Vineyard and he was sure to do it that summer. Carlos had been fretting, like so many other Latin Americans and like many other people, about the embargo on Cuba. Gabo wanted to meet Clinton, and so did Carlos. And wouldn't it be an interesting thing and profitable if indeed Gabo and he could meet Clinton and lean on him about the Cuban embargo. They thought Clinton would meet with them because he had already said he was a great admirer of *One Hundred Years of Solitude*. In fact, his daughter Chelsea had just read it and loved it very much. And so I told Carlos we'd be able to do it that summer, and that Clinton would come to our house. I said why not invite Gabo to the island. This happened in August, late August 1994, and so the dinner was arranged. Gabo came. It was a very small dinner at my house with the Clintons, Vernon Jordan and his wife, and the ex-foreign minister of Mexico, Sepúlveda, and his wife, my friend Bill Luers and his wife. Bill Luers had been the United States ambassador to Venezuela and Czechoslovakia. And so it was a small gathering. Oh, and I should add Gabo's goddaughter, Patricia Cepeda, and her husband John. She's married to John

O'Leary, who was recently the American ambassador to Chile. A prominent lawyer in Portland, Maine. Anyway, they were there too. Patricia to translate. You know Gabo . . . His English is quite good really, but I think he doesn't like to use it because it isn't perfect. Whenever I've been with him we've spoken English because I don't know enough Spanish to speak it at all. But like a lot of people who don't have perfect command of a language, he prefers to speak in his mother tongue. But Patricia is a very capable interpreter, so she was sitting at the table with Gabo and Clinton. I was sitting on the other side of the table with Hillary and could tell, though I wasn't listening closely to them, that Gabo and Carlos were engaging him in a talk about the Cuban embargo. At that time they were both very passionate about the embargo. Well, I think this was one of the reasons they approached him. But interestingly enough—and I've reconstructed this with Bill Luers, who was sitting closer to them than I was—I could tell, and Bill confirmed this, that Clinton was resisting this conversation. I suppose the reason was that his mind was already made up about Cuba and he wasn't about to be budged, even by people he admired as much as Gabo. And so Bill Luers, seeing Clinton's eyes glazed over with what I suppose was rejection—and like a complete ex-diplomat—spoke out firmly enough to change the subject of the conversation from politics in Cuba to literary matters, and that was fascinating . . . The breakthrough came when someone, I forget who, perhaps Bill Luers or perhaps Clinton, changed the conversation to ask the name of everyone's favorite novel and at this point Clinton's eyes lit up rather pleasurably and we had a sort of literary parlor game around the table. I mean politics was abandonded and everyone began to say their favorite novel. Well, I think it was because they couldn't make any headway in the Cuba matter.

GUILLERMO ANGULO: I think that basically you always want to boast about what you don't know. Gabo wants to seem a great politician and he doesn't know about politics. I think it bothers Gabo a great deal when they tell him he's a very good writer, because why should they? It's something that's very clear to him and he knows it and you don't have to tell him about it.

WILLIAM STYRON: Clinton led this sort of quiz, and I recall that Carlos said that his favorite novel was *Don Quijote*. Gabo said that among all the books, he chose *The Count of Monte Cristo*, and then he explained why. He said it was a perfect novel. It was spellbinding. It wasn't just a costume melodrama. It had great depth and was really a universal masterpiece. I said *Huckleberry Finn*, just of the top off my head. And finally Clinton said Faulkner's *The Sound and the Fury*, and immediately, to everyone's amazement, he began to recite a long, long passage from the book, word by word. And it was truly magical to see him do this because afterward he did give a little interesting lecture on the power of Faulkner and how much Faulkner had influenced him. I remember that he then had this two-way conversation with Gabo, and Gabo said that, without Faulkner, he wouldn't have been able to write a single word. That Faulkner was his direct inspiration as a writer when he was just beginning to read world literature in Colombia. And that he had made a pilgrimage to Oxford. I remember that he mentioned it to Clinton. If there was disappointment because he hadn't made any headway with Cuba, he hid it. He was animated and even exhilarated; I noticed it when they began this conversation about great novels. And so the evening was basically a great success. But it was a total failure as far as politics went.

ROSE STYRON: I recall that Bill Luers felt that perhaps Clinton had heard enough about Cuba so he switched the conversation to go from being led by Gabo to being led by Clinton, who wanted to talk about writing and literature . . . Carlos also was in the mix of that conversation about the writers Clinton had read. I mean, they were quite interested in Clinton's knowledge of Latin American literature. He began to talk about a young Mexican novelist he had been reading and thought was very good. I remember that Carlos and Gabo were quite taken aback because they both knew this young man. I don't remember his name but they were surprised that Clinton had read him. And of course Clinton quotes everything, too. They were impressed by, you know, Clinton's literary knowledge. Not necessarily of Gabo's books but of literature in general. And then I know that Chelsea was a great fan of Gabo and was reading one of his books. Later on, Gabo was invited to the White House. I think it was that same year. Or it might have been later. I think it might have been that winter that Chelsea in particular wanted him there.

WILLIAM STYRON: I think Márquez truly wanted to meet Clinton, whom he admired very much, and wanted to talk about Latin American political relations, Cuba and Colombia and Mexico and so forth, and Clinton wanted to talk about literature. So it was a wonderful evening, and Clinton seemed to have read everything, so it was very fruitful. Then, during dinner, he received a call from Mayor about trying to make peace in Ireland. So we had Cuba, Ireland, and Mexican literature sort of going, and that was the end of that. But I guess it had reverberations, because I heard about that dinner several times when I was in Latin America after that.

SANTIAGO MUTIS: That's Gabo's huge desire: to help Latin America. Intervene for Cuba and the people studying film. Intervene in political problems, help the people going through whatever. He thinks perhaps something can be resolved from there.

WILLIAM STYRON: Exactly. But that's a fairly common phenomenon in Latin America. It's not just Gabo; Carlos Fuentes too. I remember that he and I went when Salinas was president of Mexico to see him. Gabo is this kind of phenomenon par excellence, you see. Writers in general. Octavio Paz had that effect in Mexico. Hell, Vargas Llosa was close to becoming president. But as I think I said earlier, and not that it matters or anything, but the idea of a writer having this profound political and cultural influence in the United States that Gabo has in Latin America is inconceivable here.

JAIME ABELLO BANFI: Remember that after the Belisario government, he had been here during the entire time of the bombs, from '82 to '86. He was in Colombia a great deal because Belisario would call him, search him out, bring him, but something happened there, in that very complicated Belisario government, with the taking of the Palace of Justice, Armero, the abrupt end in Tlaxcala to the peace process with the FARC. Then the Barco government comes in. And the Barco government was also complicated: the struggle against narco-trafficking, the subject of extradition, the bombs. Then comes the Gaviria government. And Gaviria renews the effort to attract Gabo again. And Gaviria, in fact, asks Gabo to revise the final text of the constitution of '91. Gabo corrects it.

WILLIAM STYRON: Our dinner didn't receive a single line of ink in the North American press, but it was front-page news in every major Spanish-language newspaper in the world. I suppose for all the reasons I mentioned earlier. Yes, and that's why I think there's a huge distinction between writers in the United States and writers in Latin America. A writer in the United States might receive the respect of, to my mind, an exceptional president like Bill Clinton who himself is fascinated by writers and who has read a great deal, including my own work. I find that fascinating, but the idea that I could in any sense influence him in any major way I think is a delusion. Writers in this country are marginal. If we had been three rock stars who cornered Clinton, we would have been on the front page.

ROSE STYRON: He'd been telling us for years that we had to go to Cuba: "Please, try to come when I'm there, we can all be there together." That was just a litany of his. The pleasure, of course, was being with Gabo, who is marvelous company and a warm and affectionate human presence. You know, full of great, adventurous ideas.

We had wanted to go to Cuba and mentioned it to Arthur Miller. We thought it would be something we could do together, and we learned that Gabo would be there. He hadn't been there for years, though, because he'd been sick, for at least a year and a half. And when he heard that we would be there, he said he'd come too. I don't know whether it was pure accident that we were all there at the same time, or whether he maneuvered to be there when we were and we were encouraged to be there when he was. I don't know exactly how it happened. I don't know whether it was fortuitous or not, but I do know that the moment we knew we were going, he knew it too. And when we let him know we were going to Cuba, he already knew it and said he would be there. And in Cuba we were together, and he arranged things while we were there. He was very interested in taking us to Hemingway's place, taking us out there. He wanted us to become involved in Cuba and see the potential it had, what it had been and what it could be. He wanted to do everything he could to strengthen relations between Cuba and the United States, especially among the writers he respects. And he wanted us to have a good time.

SANTIAGO MUTIS: I don't know whether that friendship with Fidel has turned into good things for many people. I'm sure it has. But now that forms part of what the press says, that things come out of it. How much life that's not made public goes on there? One no longer knows. One's left simply as a reader of what's published.

ARISITIDES ROYO: That friendship with Fidel also allowed him to help detained people be freed and others to leave Cuba.

ROSE STYRON: He studies both real and fictitious characters very closely. This past spring when we were all in Cuba and in Castro's presence and you could see that it worried him that he wouldn't be there if we went to see Castro. And he reflected on the visit we had with Castro. He understood him so perfectly, and from every angle. I mean, he saw the good and the bad, and the reason for both. I could see this in his reactions to Castro.

WILLIAM STYRON: The fact that Gabo was there was clearly our entrée to those fascinating moments we spent with Castro.

ROSE STYRON: He wanted us to meet Castro. He wanted us to understand Castro as a human being. Castro gave us a dinner in the presidential palace. We were in Havana with Arthur Miller and his wife and a couple of other people. The Luerses and the

Janklows. Eight of us had gone, and we were all invited to the dinner. And when we walked in, Castro came out to welcome us.

And it was clear that he knew everything about each one of us because he asked each of us something a little personal, and let us know that he knew exactly who we were and what we did, things like that. And I could see Gabo simply standing there smiling behind him. But Gabo was just as interested in having Castro like us or be easy with us as in having us feel comfortable with him, so that we could understand the situation. There were no words in particular at that moment, but I remember that during the dinner I was sitting beside Gabo and he would make little drawings and, you know, pass me a note ocassionally. That was fun. That dinner lasted quite a few hours.

And then, at a certain moment, it was very late and Castro talked the way he does, wonderfully, about wars and battles. We had some funny political stuff going on but he was giving us a marvelous run-down of historical battles that had really happened. From the Peloponnesian War to the Gulf War: who the generals were and what had been their maneuvers, their successes and mistakes. And then he continued with what he thought his own errors had been, I mean, as a guerrilla, a fighter, and a leader. Gabo turned toward me and whispered: "Oh, he is really wound up now. This will go on for a long time but it'll be very good." He was also very pleased with what was happening, and without being critical he was observing, more than anything he was paying attention to everyone's reactions. I think that what I like is to observe him while he's observing others. You see what's going through his head and you can see his kindness and generosity, but no lack of judgment. This doesn't mean that he's sitting there approving or disapproving of the politics of the moment.

SANTIAGO MUTIS: But, for example, when Gabo wrote the book on Cuba, I remember he was told not to publish it because it might do harm to Cuba. It never came out. Some sections were published here in the journal *Alternativa*, and it was a book where you could see how people were living in Cuba. Gabo does it because that's how life is, but when he was about to bring it out they tell him: "Politically this is against us because you can see all the difficulties." Gabo doesn't think so, since he wrote the book. But, I don't know, you'd think it's a wonderful book, but you see a reality where they haven't been able to fix a lot of things. And it isn't advantageous politically. I think that perhaps it doesn't suit the government, but in a human way . . . Let's say it's what Gabo has to reconcile or resolve internally. And that as a reader you have to accept. Because in my opinion there are no political reasons that don't let you recount the lives of some people. Because what you want is to see what is, not how the government has made it. That's where you have to say that you no longer buy into what's politically correct.

WILLIAM STYRON: I think it's a very simple matter. It sounds complex but it really is basically very simple. I believe Gabo has become a very close friend of Castro's, and I believe it's the kind of friendship that was molded fairly early in the years of Castro's ascent. I'm using the word "ascent" here as a climb to power in Cuba. A process that has caused such a shower of violent criticism to fall on García Márquez's head. But I think their friendship is very solid and that Gabo is determined to make the best of it.

SANTIAGO MUTIS: In any case, you can't judge Gabo morally. You can judge him politically. Not judge, but show disagreements. But not morally. So if you move from literature to having a political opinion that you share publicly, people are going to give you a public response. That will lead to your having opponents. And there will be fights and awful things. Yes. Cabrera Infante has a really terrible quarrel with Gabo. And a whole stream of writers. Politically they're there because he's entering a territory where they discuss those things and it's a problem of power. Power is there to be disputed. Whether you think a writer ought to do it or not is another question.

ROSE STYRON: He is such an activist on one hand and a romantic on the other and a realist in both senses. I mean that he always really sees the injustice of the moment and goes for it, whether it's a personal injustice or a political one, whether it's Pinochet, Clinton, or Castro. Whatever it is, whether it's a person or a government driving it, he has a very grounded sense of what's just and what isn't. Besides, he's totally dedicated to fiction and to activism. Whether it's from the point of view of his fiction or his activism, I think—I'm just thinking out loud now—he has such a sense of character, such an insight into characters, which is what makes him create the reality of his own characters in his fiction. They're unforgettable. I think he sees into the character of both the good and the bad guy.

SANTIAGO MUTIS: That he's been able to contend with that . . . I don't understand. Because I believe they're things that in any case demand everything from you. I mean, when you're political, you're concerned with that and that way of living. In any case, Gabo is really a strong man. I believe they put one of those strings on other people and they burn up like rockets. How many people don't follow that? How many people? Everybody . . . competitions . . . inventing themselves to make money. Gabo continues to be untouchable, even if one says: "I don't like this or that about him." And I think that the old Gabo is much more interesting than the earlier Gabo . . . He's much more interesting because it has to do with how he became who he is and how he maintains himself. On what human values does he maintain that? And you find that in the young Gabo. It's all revealed there. From then on he begins to develop it because Gabo finds himself obliged to recount all that.

WILLIAM STYRON: I think he admires Fidel for his intellectual brilliance. And I do think Castro has an eccentric aspect that sets him apart from other dictators. He has got a fascinating and supple and intricate mind, and I think that attracts Gabo, that part of Castro. I remember an interesting anecdote that Gabo told me. He said once, during a very, very delicate crisis that brought the world's journalists to Cuba, he flew to Havana. I believe from Mexico City. There were hundreds of reporters gathered at the airport. And Fidel met Gabo and they walked together to an anteroom in the airport, and were there for half an hour or more while the reporters from all the agencies in the world clustered around, waiting to see what Fidel had said to Gabo, and vice versa. Finally they came out, and the reporters confronted them. The first question was for Gabo: "May we ask what you were talking about?" Gabo answered: "We were talking about the best way to cook red snapper."

So I always love that little item because I'm sure it's true: how to cook *huachinango*.

García Márquez with a black eye.

31

Knockout

In which we finally talk about how Mario Vargas Llosa
punched García Márquez in 1976

RODRIGO MOYA: It was about eleven or twelve in the morning and I was in my house in Colonia Nápoles, where I had an office, a big house with an editorial office in one part, and in the other part I lived with my girlfriend and my two children. There's a knock at the door and it's Gabo and Mercedes. I was very happy and very surprised to see him. Gabo was already a friend of mine, but there are hierarchies in friendships. It was a friendship of guarded proportions. I was a newspaper photographer and he was what he is. Back then I didn't presume to call him Gabo. Calling him Gabito was for me like calling Cervantes Miguelito. For me, he's Gabriel García Márquez. They came for the photographs. He told me: "I want you to take some pictures of my black eye." They came to my house because they trust me.

He wore a jacket. It wasn't the plaid one. It was another one. And she was in black with large sunglasses. And I said to him: "What happened?" He made a joke, like: "I was boxing and I lost." The one who spoke up was Mercedes. She said that Vargas Llosa had sucker-punched him. "And why was that?" "I don't know. I went up to him with my arms wide open to greet him. We hadn't seen each other for some time." I already knew they had been very good friends in Barcelona and everything, and the two couples got along because he had talked about that with our mutual friend Guillermo Angulo. I mean, it was something everybody knew; when I found out it was Mario Vargas Llosa who had hit him, I was very surprised. They sat down in the living room and began to talk to me.

GUILLERMO ANGULO: I know the truth about that fight. I'll tell you. Look: Mario has been a great womanizer and he's a very good-looking man. Women die for Mario. So Mario, on a trip he made by ship from Barcelona to El Callao, met a very beautiful woman. They fell in love. He left his wife and went off with her. And the marriage was over and all that. His wife went back to pack up the house and, of course, she began to see friends. Then they got back together and his wife told Vargas Llosa: "Don't think I'm not attractive. Friends of yours like Gabo were after me . . ." One day they met in a theater in Mexico City, and Gabo went toward him with open arms. Vargas Llosa made a fist and said: "For what you tried to do to my wife," and knocked him to the ground. Then Ms. Gaba said: "What you're saying can't be true because my husband likes women, but only very good-looking women."

RODRIGO MOYA: It had happened two days earlier. The day before he was sick. The punch happened at night. You know the story, don't you? It was at a film preview, the one about the survivors in the Andes. So Gabo arrived and said "Mario" and Mario turned and *wham!*, he hit him with a right and knocked him to the floor, he was bleeding when he fell because the lens in his glasses broke right on the bridge of his nose and the bruise was pretty bad. First aid helped alleviate that, which is what they talk about, I don't know whether it was China Mendoza or Elena Poniatowska who went to buy meat to put on his eye. And that's really true. I boxed a little since I was a kid, and you put steak on a black eye. I don't know how, but it takes away the bruise. Now they use arnica.

GUILLERMO ANGULO: Well, my secret is this: Gabo told me what had happened before the fight. I mean, if he had told me afterward it would be worthless. He said: "No, look, she's coming on to me but I'm so fond of Mario that, even though they're separated . . ." So imagine, I couldn't tell Mario that, I'm a friend of his too, but I'd destroy the marriage. That was one of her tricks to tell him: "I have my own public," right? And she knows she lied. Besides, afterward I was finding out how things had happened when she was in Barcelona. If they saw each other it was with all their friends, they were always together. There were always two or three friends with them. See? They were never alone when they saw each other.

RODRIGO MOYA: What I do remember very well is that Mercedes interrupted twice and said: "The fact is that Mario is a jealous fool. He's a jealous fool."

GREGORY RABASSA: The story I heard is that Mario was seeing someone else and Patricia went to Gabo, a good friend, and he told her: "Leave him." And Mario found out and hit Gabo.

RODRIGO MOYA: Everybody sees a sexual or erotic issue, and that may or may not have been true. But the three of them are the only ones who know that. More than a political dispute they had a separation. Vargas Llosa had already moved surprisingly to the right. I think the clash must have been because there was that separation, and certainly there must have been other things as well that made

Vargas Llosa explode. The punch was certainly violent. I know about punches. It was a right. He was in the row in front of him. It seems he came from the side and Vargas Llosa stood up and hit him. I don't know from what angle, but it was a hard punch.

PLINIO APULEYO MENDOZA: Patricia was on the ship with Mario when he falls in love. When they get to Chile, Patricia has to go back to Barcelona and pack up the house. Gabo and Mercedes were with her the whole time. They were very close. I know this because Gabo told me about it. When Patricia has to go back, Gabo takes her to the airport, but they were running late, and Gabo told her in an offhand way: "If the plane takes off without you, great, we'll have a party." Gabo's Caribbean and it was in that spirit that he said it, and she misunderstood.

RODRIGO MOYA: But what worried me was that he was pretending to be in good humor, but the photos tell you that he was depressed. I took half a roll. When he arrived, I didn't have any film in my house. I was doing a piece for an international magazine on fishing. So I ran to the office that I had in my house. It was quick. There was a small garden. I ran out and said to the technician: "Chino, don't you have any film?" And he said, "No, I don't have any, but there's a little tail end in the camera." So I said to him: "Make me a roll right away."

I was concerned about his melodramatic face, and I thought about it very quickly. It would satisfy Vargas Llosa to see his victim wounded, destroyed. What I wanted was to make him laugh, and he wouldn't give me a damn laugh even at a joke. He wasn't laughing at all, and I played the fool and said to him: "Listen, that was some kick he gave you. How does it feel?" And he answered, but very dry. Then suddenly something happened, I said something and he laughed and I took two photographs. One is the one I circulate because, since I really love him, I didn't want to pass that photo off as tragic. Now, whenever they ask me for that photograph, I send the one where he's laughing so that the reaction is, "He hit me but it's nothing. I don't give a damn," as we say in Mexico, right?

GUILLERMO ANGULO: *History of a Deicide** is not available because Mario doesn't want it printed. My copy of the book was signed by Mario, and with thanks, besides, because I helped him with the research. Then, yes, the idea of the book is that the writer is a god because he gives life to the characters, kills them, and everything. That's *History of a Deicide*. The writer ends up killing God and taking his place. That's the real story.

GREGORY RABASSA: I have it in Spanish. Mario didn't allow it to be translated. Cass Canfield had already talked to the two of us. Harper was publishing both of them but he said no.

RODRIGO MOYA: That photo wasn't circulated because he said to me . . . and I've been very loyal about that. He said to me: "Send me a set and keep the negatives." So I made him a set and sent it to him and in a few days, I don't know whether with Angulo or somebody else, he returned it to me with his notes. Not this one. This

---

* As a student, Mario Vargas Llosa was so taken with *One Hundred Years of Solitude* when it came out that he wrote his doctoral thesis from Madrid's Complutense University about it. It was published by Barral Editores in Spain in 1971 as *History of a Deicide*—my translation, as the book was never translated into English. Vargas Llosa claims that writers are God-like: a writer can change the course of reality. By having the absolute power to recount things, the writer is killing God and assuming his power. The two writers were best of friends until 1976. They had a fight and never spoke after that. Vargas Llosa is said to have stopped the book from being published. It is, in fact, a very hard book to find.

one. Two copies of this. And then I sent him the printed photos, all of them eight-by-ten. A select set, fifteen or sixteen photos, whatever was on the roll. He must have sent me some money, I don't remember. I sent him the photographs and the curious thing is that I kept them in the file and no one saw them. He told me it was for documentation and Mercedes agreed and told me: "Gabo has his files of everything important that happens to him." And at bottom there's a touch of vanity in liking the photo. I have it, I have something fairly complicated that's called the "ego-brary."

I always had a small photo from that shoot tacked up in my lab because he really revolutionized my concept of literature and of America when *One Hundred Years* came out, and I've read it four times. And I lived with that tiny photo that I had. Every time I sat at my desk to work I saw it. Then a friend of mine saw it about the time Gabo was going to turn eighty, and he said to me: "Listen, I want that photograph. I'll buy it from you." I said: "No, I can't sell that photo or anything." And I told him the story of how that photo came about. Gabo said to send him a set and to keep them. That was in '76, but when Gabo turned eighty my friend who knew the story told a reporter: "Listen, Rodrigo Moya has an incredible photograph of Gabo with a black eye." And so the magazines wanted to talk to me. So I thought: They're publishing photos of Gabo, who's going to turn eighty. I can break the promise that really wasn't a promise. It was an assignment to keep them. I kept them and now I'm going to bring them out. I've never made so much money from a photograph.

JAIME ABELLO BANFI: He's always been very loyal, but at the same time implacable when he breaks with you. There are people he's broken with and never spoken to again. Obviously, that was the case with Vargas Llosa.

32

Cod-Liver Oil

In which everybody lucubrates on the
brilliance of García Márquez

ROSE STYRON: He's a wonderful storyteller and talks about how his grandmother was the great storyteller in his family, and he learned from her. He lived with her when he was a boy. And he said that his mother became a storyteller as she aged but wasn't one earlier. It was having lived with his grandmother. He also says that knowing how to tell stories is something congenital and hereditary. That is, that it's natural that many of us think our grandmothers are the ones who told us stories and turned us into the storytellers we are.

GUILLERMO ANGULO: He told me one day: "Do you know what it means to be a good writer?" I said no. "A writer is someone who writes a line and makes the reader want to read the one that follows." Because Gabo, even in the bad things he has, has that thing of controlling the prose so that you say: "How marvelous! How did he say that?"

ELIGIO "YIYO" GARCÍA MÁRQUEZ: My mother says that Gabito turned out so intelligent because when she was pregnant with Gabito, she took a lot of Scott's Emulsion. It was the only one of her twelve pregnancies when she took that cod-liver oil. And

Gabito came out so intelligent because of the pure cod-liver oil. She says that he was born smelling of Scott's Emulsion.

RAFAEL ULLOA: I really believe what the old man Gabriel Eligio says. That Gabo is bicephalic. That he has two brains.

ROSE STYRON: I don't know whether it was true for the rest of the world or not. But the fact is that Macondo was so real for me that it influenced my vision of Latin America. But of course I had another Latin American political experience, I mean, I could see it from the outside, perhaps because of my experience in Argentina, Chile, or Uruguay. The fact that I had been a human rights activist allowed me to see it from the outside, from another perspective, in the same way I saw Central America. So then I wouldn't say that Macondo turned into all of Latin America for me, but it certainly did for those who had not been in Latin America. But when Bill and I were in Cartagena, during the film festival, to my surprise and delight, I walked along the streets and realized that I already knew them through Gabo's books . . . even the jars filled with sweets in the market. It's all so detailed. He had depicted it as a reality. It was a reality. It wasn't a surprise.

I'm from Baltimore. Not so far south. I mean, southern intensity and lightness are there. I can see that Gabo had read Faulkner. It's interesting, but for me, Gabo's town, his city, is much more vivid than the one Faulkner had created.

PATRICIA CASTAÑO: There's something very interesting that has to be looked at. Do you remember that there's a story by Gabo when he was writing in *El Espectador*? He says there, speaking of the magic that surrounds him, that one day he was with a

Catalan writer or editor who came to visit him in Cartagena. He recounts everything that happened in those two days, and that the gentleman said to him: "No, well, excuse me, but you don't even have an imagination. What one experiences in these countries is madness." Then he narrates everything that happened to that gentleman. But the most impressive thing is that they were having lunch one Sunday in his mother's house in Cartagena, and suddenly a lady in a Guajiran tunic rang the doorbell. She comes in and says she's cousin so-and-so and that she came to die. She dreamed she was going to die, and so she came to say goodbye.

ROSE STYRON: When you read Gabo it's like reading all of Latin America. Or, suddenly you understand it all. Or you think you understand it.

EDMUNDO PAZ SOLDÁN: When you talk about García Márquez, he's the one who has narrated the continent for us. This is Latin America. And I didn't feel it was the Latin America where I grew up. My world has been very urban, for better and for worse. So I always saw the world of the tropics from a distance. That wasn't the Latin America where I grew up.

ILAN STAVANS: Our generation has had to define itself in opposition to García Márquez.

ALBERTO FUGUET: I've been in literary workshops and all my classmates, except me, were infected by the García Márquez virus. I mean, it's not only admiration, but they cling to the story. So I feel that reading García Márquez at a certain age can do you a lot of harm. In other words, I'd prohibit it. As a Latin American. It can affect you very badly and you're damaged forever.

The other day, in a talk in Lima, Ignacio Padilla wrote a story by García Márquez. I mean, a page. Before coming up onstage, he went to the last seat and wrote for ten minutes, read it aloud, and it was incredible. It was like . . . The captain, his name like Evaristo So-and-so, and it went on and on and on. And you said: "But . . . it was magical realism." And it totally was. It's almost like a software you install and it takes off.

ILAN STAVANS: There's a formula. But also poor García Márquez. It's not his fault. It's been pinned on him. Earlier it was Kafka and Sinclair Lewis as magical realists. It comes from Carpentier. I believe García Márquez changed Latin American culture, totally. He changed how Latin America is viewed in the rest of the world. I believe not always beneficially. Like the number of tourists who go to Latin America looking for butterflies, prostitutes. But it isn't his fault.

ALBERTO FUGUET: I read García Márquez years before I wanted to be a writer. I read him because—and this always annoyed me a little—because it was official reading. And I felt a little more rebellious. It was what we had to read in secondary school. It was literature that was already official, that came from the Ministry of Education. For me it was associated with the establishment. For me, García Márquez was always establishment. Soon afterward he won the Nobel. It was a little adolescent of me, but it was how I felt.

GUILLERMO ANGULO: There's something very important about Gabo, and it must be said because it's useful to everybody. Gabo has something that doesn't exist in Colombia: discipline. Fernando Botero has it, too. Rogelio Salmona has it, the man who designed these buildings. And Gabo has it. There must be more people, but I know only these three. And I can give you in more graphic form what Gabo's discipline is, which is incredible in a Latin American. Before he was married, I had an unlucky night. I was with two women. It's the worst thing that can happen to you. You can't do anything. So then I said: "No, my solution is Gabo. Two men and two women, now that's another kettle of fish." I went to Gabo: "Brother, this is my situation." This is a nice story. He says to me: "I have to correct the third chapter of *In Evil Hour*." "And do you have a contract or what?" "I gave myself the assignment that I would correct that third chapter tonight." There was no way. No way. It would have been the easiest thing in the world to say: "I'll do it tomorrow. I'll do it later." There was no way.

JOSÉ SALGAR: I remember that with *Autumn of the Patriarch*, Gabo would start to work from five in the morning until not very late because he would always stop writing and start to drink with his friends and talk, but they were very intense and productive working days.

GUILLERMO ANGULO: And he has his life divided with his friends. Work in the morning. In the afternoon he's with his friends. But in the morning he doesn't talk to anybody. He's just working. He's in his element.

JUANCHO JINETE: When he wrote that thing about Bolívar . . . What's it called? [*The General in His Labyrinth*.] So one day Alfonso says to me: "I need to take a trip to Soledad, maestro.

I know you have connections in that town." So then we went there and he said to me: "I have to do this and that and the other. Take me to the city hall, I understand that Simón Bolívar slept there." I have entrance privileges at the city hall because I helped out when I was manager of the Banco Popular in Soledad. I gave them a few gifts to the guards there. So then they let me go in. Listen to this story. So then I say to him, "Maestro, what do you want to find out?" "You'll see." Finally I got to the city hall and I said: "This is Maestro Fuenmayor. Look, I need to know which is the room where Bolívar slept." So then I swear, the guy says: "Here they say it was this one, this one, this one." We went up there. "Aha, and what is it that you want, Alfonso?" He says to me: "No, I need to see if when Bolívar would hang his hammock here he could see the square, the square that's in front of that church there."

We made two trips like that. Finally I told him: "Well, what is it, what do we come here for?" "No, *hombre*, it's just that Gabo's writing."

Gabito relied on Alfonso, and Alfonso was the one who corrected all those things for him. What you say is true: in his novels, the things that appear can't be contradicted. It's true that Alvaro got down to Soledad and that he looked out from the room so that Gabito could say that Bolívar thought who knows what. Whew! All that was missing was our hanging up his hammock!

JOSÉ SALGAR: He calls and asks me: "Don't you remember? Where can I get that thing?" So then he gets people to go to the library, to go and get this, and see where that negative is. And he has to have it perfect. Things like the colors, the atmosphere, the music, it has to be exact. If he says: "There was a murmur of Vivaldi," it was Vivaldi. So my conclusion has always been—and I've said this—that it was a human privilege to have successfully beautified journalistic reality, which is so harsh, every day; beautify it with those devices of literature, of music and poetry.

EDUARDO MÁRCELES DACONTE: There's an example he gives that I think is the best one to illustrate this for us. He says that when he was little, the cook in the house, the maid, once disappeared. Somebody asked: "And what happened to So-and-so?" "Imagine, she was hanging the sheets there outside." It occurred to someone to say that to mislead him. Do you understand me? "And then . . . uuuhhh . . . she went flying away." That image was etched in his mind.

RAFAEL ULLOA: Gabo has some marvelous things that leave me surprised. Not long ago he was talking with some friends and we were remembering that thing about the mourners, the old women they hire to cry over the dead. The weepers. And so Pachita Pérez came up, the champion weeper, and he says that old woman was so good at crying that she was capable of synthesizing the entire history of the dead person in a single howl. His words captured the idea of the weeps perfectly. Brilliant. So I like these things.

EDUARDO MÁRCELES DACONTE: That's true, definitely, García Márquez's memory is incredible. Because I'll tell you something: do you remember the stories they told you when you were eight years old? He's been working on them in his mind for his whole life. This isn't a question of something coming out just like that . . . It's an entire process.

JOSÉ SALGAR: *Life* magazine, when it was still in circulation . . . When Pope John Paul II had just been elected . . . Gabo was in Cuba and they gave him the assignment of going to talk to the Pope so he'd go there to free some prisoners in Cuba. So he couldn't arrange the visit with the Pope and some very strange tricks were devised. A Polish countess in Rome appeared and called him and said: "Be ready, at any moment I'll call you to come to Rome, and I'll arrange your visit with the Pope." To make a very long story short, the countess calls Gabo at five in the morning when Gabo is in Paris and says: "Come immediately, I have an appointment for you with the Pope at seven in the morning." And so the man left Paris for Rome and the first thing that occurred to him was to get some decent clothes, a blazer. So he went to a friend who lent him one, but it was too small. Well, the key moment finally came and he arrives there and . . . Brother, let me tell you. The Pope, in white, up there, and the man didn't know what to do except motion like this with his right hand. The Pope, up there, motions like this and Gabo motioned back. They make a connection, but the Pope didn't know all the secrets. He came in, and there was a very shiny wooden floor there, and in the middle a table. They both went in. The Pope closed the door and they were alone. Gabo says that at that moment, he thinks: "What would my mother say if she could see me now?" And the story begins and they talk. What's true is that he managed to raise the question of the men with the Pope, and he left the interview. That night, Mercedes asks him: "Well, how was it?" "The thing with the Pope was perfect. It went very well." "Nothing strange happened?" "Wait. Since I had to go to something else, I don't remember, but wait . . . Of course, the button!" "What about the button?" "Wait, because I went in with the blazer I had bought, and we both went in, and at the moment we went in I went up in the air and *bam!* The button fell off the blazer and went clattering under the table in the middle. Then the only thing I saw was that the Pope went ahead of me, kneeled down, and I saw his slipper. The Pope stood up, took the button, and gave it to me." And then another few details like, for example, that when they went out, the Pope didn't know how to open the door or call the Swiss Guards, so the two of them were locked in and couldn't get out. But at that moment he couldn't remember all the details. It turned into a very long story because now he remembered all about the countess and everything. So, on the basis of something that passes in the moment, the man turns it into another *Hundred Years of Solitude.*

ROSE STYRON: His characters are extremely romantic, and even when you end up in an excavation, in a convent, or in something like *News of a Kidnapping*, there's still that purely romantic part that remains. In other words, he's a man who loves people. Who loves life!

JOSÉ SALGAR: I think there aren't people these days who spend so much money on the telephone, because he doesn't care how much the phone call costs. Wherever he was, in all those times, he would call. He says so himself. When he had some special thing to tell, he would call Guillermo Cano* or me for any reason. And it

---

* Guillermo Cano, son of Fidel Cano Gutiérrez, founder of *El Espectador*. When García Márquez started working there as a reporter, he was twenty-seven at the most and the paper's editor. When Guillermo Cano was murdered in 1986 by two hit men linked to drug cartels in reprisal for denouncing the ties between traffickers and politicians, García Márquez wrote a heartfelt and hyperbolic column describing how young Cano had a visceral sense of what made news. He recalls the time Cano made them cover a three-hour-long rainfall; his insistence that he interview the sailor that ended up giving García Márquez his first scoop and is now *News of a Shipwreck*, part of the canon. It was under Cano that the paper started doing film reviews, many written by García Márquez, who was then seriously considering becoming a filmmaker.

was a long conversation. He doesn't measure the time. But he has a way of paying for the phone. He doesn't pay the bill, but surely Mercedes must pay it, or that old woman, his agent. So then he says: "Listen, we didn't realize we were talking for a long time." From Europe it must be a fortune. He realizes about the time but isn't happy until he gets to the bottom of the last detail about that button.

ROSE STYRON: I remember that he says it's his job to be a magician for his readers, but that magicians always begin with reality and return to reality. Though as a novelist he might fly between them and be as magical, as surreal, as he likes, as long as he writes well enough and with enough magic to convince the reader.

SANTIAGO MUTIS: Gabo has a background of alchemical knowledge. And alchemy is what they call magical realism. When the boy goes into the kitchen and says to his mother: "That pot's going to fall." The pot's firmly placed on the table but it slips and breaks when it falls. Colombia has a lot of that, it's a country where the people believe in that. When you go to a party at a fair or market in Villa de Leyva, the people sprinkle holy water on the bus so it doesn't drive out of control on the road. That's how he was. There's a huge religious background. That is, it's a religious culture . . . In Gabo it's the culture. Before that, it was religion.

IMPERIA DACONTE: In Aracataca they say that one night they saw him driving around town in a car with some friends. But he says he hasn't gone back there.

SANTIAGO MUTIS: I think this happens with Gabo: the country

had its oral tradition. I mean, literature didn't occupy an important place and the oral tradition begins to be pushed back a little. Cities begin to have great importance, things begin to appear that come from a totally different place, and as popular culture begins to rust, to feel threatened, to stop being oral, Gabo takes it in. And it begins to turn into literature.

RAMÓN ILLÁN BACCA: With García Márquez the world has come to know things that everybody knew here. What happened is that they were internationalized. Everybody handled them. The story about the capon . . . that's something that's always belonged to us.

RAFAEL ULLOA: What I think is that his greatness is in his imagination. Without that imagination, he would throw a few topics out into the world that would seem unbelievable. But the way he says them . . . Like when he says: "A metal grasshopper leaping from town to town along the banks of the Magdalena," to describe those anvils. And he calls them metal grasshoppers. That is, things that connect technical things and crickets. The simpler the better.

RAMÓN ILLÁN BACCA: In the story about the curlews, García Márquez puts in *Terry and the Pirates* and everybody says: "Look, that's an invention of García Márquez." No, it isn't. That's a lie. *Terry and the Pirates* was the comic strip that came out in the Sunday papers. The first Sunday papers in color were printed in Barranquilla, in 1929, and they were the Sunday papers that practically everybody bought on Saturday for five cents. I remember that I bought them. There was *Little Orphan Annie. Winnie Winkle. Tarzan.* He puts *Terry and the Pirates* into a story.

JOSÉ SALGAR: The story of the Beautiful Remedios* in *One Hundred Years of Solitude*: an image, a symbol he gave to an ordinary girl which must have been like what happened with the Virgin Mary at first. He made her sublime through literature. It's not exactly the Beautiful Remedios ascending to heaven, but it's an image he created that, in the concept of the characters in the novel, had that meaning. It's a way of beautifying the story. Of telling the story well when the facts fall short. Same thing in *Love in the Time of Cholera* . . . He knew the characters directly. Basically, it's the story of Gabo's father and mother, but it's the story he heard from his grandfather. And he begins to remember and to assimilate, and then he starts to put it together. Things his grandfather never thought about again or anything, but he reconstructs it, like the Pope's button. So then, the real genius of the man lies in having a prodigious memory and in confirming the facts responsibly so he won't stray too far from reality. And in the beauty of his language. Because the man has mastery. First he devoted himself to the classics in order to write well. And to realism. And to poetry. And to music. Gabo is also fanatical about music. So with music and poetry in his head, a nice story comes to him and he knows how to tell it. And he tells the story without straying too far because there's also his journalistic responsibility. You can't start creating fantasies. You have to say exactly what's there.

ROSE STYRON: It's fantastic, because having begun as a reporter, I think he always takes that into account. He sees journalism as

---

* Beautiful Remedios, or Remedios la bella, is one of the most iconic characters of *One Hundred Years of Solitude*. The innocent girl-woman, unaware that she is the most beautiful woman in the world, leaves behind a trail of men who die after trying to seduce her. Remedio's story of ascension to the heavens while laying out bedsheets to be dried is one of the most studied cases of García Márquez magical realism. He claims that image has been in his head because that's how the women around him explained the disappearance of a young woman who eloped.

a literary genre. Just like fiction. The way he writes, everything seems like a news item, even when people go flying away.

RAMÓN ILLÁN BACCA: Magical realism makes up only half of his work. Perhaps scholars study that aspect of magical realism in García Márquez a great deal. The only thing I can tell you about magical realism is that here on the coast, one hears so many things that really are magical realism and that grow very well around here. For example, I'm going to tell you the story of Professor Darío Hernández, in Santa Marta. I tell it in *Deborah Kruel* and I've told it to everybody. Professor Darío Hernández was in Brussels, as is proper for all decent people from Santa Marta. He wasn't very rich, but there he was, in Brussels. He studied piano. He played for Queen Astrid. He comes back because in '31, '32, I don't really know how, in what year, there's agitation because of the stock market crash in New York, that whole story. So then a lot of people had to come running back because banana shipments fell, all those things that made up the Great Depression. So then Darío came, he returns to Santa Marta. Naturally, in the recently opened Santa Marta Club, they say: "Play something, Darío." So then he comes and plays *Moonlight Sonata* by Beethoven. "Aha, Darío, play something else." Chopin's *Polonaise*. Liszt's *Liebestraum*. "Listen, is that what you went there to learn? You don't know how to play the *cumbia Puya Puyarás*, for example?" Then Darío, indignant, slammed down the piano lid and said: "This town is never going to see me play a single note again." Darío lived to the age of ninety. When this happened, he was thirty. So then he lived sixty more years. He was conductor of the municipal band. Then he was the director of Fine Arts, and pianists like Carol Bermúdez and Andrés Lineros came out of there, and they're very popular pianists. And nobody ever heard him play another note. And those who passed his house, which was an old house where he lived with two mummified aunts, older than he was, said he had put cotton between the piano strings; that is, people heard nothing but a *clap clap clan clan* when he practiced every morning. If that isn't a story of magical realism, I don't know what is. And it was Darío, and we saw him every day.

MARGARITA DE LA VEGA: I used to give paperback editions of *One Hundred Years of Solitude* with an awful cover as gifts. Later on it was the naked couple in the flowers. It was also very gaudy. I bought five or six copies, and when I was invited to dinner, instead of bringing a bottle of wine, some cookies, whatever, I would bring *One Hundred Years of Solitude*. I remember that one lady I had given it to called and invited me to lunch. She presented it to me with fifteen annotated pages, such and such a page, such and such a line, detailing all the things in *One Hundred Years of Solitude* that couldn't exist for scientific reasons, like the duration of the rains. And the first Aureliano, the one who founds Macondo with Úrsula, lives a very long time. And besides that, he survives tied to a papaya tree in the courtyard. But I knew people who tied up idiots in the courtyard.

And the fact is that the word "marvelous" and the word "magical" are not the same. Carpentier talks about marvelous realism with a very clear explanation, because Carpentier, who is a great writer and does that kind of thing, is also a theoretician. He had studied. He was an ethnomusicologist. And he, one of his things, is that marvelous realism is produced because in Latin America— to use the term that's, well, popular today—what happens is that not only several climates, several civilizations, but also several periods all meet at the same time, in the same situation, and in the same era. So that feudalism is right beside modernism.

The airplane is beside the burro. There's the chain saw and the Uzi machine gun and arrows, too. All at the same time. So then, there's this interweaving that many people, especially Cuban theoreticians like Fernando Ortiz, have worked on: he does so in his book *Cuban Counterpoint: Tobacco and Sugar*, where he explains transculturation, a term he coined that comes about when you mix the three cultures: the indigenous, the Spanish, and the African. And just like this lady made me the list of what didn't work, I remember that I sat down and said: "I should have told her point by point everything that is true, but then how boring. The magic is reading it and entering that world and not questioning this side or the other."

RAMÓN ILLÁN BACCA: Generally on Tuesday I would go to have lunch with Germán [Vargas]—some coffee, some cheese, whatever—and we'd talk a long time about literature. But whenever Gabo came to Colombia, Germán became nervous that day. One day he said to me: "You can't come for lunch today because today I'm going to eat with Guillo Marín." On that day he was more nervous than ever. His wife Susy was nervous. Tita Cepeda arrived in her big car and sounded her horn—in their agreed way. *Paparapapá!* I already knew that Guillo Marín was Gabo, and I disappeared. Well, so then something like nine years went by. Then he says to me once: "But, haven't you met Gabriel García Márquez?" I tell him: "But you've introduced him to every gringo professor who's passed through here and you haven't wanted to introduce him to me." So then he says: "No, now when we go to Cartagena I have to introduce you to him. The two of you would get along."

And then Germán and I happen to be in Cartagena at the same time, because I was at the premiere of *My Macondo*, a film some Englishmen made, and García Márquez appeared in it. And I had a small speaking part. And so on and so forth. So then I was with Guillermo Henríquez, who hates García Márquez now, and Julio Roca. We were there when the Englishmen say to us: "Well, then, let's go to the birthday party, it's a *vallenato* party." So then, for the whole day, all the papers in Cartagena had been dedicated to saying let's hope there are no party crashers, no party crashers accepted, and I don't know what about party crashers. Then Guillermo says: "No, Ramón and I aren't going. We don't like *vallenato* parties." And then, not to be left behind, I said: "We don't like *vallenato* parties." And when I go back Germán says to me: "Faggot, why didn't you go? It would have been perfect. Well, some other time." And *wham!* Germán died. I couldn't meet him.

MIGUEL FALQUEZ-CERTAIN: He's already met him, but the time he was put on display was when Tita Cepeda gave a party in her house when García Márquez returned to Barranquilla. That was in the eighties, and so she had a party with a waiter and everything. And when Ramón came to the door, the porter stopped him and said he couldn't go up. "But what do you mean? I've been invited." "No, sir." He got sick that day. Oof! He almost cried. He left with his tail between his legs. I imagine that it was very exclusive to have García Márquez in your party then because he had just returned to Colombia. It was like: only intimate, intimate, intimate friends. So from that time on it was a joke: "Poor me, I'm the only person left in Barranquilla who doesn't know García Márquez." Every lizard, everybody gave a party and invited him. He was the only one left to meet him.

GUILLERMO ANGULO: Look, I can tell you my part and it's tremendously disheartening. I haven't found anything based on me in all of Gabo's work, except for one thing he said in an article. It turns out I had a friend who was building a water tank in Aracataca. He told me: "The heat was so bad we had to work at night and pick up the metal sheets wearing gloves because they were still too hot to touch." [Gabo] recounted that in an article.

EDUARDO MÁRCELES DACONTE: Once there was a writers' conference in Sincelejo. I'm talking about '84, '85, somewhere in there. And García Márquez was living in Cartagena at that time, and I was in Barranquilla, and I was going to Sincelejo. And when I passed through Cartagena, I stopped and called him on the phone. I say: "Gabo, I'm here." He says: "Come for lunch." Okay, so I go for lunch. At that time he usually stayed in his sister's house, in Bocagrande, because he had barely settled in. And I went to have lunch with him and he says: "Eduardo, what's the news? What's happening in Aracataca?" And I say: "Well, no, about Aracataca no, but what I can tell you is that my uncle Galileo Daconte . . ." My uncle Galileo Daconte had just died. "Ay, damn it!" And he was his best friend in my family; when they were little he and that uncle of mine had been the same age. And then he dies. I ask him what he was writing and he tells me a little of what he was writing, which was *Love in the Time of Cholera*. So then, what happens? When I'm reading *Love* sometime afterward . . . One of the characters is named Galileo Daconte. He's, what do you call it? The coachman of that character, the doctor who falls and kills himself. The coachman's name is Galileo Daconte. So then I imagine that since he was writing that part at the time I visited him . . . and since I told him he had died, *bam!* He put him in. And even more in *The Trail of Your Blood in the Snow*, where the character is named Nena Daconte, who's my mother's sister who was always called the Nena, Nena Daconte.

When we told her: "Look, aunt, Gabo . . ." and she: "Ah yes, that Gabito . . . Look. That Gabito has a memory . . ." No. She really doesn't resemble the character. She's simply the name and idea of what she could be.

MARGARITA DE LA VEGA: He writes *Love* between '82 and '85. García Márquez presents a person from the old families of Cartagena who leaves the country to study and returns. Gabo takes the experience of my father, who left Cartagena to study in Paris and returned, and how he survived. He's Juvenal Urbino. Now, the love story has nothing to do with my father. It's the part about being a person from Cartagena from a traditional family, insofar as the families of Cartagena were traditional, because when I look at the families of my friends and others, there was always a little bit of everything. When I saw him, I said: "No, but that character from *Love in the Time of Cholera* isn't my father." Then he said to me: "No, Florentino is my father. We won't take that away from him." Then he said to me: "I was interested in somehow transforming the love story of my father and mother." And I think that's the time when his father's sick. Florentino Ariza is his father and the lady he places as the doctor's wife is his mother, Fermina Daza. Juvenal, my father, marries Fermina, his mother. My mother doesn't go out for the afternoon promenade. He transformed all that with the love story and that comes from nineteenth-century stories. That's why I say that I see my father's influence more in the style of the novel, which is a nineteenth-century novel with lots of characters, written in the style of Balzac. It has a huge number of characters. It's the portrait of an age. The love story is important, but it isn't fundamental. It was his source of inspiration. He always wanted to write something new and different.

My father didn't die like Dr. Urbino because of a parrot, but he absolutely would have risked his life for an animal, because people gave him parrots and parakeets and whatever as presents. We had a macaw that wandered through the house and was named Gonzalo; he danced and everything.

GUILLERMO ANGULO: Somewhere his literary agent tells me that the photograph in *Innocent Eréndira* is of me, but no . . . I mean, the only thing is that I'm a photographer and he was a photographer, but there's nothing I said, or told him, no. So the elaboration has to exist, but it's so complex that, as I've said, you can't follow it.

CARMELO MARTÍNEZ: I appear as Cristo, a friend of Cayetano's, but Gabito doesn't describe him in the novel, he leaves some doubt. He could have been me or a cousin of Cayetano's who died of brain cancer.

GUILLERMO ANGULO: You have to be very careful when you think: "I inspired the work." You have to discount all that because I think his great inspiration was his grandmother and his mother and his family. I remember the things he would tell me, that the family talked about, that are written by Gabo. Of course, Gabo is telling them to you. About how a female relative of his was combing her hair and the grandmother said: "Don't comb your hair at night because ships get lost when you do . . ." The colonel's in his family. It's an entire family fortune that he accumulates and keeps spending for his whole life.

I haven't found anything directly having to do with his friends, and I think I know them very well, all of them very well. He's stolen ideas from them, but openly. I mean, Mutis began to write *The General in His Labyrinth*. He took one thing and then he said: "No, you're not going to do anything with that. I'm going to steal it from you." But that's all. I mean, it's circumstantial because the other man also talks about Bolívar when he's going to die, is going toward death, but you can read both things, the two things coexist, and you can't say: "Look, Gabo, you copied this." The elaboration is so complex that it's no longer an elaboration.

RAFAEL ULLOA: That guy he presents there, that Gypsy who arrives and changes, that guy resembles his father, who did all those things. Or that other madman he presents in the story about Blacamán. I'm telling you it was Jorgito, from there in Sincé, who would have a snake bite him. And there's one in "Blacamán, Seller of Miracles," who has something of Jorgito. Because Jorgito, as I say, would smear himself with pomade . . . "And now you'll see that a fer-de-lance . . ." Of course, the serpent's fangs had been removed.

JOSÉ SALGAR: *One Hundred Years* isn't a newspaper story but it has a newspaper background, which is the tragedy of La Guajira, which is the life of coastal people, which is the imagination of the people, because all the characters are real. Because the Gypsy sold things there. Úrsula. All the characters have a real background that makes them newspaper characters. And it ends with the tragedy of the banana plantations, and basically, many of the characters of *One Hundred Years* must have died on the banana plantations. Then too, he puts in many people from La Cueva and uses their real names. He gathers together. It's a kind of compilation of the most beautiful memories of his youth.

EMMANUEL CARBALLO: I thought it was something . . . I knew it was how they talked in Barranquilla, but he had invented a way of putting words together and making a style different from the different styles at that time. And he brought in a new fashion with that language. And not only that language: that ability to imagine! A power of creation. For me it was invention. For me there was no Colombian word or Mexican word; there were words that sounded good and said important things.

ROSE STYRON: I think he's a man of great, great profundity, that he's a creative man. I've heard him say that to explain the mystery of creation, he would do anything. And so he sits down to talk with a film student or whoever. He says you never get to the heart of the mystery of creation, but that he's always ready to rummage around and go deeper into it.

JOSÉ SALGAR: He's a tape recorder, but a magnificent one. Everything stays with the man. A subject emerges and he turns it around. He has a certain cadence, a very pleasant something for telling stories. He's listening and suddenly he asks you a question. There's always an exchange. He goes back to the central facts in the life of the person who is his interlocutor, I believe. He asks you: "Aha, do you remember Sánchez?" (A photographer.) "Where did he come from? Who gave him the name Dog? Why is he the Dog?" And he begins to find out about his life. I don't know if he does it unconsciously, but he's creating the novel of the *el Perro* Sánchez. He's a tremendous presence.

SANTIAGO MUTIS: The Gabo of today is a Gabo who works things out. He tells his story. Which is literary. It doesn't mean it isn't true. It's literary.

GUILLERMO ANGULO: He's a character in search of an author. And he found him.

GERALD MARTIN: The first time I saw him was in Havana in the year 1990. In his house in Havana. I felt I had lived for that moment. It was out of this world how well we got along. We talked for four straight hours. When he wants to be, he's marvelous. A delicious conversationalist. At the end of the day he said: "And what time will you be here tomorrow?" Imagine! I left there flying with happiness. The next day I returned and found a different person. When I sat down he said: "Do you know something? I couldn't sleep last night, I was traveling through the labyrinth of Latin American literature." I realized right away, and was very frightened, that he was talking about my book *Journeys Through the Labyrinth* that had been published the year before, and that some friend (in English we'd say, ironically, a well-wisher) must have lent it to him; in it I criticize *Autumn of the Patriarch*. "I'm the patriarch," he said to me. "It's my self-portrait. If you don't understand that and if you don't like the patriarch, how will you be my biographer?" Gabo had realized that night that it's difficult to be friends with your biographer, but even so we continued to get along well, but we were no longer soul brothers. We never again had the relationship we'd had at that first meeting; but we never forgot it either, it was always there.

SANTIAGO MUTIS: Yes, Gabo has had really lovely people. Generous and beautiful, and that's why Gabo is a person filled with gratitude. Because he has people to be grateful to. And being grateful isn't anything different from being humane, but a torrent of humaneness. And Gabo, I believe, is humane. And his books are humane.

CARMEN BALCELLS: When he brought me a copy of the manuscript for *Of Love and Other Demons* in the year '94, it was a little difficult for me to understand that he had dedicated the book to me. And the dedication said: "To Carmen bathed in tears." That dedication was the one he had put in my copy of *Autumn of the Patriarch* because of the story of the publication of that book, which was a disaster. He put that dedication in the presentation copy of the first edition, which was falling apart. When I saw that text I didn't understand completely, or with the speed that would have been necessary, that he was dedicating the book to me. To Carmen Balcells. And it was so special a moment that today I still remember physically the details of his presence, of the manuscript, of everything just as it happened, and the truth is I don't know whether I was capable of expressing or translating the emotion I felt. I don't think so. And I didn't. I didn't express it well.

GUSTAVO GARCÍA MÁRQUEZ: I said at the start that Gabito and I have a rivalry as to who has the better memory. For example, he doesn't remember when, in Cartagena, around 1951, a representative of Losada Publishers came looking for writers and he asked Gabito if he had a novel. So then Gabito said to me: "Listen, help me out here," and he took out the originals of *Leaf Storm* to read them. We were in the middle of reading them when Gabito stopped and said: "This is good, but I'm going to write something that people will read more than the *Quijote*."

MARÍA LUISA ELÍO: Here in this photograph I'm with Gabriel and Diego. He's my son. In Gabo's house. A very amusing day. He was writing and he had us come in; something very unusual for him. I don't know which novel he was writing at that moment.

He says to me: "I've written the whole book on this thing, this machine." It was a computer. And he says: "But, just in case, look." He opens a drawer and he had it all typed out.

Álvaro Mutis and García Márquez.

33

The Start

In which Quique and Juancho are already drunk but insist on having "the start," as they call the last whiskey in Barranquilla, which is always one too many

JUANCHO JINETE: Maestro Obregón called me one day and said: "Juan, come over, because tomorrow I'm going to a dinner and someone who's here and I want you to come." So I went and it was Gabo there with Mercedes and their two sons. So then I don't know what happened and he said to me: "I got the Nobel Prize," and like that. Damn! I got up and left and Alejandro went out with me.

QUIQUE SCOPELL: In Cartagena, when Alejandro was alive, I saw him. Later, when Alejandro died, not anymore . . . The pranksters from La Cueva: one is Alfonso Fuenmayor and another is Álvaro Cepeda. The other is . . .

JUANCHO JINETE: Germán . . . He names them a lot. When he says that Big Mama died, he says they went there, that the *mamagallistas* from La Cueva were there. So look: Álvaro died so long ago. He died young. He was forty-two. Alfonso Fuenmayor: from La Cueva to heaven. Alejandro, another buddy. Gabriel García Márquez—Gabito—turned them into characters in *One Hundred Years of Solitude.*

QUIQUE SCOPELL: Alfonso, for me . . . Let's define the word "friend." A friend is . . . There are very few. You may have four or five friends, you won't have more. And Alfonso was one of the few true friends that Gabito had. Because Alejandro and Álvaro and Germán weren't Gabito's friends the way Alfonso was. Alfonso was Gabito's friend. You're a person's friend, why? Because . . . When you fall in love, you fall in love with a person, why? Because you fell in love. Why did you fall in love? You don't know. You fell in love.

JUANCHO JINETE: It's what I was saying. Listen, Quique: he heard our stories and ra, ra, ra he wrote them down. That's why Cepeda would say to me: "Fuck me, fuck me." In one of them there's even a saying I had that came from my grandfather: "To hell with a fan, for time is a breeze." That's in the book about the loves of old people. When the old man walks through the town. "To hell with a fan, for time is a breeze."

Before he used to come a lot, because of Fuenmayor. When Fuenmayor died, not anymore. Whenever they say something about Fuenmayor, they put in Gabo. He died in '94. "Gabo's friend died." This is something from *El Tiempo*. It says: "Fuenmayor along with García Márquez, Álvaro Cepeda Samudio, Germán Varas Cantillo, the painter Alejandro Obregón, and also the industrialist Julio Mario Santo Domingo were in the habit of going to La Cueva to talk and learn about literature."

QUIQUE SCOPELL: Because at that time Gabito was flat broke, he didn't have means, he didn't have shit, he didn't have culture. Because nowadays he has a lot of culture, it's true, but he wasn't born with that culture; because of something that isn't reproachable in life. Because he was a poor man. He has too much merit to have reached the top by his own merits. Because the man has gotten there by his own merits. Nobody gave him a toothpick so he could live. He's earned that position through his own efforts, through obstinacy. Because he's as obstinate as a sonuvabitch. That man earned his position through obstinacy. He deserves it because he earned it. Because when a man works the way he's worked, he deserves it. He deserves it because he's worked for that thing his whole life. And he's been . . .

GERALD MARTIN: This fight that Quique Scopell and Juancho Jinete have about his stealing things from Álvaro [Cepeda Samudio] is simply because they were closer to Álvaro than to Gabo. Álvaro had an irresistible personality and he was a very talented writer, but he obviously isn't a more important writer than García Márquez. What happens is that they were both feeding on the same thing. Gabo absorbs it all. All. I'm sure he took from Álvaro and from Rojas Herazo. He takes what has to be taken and makes it his own. That isn't called plagiarism; it's called genius.

QUIQUE SCOPELL: Nowadays they go so far as to compare him to Shakespeare and to Cervantes. With that, you don't fuck around! So what else do you want? No! No! I'll have this drink and we're leaving.

Epilogue

The Day We All Woke Up Old

GLORIA TRIANA: When he turned eighty, we were having lunch at the house of Alberto Abello, the Samarian. He was on a sofa and we were on cushions on the floor. He hadn't said anything in all that time, and someone mentioned that Santiago Mutis, the son of Álvaro Mutis, his lifelong friend, was negotiating his pension. So then that was the subject and I said: "The fact is that when you stop seeing people, they freeze in the moment that you last saw them." I said: "Santiago, so young, already on a pension." Then he, who in those last days didn't maintain a long dialogue or argue or anything, but he would say . . . they were like proverbs. Of course the proverbs he said were all in his style and the style of his books. Then when he commented on that he says in that tone of his, the way he talked: "The truth is I don't know what happened but from one day to the next we all woke up old."

JAIME ABELLO BANFI: He always maintained his routine until his last day. He would dress, always elegantly, and go down to his office, where his life-long secretary, Mónica Alonso, was waiting for him. There I don't know what he did. He would read, I suppose. I don't know what he read. Then they had lunch, or as they say in Mexico, they ate. They always had a delicious lunch, lunches were very important. First an aperitif. Mercedes, a tequila. Gabo, champagne. In the afternoon they took care of domestic matters and at night they watched a movie like any other couple in the world.

GLORIA TRIANA: On his last visits to Cartagena he was dressed in absolutely perfect white and you could feel his serenity. He produced tenderness in me because he would say things. He would greet you with great warmth but it seemed to me he didn't know whom he was greeting.

DANIEL PASTOR: On the day of Mercedes's eightieth birthday he looked very happy. He was wearing a Greek sailor's cap. I've been a friend of his son Gonzalo since we were teenagers. I don't think Gabo recognized me but he took my hand very sweetly and kissed it and said: "How good to be here with real friends."

GLORIA TRIANA: One afternoon I went to their house in Cartagena, and he was there with Mercedes, and in front of Mercedes he took my hand and said to me: "Do you know I think of you every day?" And then I said to him: "So do I, Gabo." And he said: "And why haven't you told me?" Then I said to him, since she was standing right there: "Well, because I thought Mercedes wouldn't like my telling you that." And then he said: "No, no, no. She doesn't say anything." He was like that, first with that warmth, but at the same time as serene as a child. You never saw him embittered or anything.

CARLITOS GONZÁLEZ ROMERO: Gabo is flying like an eagle. He's pure sweetness. With his half-boots and his plaid jackets, he must have dozens of them. I just saw him sitting in his office in Mexico City. He looks handsomer than ever in that afternoon light, in his golden age. He wants to dance. He kept saying: "And who's going dancing? You look like you'll go dancing. Take me dancing!" . . . To those who say he's losing his memory, I want to say: What do you expect, with how hard he set his mind to working to be able to write all those books he gave us?

RODRIGO MOYA: I saw him a year ago at lunch in his house. He sat with me and dedicated the special edition of *One Hundred Years*: "To Don Rodrigo from Don Gabo." But there was no more conversation. The person he liked very much was Susana, my wife. He adored Susana. Susana was sitting beside him, on his right, and there was a moment when he had to get up because they were going to give him a massage or something; then Susana helped him up and he, as if he were surprised, turned around. When he saw who had helped him up, he kept looking at her, gave a big smile, and said: "Ay, how delicious."

GLORIA TRIANA: I gave Gabo his last farewell party in Cartagena. They were going to return to Mexico City and had spent three or four months here, and I told Mercedes that I wanted to give them a party. Make a lunch for him; she knows my lunches have live music, *porro* and *vallenato*, his favorites, and *cumbia*. She said: "Wait, because Gonzalo and my grandchildren are coming, and I want them to be there." I told the musicians: "The moment he comes in, you begin to play." He came in dancing a *porro*. He was absolutely ecstatic. That's the last image I have of him. It was the last time I saw him.

CARMEN BALCELLS: I remember that perfectly. The last time I saw him in Barcelona. And in my house. I have a memory that I hope stays with me until the last day of my life.

JAIME ABELLO BANFI: I arrived in Mexico City on Monday, April 15, for a conference on journalism. I called Mercedes and she sounded calm. Gabo was weak but stable. We made plans for me to visit them when I was finished with my work. I called again on Wednesday and I felt something else. "How's everything going?" I asked. "Badly," she replied, plain and simple. I immediately communicated with my team in Cartagena so they could be prepared.

GUILLERMO ANGULO: I took a plane. I arrived at the house in Pedregal at 1:15 in the afternoon. Gabito had died at 12:08. Rodrigo, the older of the Gabos, said to me: "How good you came, brother. The more of us there are, the better we can share the blows."

JAIME ABELLO BANFI: The house was surrounded by reporters, cameras, admirers holding yellow flowers, and it was difficult to gain access. I was coming from Calle de Fuego in a taxi when the police stopped me. I showed them my card. I told them I was the director of the Gabriel García Márquez Foundation and they let me through. When I finally could go in I realized that nothing was prepared. Everything was being resolved very quickly but in a coherent way, and with their style. Mexico announced that they would pay him civil tribute in the Palace of Fine Arts. I spoke to his son Gonzalo at about five on Friday afternoon, and he said that in addition to the chamber music by Bartók and other composers that Gabo liked, he also wanted there to be a *vallenato* group to accompany the people who would wait in line to enter the Teatro Bellas Artes.

GUILLERMO ANGULO: I was the only one besides the family who saw Gabo dead. He looked very well, very peaceful, I gave him a goodbye kiss on the cheek. The *vallenatos* that had been playing until his death were silent.

CARLITOS GONZÁLEZ ROMERO: That day I found Mercedes in the kitchen surrounded by her sons, daughters-in-law, and grandchildren, and Maestro Angulo. She was serene and tranquil, dressed in the blouse and shoes of a tigress, holding a cigarette and a glass of white tequila, taking phone calls. All the calls were short, she listened, not speaking very much, and at the end she would say: Thank you. When I went back the next day, she already had the box of ashes in her study. I approached and placed a red rose on it. Mónica, his secretary, was there, just beside the urn, and we talked for quite a while.

GUILLERMO ANGULO: Before we went out, Mercedes said to all of us going to Bellas Artes: "Nobody cries here. Here everything's pure macho from Jalisco."

CARLITOS GONZÁLEZ ROMERO: I have my pockets full of butterflies made of paper, yellow butterflies they brought from Colombia. Now the presidents have spoken. Let's do away with the seriousness. There are some electric fans that will make them fly.

KATYA GONZÁLEZ RIPOLL: Look outside. They're flying. Let's go there.
Viva Gabo! Viva Gabo!

CECILIA BUSTAMANTE: Viva Gabo!

TANIA LIBERTAD: Viva Gabo!

UNKNOWN VOICE: Viva Gabo!

Notes on the Most Important Voices

JAIME ABELLO BANFI: Director and cofounder of the Foundation for a New Ibero-American Journalism (FNPI), today the Gabriel García Márquez Foundation, created by Gabo in 1994 to contribute to the renovation of journalism in the countries of Latin America. A purebred Barranquillero and lover of Carnival.

ELISEO "LICHI" ALBERTO: The son of the Cuban poet Eliseo Diego, he was also a poet as well as a screenwriter and novelist. Diego always had a stormy relationship with Castro's regime, and went into exile in Mexico in 1990. It is said that García Márquez helped him leave Cuba and settle in Mexico. In 1997 he published *Report Against Myself,* accusing the Cuban government of obliging him to spy on his father. He received the Alfaguara Novel Prize in 1998 for *Caracol Beach.* He died in Mexico City in 2012 at the age of sixty.

GUILLERMO ANGULO: Colombian photographer, writer, documentarian, and orchid grower. A close friend of García Márquez since their poverty-stricken Parisian days. He's called Maestro Angulo. He lives in Bogotá and cultivates orchids outside the city.

RAMÓN ILLÁN BACCA: Recognized, prizewinning author and professor of literature living in Barranquilla, related to Samarian families of good name. Although his aunts knew Luisa Santiaga, García Márquez's mother, it was difficult for him to get to know him.

CARMEN BALCELLS: The most powerful literary agent in the Spanish language, credited with having created the "boom." In the days after Gabo died, she predicted that Gabismo would become a religion. The "Mamá Grande" as Gabo dubbed her, she died in Barcelona in 2015 at eighty-five.

CECILIA BUSTAMANTE: Colombian poet, a friend of García Márquez.

EMMANUEL CARBALLO: Mexican editor and writer with a long career. He was part of the group of intellectuals who embraced Gabriel García Márquez when he settled in Mexico City in 1963, with his wife Mercedes and son Rodrigo. He was the editor of ERA and founded a literary magazine with Carlos Fuentes. He died in 2014.

PATRICIA CASTAÑO: Documentary filmmaker and producer from Bogotá who served as guide and interpreter for Gerald Martin, the biographer of García

Márquez, when he traveled to the Atlantic Coast to interview the writer's maternal relatives.

IMPERIA DACONTE: The daughter of Antonio Daconte, an Italian immigrant who made a small fortune in Aracataca, where García Márquez lived with his paternal grandparents until he was eight years old. Colonel Nicolás Márquez was a good friend of Daconte's and visited him frequently with his grandson. Imperia remembers García Márquez as a "cute little blondie" when they were children. She is ninety-seven.

MARGARITA DE LA VEGA: A Cartagenan academic, film producer, and critic who has lived in the United States since 1974. The daughter of Dr. Henrique de la Vega, who was a specialist in ailments of the head and a very good friend of García Márquez.

ALBINA DU BOISROUVRAY: French film producer, activist, and granddaughter of Bolivian tin king Simón Patiño. She met García Márquez during the golden days of the boom when together with Juan Goytisolo in Paris she created *Libre*, a magazine that published Latin American writers.

MARÍA LUISA ELÍO: She came to Mexico City as a refugee, the child of Spanish Republicans. She married Jomí García Ascot, a poet and filmmaker, the son of a Republican diplomat, and they were an integral part of the group of intellectuals, writers, and filmmakers in Mexico in the 1960s. The film *On the Empty Balcony*, which deals with the subject of exile and was directed by her husband, is based on one of her stories. *One Hundred Years of Solitude* is dedicated to her and her husband. She died in Mexico City in 2009.

MIGUEL FALQUEZ-CERTAIN: Poet, playwright, writer, and translator from Barranquilla, he has lived in New York since the 1980s.

HERIBERTO FIORILLO: Writer, filmmaker, and journalist, he has written eight books of essays and fiction, three films, and four newsreels. Creator and director of the La Cueva Foundation and the International Carnival of Arts.

ALBERTO FUGUET: Chilean filmmaker and writer. He was one of the leaders of the movement known as McOndo, which declared the end of magical realism. He was selected by *Time* magazine and CNN as one of fifty Latin American leaders in the new millennium.

ODERAY GAME: Ecuadorian filmmaker and producer who lived for many years in Paris and Madrid. She now lives in Quito.

AIDA GARCÍA MÁRQUEZ: Aida is the second of the García Márquez sisters and the fourth in order of birth. A teacher and a Salesian nun until 1979, she wrote a book about the childhood of the twelve García Márquez children.

ELIGIO "YIYO" GARCÍA MÁRQUEZ: The youngest of the eleven siblings of García Márquez, and like him, a writer and journalist. Among his books is *Behind the Keys of Melquíades*, a journalistic investigation into *One Hundred Years of Solitude* published in 2001. In that same year he died of a brain tumor at the age of fifty-three.

GUSTAVO GARCÍA MÁRQUEZ: A Colombian diplomat and brother of García Márquez. He died in March 2014 at the age of seventy-eight, waiting for a disability pension that never arrived, an echo of *Nobody Writes to the Colonel*.

JAIME GARCÍA MÁRQUEZ: The eighth of the twelve García Márquez siblings, a great teller of stories about the life and culture of the Colombian Caribbean. He is one of the original members of the Foundation for a New Ibero-American Journalism, the foundation García Márquez founded in 1994.

MARGOT GARCÍA MÁRQUEZ: The oldest of the García Márquez sisters who, like Gabriel, because of the closeness in their ages, was brought up in the house of their grandparents in Aracataca. García Márquez has said that she was the spine of the family, and that the character of Amaranta in *One Hundred Years of Solitude* was inspired by her.

KATYA GONZÁLEZ RIPOLL: A Colombian architect born in Barranquilla, "carnival queen" and García Márquez's goddaughter.

CARLITOS GONZÁLEZ ROMERO: A multifaceted and creative Barranquillero, a designer of costumes and masks for the Barranquilla Carnival. He made Gabo and Mercedes their hooded cloaks when they considered the possibility of returning incognito to celebrate Carnival.

JUANCHO JINETE: More than anything else, he dedicated his life to being a great friend and organizer of whatever he was asked to do, above all by the four friends García Márquez immortalized as "the jokers of La Cueva" in *Big Mama's Funeral* and then in *One Hundred Years of Solitude*. When French intellectuals and world journalists set out to find the origins of Macondo, Juancho acted as their guide. He died in 2010.

TANIA LIBERTAD: A Peruvian singer, a close friend of the García Márquez family.

NEREO LÓPEZ: He is one of the best-known photographers in Colombia. He has received all the possible prizes, for he has been documenting Colombia since the time of the Violence. He was part of the La Cueva group when he lived in Barranquilla as a graphic reporter for *El Espectador*. He was the official photographer for the committee that accompanied García Márquez to Stockholm to receive the Nobel. In 1997, at the age of eighty, he moved to New York to "open new horizons." He died in New York in 2015 at ninety-four, leaving a bevy of unfinished photography projects.

EDUARDO MÁRCELES DACONTE: A writer and art critic born in Aracataca, the grandson of Antonio Daconte, the Italian friend of García Márquez's grandfather. It was thanks to his grandfather, who brought the gramophone and movies to Aracataca, that García Márquez listened to music and saw his first film as a boy.

GERALD MARTIN: An English academic and writer, he spent seventeen years writing the biography of García Márquez, who called him "my English biographer."

CARMELO MARTÍNEZ: He was a judge in Colombia. A native of Sincé, where the event occurred that García Márquez re-created in *Chronicle of a Death Foretold*. He has known García Márquez since they were both thirteen years old, when the writer came to live with his parents for the first time. Martínez was the best friend of Cayetano Gentile, the boy whom two brothers murdered over a question of honor. Carmelo was with him that day. García Márquez asked him to recount what happened. He died in Cartagena.

PLINIO APULEYO MENDOZA: A Colombian novelist, journalist, diplomat, and editor of *Libre*. Among the many books he has written are three about the time he spent with García Márquez. In them he recounts how poor García Márquez was in Bogotá and in Paris. They were intimate friends and companions. He was the one who arranged for him to work in Caracas and for *Prensa Latina*. In that period, they were both fervent believers in the revolution of Fidel Castro. Their political ideals separated them when García Márquez did not denounce the arrest of the Cuban poet Heberto Padilla in 1971, which is known as "the Padilla Case." He is the author, along with Álvaro Vargas Llosa and Carlos Alberto Montaner, of the "Manual of the Perfect Latin American Idiot," an essay that satirizes sympathizers from leftist groups in Latin America. He lives in Bogotá, where he writes a political column for the newspaper *El Tiempo*.

RODRIGO MOYA: A Colombian photographer residing in Mexico, and a close friend of García Márquez.

SANTIAGO MUTIS: A Colombian poet, the godson of García Márquez, and the son of Álvaro Mutis, who lives in Bogotá. A professor and editor of literary journals at the Universidad Nacional in Colombia. In 1997 he organized a traveling exhibit on García Márquez.

JOSÉ ANTONIO PATERNOSTRO: An economist from Barranquilla, a Barranquilloso, and father of the author.

EDMUNDO PAZ SOLDÁN: A Bolivian writer, one of the most representative of the Latin American generation of the nineties, known as McOndo. His work includes essays, stories, and novels.

KAREN PONIACHIK: A Chilean journalist and consultant who has worked in governmental posts in her country. She served as Minister of Mines and Energy during the first presidency of Michelle Bachelet.

GREGORY RABASSA: Translator of Spanish and Portuguese into English, who introduced the North American public to the works of the so-called Latin American boom. The translator into English of *One Hundred Years of Solitude* and four other books by García Márquez. With his translation of *Hopscotch* he won the National Book Award. It was Julio Cortázar who suggested to García Márquez that he use Rabassa as his translator. Among other authors he has translated are Jorge Amado, José Lezama Lima, Clarice Lispector, and Mario Vargas Llosa. His last years were dedicated to only translating dead poets. He died in New York in 2016.

FERNANDO RESTREPO: A pioneer of television in Colombia, who, with Fernando Gómez Agudelo, coordinated the operations that brought television to the entire country. Nine years later, in 1963, they founded RTI, the first programmer of the state television channels. In 1973 they transmitted the first television program in color. It is the first enterprise to produce its own soap operas and dramatic programs, among them *Time to Die*, in 1984, with a script written by García Márquez. He is the epitome of a Bogotá gentleman, a slicker.

HÉCTOR ROJAS HERAZO: A Colombian poet, novelist, journalist, and painter, he was García Márquez's friend when they both worked for the newspaper *El Universal* in Cartagena, the city to which García Márquez returned after abandoning the study of law and a Bogotá inflamed by the assassination of Jorge Eliézer Gaitán on April 9, 1948. At that time Rojas Herazo was a reporter and columnist on the staff of the paper. He died in Bogotá in 2002.

ARISTIDES ROYO SÁNCHEZ: A Panamanian lawyer and former diplomat and minister of education who helped negotiate the Torrijos-Carter Treaties in 1977. He also served as president of Panama from October 11, 1978, to July 31, 1982, when he was pressured to resign by the military. From 1968 to 1989, Panama was ruled by a military dictatorship that started with General Omar Torrijos and ended with the overthrow of Manuel Noriega with the help of the United States. Torrijos had named Royo and the military deposed him exactly a year after the general died in a helicopter accident. He currently serves as the director of the Academy of Letters of Panama.

JOSÉ SALGAR: Editor, journalist, and director of newspapers in Colombia, he was the head of the editorial room at *El Espectador* when García Márquez arrived in Bogotá to work as a reporter. He died in 2013 after having worked in journalism for more than sixty-five years.

ENRIQUE "QUIQUE" SCOPELL: A Colombian photographer, the son of Cuban immigrants, he was the other Barranquillero still alive when I began this series of interviews in 1999. He was one of the group García Márquez joined when he came to work at *El Heraldo* in 1951. He called himself a professional drunkard. He died in 2014 in Los Angeles at age ninety-one and he made sure his body was laid to rest in Barranquilla.

ILAN STAVANS: Mexican writer and professor living in the United States. A student of Hispanic culture in the United States and Jewish culture in the Hispanic world. Among his books are a dictionary of Spanglish and one on the first forty years of Gabriel García Márquez's life.

ROSE STYRON: A poet and human rights activist from the United States, she was the wife of the writer William Styron; García Márquez was a good friend of both of them. Since 1970, she has been part of the founding board of Amnesty International and many other nongovernmental organizations that fight for human rights. She worked with García Márquez in several Latin American causes, such as the case of Allende in Chile and the United States embargo on Cuba.

WILLIAM STYRON: An important author from the southern United States. He is famous for *Sophie's Choice*, a novel about the life of a woman who survived Auschwitz, and for writing in the first person about his own alcoholism and depression. Because of his southern subject matter, in his earlier novels he was known as the heir to William Faulkner. Winner of the Pulitzer Prize, among many other awards. He had a circle of very influential literary and political friends, among them two Latin Americans: Carlos Fuentes and Gabriel García Márquez. He died in 2006 at the age of eighty-one.

BRAM TOWBIN: A born and raised Upper East Side New Yorker turned flower grower in Vermont.

GLORIA TRIANA: Director of the Festivities and Folklore section of Colcultura, a key element in making the award of the Nobel Prize to García Márquez a fiesta.

RAFAEL ULLOA PATERNINA: A distant cousin of García Márquez on his father's side, he is a chemical engineer whose vocation is writing short stories about the Colombian coast. He was born in Sincé, the river town where García Márquez's father was also born. He cuts out and saves everything the press publishes about "his kinsman." He died in Barranquilla.

ARMANDO ZABALETA: One of the most respected composers and singers of the *vallenato*, a very popular musical genre along the Caribbean coast. Among his best-loved songs is "I'm Not Returning to Patillal," written as an homage to Freddy Molina, his spiritual brother, another troubadour like him, when he died suddenly. In 1973, Zabaleta composed a protest song against García Márquez when he learned that he had given some prize money to a group of guerrillas in Venezuela and not to Aracataca. He died in 2010 at age eighty-three, thankful for the love he received for his compositions.

List of Images